The American Ethos

A Twentieth Century Fund Report

The Twentieth Century Fund is an independent research foundation which undertakes policy studies of economic, political, and social institutions and issues. The Fund was founded in 1919 and endowed by Edward A. Filene.

The American Ethos

Public Attitudes toward Capitalism
and Democracy

Herbert McClosky ★ John Zaller

A Twentieth Century Fund Report

Harvard University Press
Cambridge, Massachusetts, and London, England   1984

Library of Congress Cataloging in Publication Data

McClosky, Herbert.
    The American ethos.

    (A Twentieth Century Fund report)
    Includes bibliographical references and index.
    1. Public opinion—United States.   2. Capitalism—Public opin-
ion.   3. Democracy—Public opinion.
I. Zaller, John, 1949–   .   II. Title.   III. Series.
HN90.P8M4   1984   330.12′2   84-12793
ISBN 0-674-02330-7

To Mitzi
and
To Debbie

Foreword

What are the enduring values in the American polity? This question began to be asked following the political and social turmoil of the 1960s and the traumas of Vietnam. One persistent questioner was Herbert McClosky, a distinguished political scientist at the Survey Research Center at the University of California at Berkeley. For more than twenty years he has been a trenchant analyst of the American public's political attitudes and participation in politics, often taking issue with the orthodox view that our constitutional system has been able to accommodate a wide range of opinion on policy issues because of deeply rooted agreement on values.

As an operating foundation, the Twentieth Century Fund formulates its own program of research on public policy and solicits scholars to write books on critical issues. In McClosky's case, he came to us just after completing a survey on the political attitudes and values of opinion leaders and the public. Since we had recently completed two studies focusing on this area—*The Changing American Voter* by Norman Nie, Sidney Verba, and John Petrocik and *The Presidential Elite* by Jeane Kirkpatrick—we were interested in McClosky's ideas. He was particularly intent on examining the tension between two traditional American systems—capitalism, which offers rewards to individuals with imagination, talent, and industriousness and encourages the amassing of material wealth, and democracy, which seeks to ensure equality and a decent living for all—as a means of determining how these conflicting beliefs affect political behavior. Although McClosky's proposed book was not as directly related to public policy as those we usually sponsor, the Fund has a commitment to intellectual risk taking and a flexible approach to what it sponsors. We considered this self-imposed task a difficult and daunting one, but one that could, if successful, prove enormously informative and enlightening for the body politic, and especially for policymakers.

Even before McClosky could analyze the data already collected, he decided to undertake further survey work focused on opinion elites, the relatively few who influence the political thinking of the many. Once those results were in hand, he then began the long and arduous task of evaluating his data. For this assignment he took on a collaborator, John Zaller, then at the Survey Research Center and now on the faculty at Princeton University.

It has taken more than eight years from the inception of the project to its successful conclusion. The result of this work is a remarkably rich and solid analysis of the nation's political culture—how our major values developed, the depth with which they are held, and the support they enjoy. This book promises to be an important and perhaps even indispensable source for everyone interested in the basic beliefs of our society: its strength, its weaknesses, its potential.

M. J. Rossant, Director
The Twentieth Century Fund

Acknowledgments

Our aim in this book has been not only to report what we have learned about the values of the American people today, as evidenced from their responses to the questions asked in several national surveys that we conducted, but to assess the meaning and significance of those values in light of their history in the American experience. We have also sought to explain how the traditional values of the American ethos have affected ideological and partisan divisions in this country and influenced the course of American politics in our own day.

In preparing a work of this scope, we have inevitably accumulated many debts. Most of all, we are indebted to the Twentieth Century Fund and to its officers and staff. The Fund generously provided financial assistance to help us collect, process, and analyze some of the data turned up by our surveys of American values, and to cover the costs incurred in the preparation of the manuscript. The Fund's director, Murray J. Rossant, and its staff members James A. Smith and especially Carol M. Barker not only gave their unstinting support to the project but offered advice and criticism that influenced its intellectual focus and substance. We have also benefited greatly from the outstanding editorial assistance furnished by one of the Fund's assistant directors, Beverly Goldberg, and from the numerous suggestions proposed by William Bischoff, who edited the manuscript. For her help in expediting publication, we wish to thank Brenda Melissaratos at the Fund. We are also grateful to Mary Ellen Geer at

Harvard University Press for her careful and perceptive editing of the final manuscript.

Support for the research on which this book is based was also provided by the University of California, Berkeley, and by the university's Survey Research Center. J. Merrill Shanks, former director of the Center, was an invaluable ally, adviser, and benefactor at every stage of the project; without his generous assistance and counsel, the research could never have been launched or sustained. Percy Tannenbaum, the current director, also gave support to the project by continuing to make available the Center's facilities for the analysis of data and the preparation of the manuscript.

We are also indebted to a number of people at the Survey Research Center who worked or consulted with us during the conduct of the research and the course of the writing. Chief among these were E. Deborah Jay and Russell Neuman, research assistants on the project, who played vital roles in the design and administration of the Opinions and Values surveys, from which we have drawn most of the data reported in this volume. Michael Goldstein also contributed greatly as a research assistant, helping us to formulate and assess some of the ideas explored in the book. Dennis Chong and Barbara Geddes, research assistants on a related project, read the manuscript at various stages and were frequently consulted by us for their perceptive observations and suggestions. On more than one occasion we also had need to consult Samuel Haber for advice on American history and Christopher Achen for advice on questions of research methodology, measurement, and inference, and we found their counsel invariably wise and instructive. Charles Bann contributed at various stages to the analysis of findings, and, along with Margaret Baker and other members of the Center's technical staff, assisted in the preparation of computer tapes and codebooks and the processing of data. We also profited greatly from the many discerning comments on the manuscript we received from Larry Bartels, Robert Kagan, Austin Ranney, Eric Smith, Mark Westlye, and Joseph White.

The formidable job of converting computer output into finished tables, and of typing countless research memoranda, notes, and manuscript drafts, fell chiefly to Roberta Friedman, who handled these tasks with exceptional skill, speed, and intelligence. We are equally grateful to Carol McKevitt, who had major responsibility for the maintenance of files, record keeping, the preparation of graphs, and the management of library materials. Carol Cantor has also been helpful in checking and typing tables, footnotes, and other materials in the course of publication.

Parts of Chapter 8 appeared in modified form in "Patterns of Support for Democratic and Capitalist Values" (written with Dennis Chong), *British Journal of Political Science* 13 (October 1983), 401–440.

We owe a particular debt to the Gallup Organization, to its former president, Irving Crespi, and to his successor, Arthur Keiser, for their cooperation in selecting national cross-section samples of the general population for three of our surveys and delivering a copy of our questionnaire to each of the respondents in these samples. The Gallup Organization also helped to identify and enlist the cooperation of a large sample of opinion leaders from some 300 communities across the nation. Some of the data reported in this volume are drawn from a survey of attitudes toward civil liberties that was conducted, with the assistance of the Gallup Organization, under a grant made to Herbert McClosky by the Russell Sage Foundation.

None of these benefactors should be held to account for any failings that readers may encounter in this volume. We alone bear that responsibility.

Herbert McClosky
John Zaller

Contents

Figures

Tables

1 The Foundations of the American Ethos: Capitalism and Democracy

Two major traditions of belief, capitalism and democracy, have dominated the life of the American nation from its inception. Whether these beliefs are described as the *American creed,* the *Lockean settlement,* the *American consensus,* or, as we prefer, the *American ethos,* it is clear that capitalist and democratic values have strongly influenced the course and character of American development, and that they continue to serve as the authoritative values of the nation's political culture.

Yet, despite their central importance in American life, the values of the ethos are often in conflict. Some of the conflicts arise within the same strand of the ethos—for example, the conflict between the democratic values of majority rule and minority rights. Most, however, occur between the two major strands of the ethos—between the values of capitalism on the one side and democracy on the other. In our view, the tension that exists between capitalist and democratic values is a definitive feature of American life that has helped to shape the ideological divisions of the nation's politics.

Our aim in this book is to trace the evolution of capitalist and democratic values in American history, to explain the conflicts that have developed around them, and, by drawing on several decades of public opinion research, to show what modern Americans think about capitalism and democracy. We shall also try to illuminate the vital role played by "opinion elites"—the politically active or influential—in clarifying the values of the ethos, in resolving conflicts among these values, and in setting normative standards that members of the general public can learn and adopt as their own.

The values embodied in capitalism and democracy are, in their general form at least, so familiar to most of us that they require little exposition. Both the theory and the practice of democracy rest on the notion that all people possess equal worth and have the right to share in their own governance—to rule themselves either directly or through leaders of their own choosing. The ruled, in short, must consent to their rulers, who are in turn accountable to the governed. Democracy also aims to protect the governed against arbitrary authority and requires that rulers observe "due process" in the enforcement of law. It also, of course, includes respect for freedom of speech, press, assembly, and worship. These rights are valued not only as manifestations of each individual's worth, but as liberties essential to the process by which consent and accountability are exercised. All—the ruled as well as the rulers—are equal before the law and are supposed to enjoy equal rights and, as far as possible, equal opportunities.

The values and practices associated with capitalism are equally familiar: they include private ownership of the means of production, the pursuit of profit by self-interested entrepreneurs, and the right to unlimited gain through economic effort. In its "ideal" formulation, capitalism also stresses competition among producers, a substantial measure of laissez-faire, and market determination of production, distribution, and economic reward. Certain notions from individualist doctrine and the so-called Protestant ethic, such as an emphasis on achievement and hard work, are also widely regarded as part of the capitalist creed.

Despite their differences, capitalism and democracy evolved side by side as part of a common protest against the inequities and petty tyrannies of Old World monarchism, mercantilism, and the remnants of feudalism. Both aimed to free the individual from the dead hand of traditional restraints and to limit the power of the rich and well-born to exploit the less privileged. In part because of their common origins, the two traditions share many values, foremost among them a commitment to freedom and individualism, limited government, equality before the law, and rational—as opposed to feudal or merely traditional—modes of

decision making. Despite the transformation of the United States
from a dependent colony to a free and independent nation, from
a largely rural and sparsely populated society to one that is predominantly urban, industrial, and heavily populated, and despite
the recurrent traumas of having to absorb into the economy and
the body politic millions of immigrant aliens from almost every
part of the world, the traditions of democracy and capitalism
have maintained their role as the major constituents of the
American civic culture.

Louis Hartz, for example, has argued that capitalism and democracy constitute a "liberal tradition" that is fundamental to
American history and experience: "... where the aristocracies,
peasantries, and proletariats of Europe are missing, where virtually everyone ... has the mentality of an independent entrepreneur, two national impulses are bound to make themselves felt:
the impulse toward democracy and the impulse toward capitalism."[1] Clinton Rossiter has described the American political tradition in essentially similar terms, except that he emphasizes the
paramount influence of democratic values in American society:
"There has been in a doctrinal sense, only one America. We have
debated fiercely, but as men who agreed on fundamentals ...
The American political tradition is basically a liberal tradition
... its articles of faith, a sort of American Holy Writ, are per-
fectability, progress, liberty, equality, democracy, and individualism."[2]

Richard Hofstadter agrees that American society is essentially
democratic, but he emphasizes to a greater extent than Rossiter
the importance of capitalist influences in the nation's political
tradition:

> The fierceness of the political struggles in American history
> has often been misleading; for the range of vision embraced
> by the primary contestants in the major parties has always
> been bounded by the horizons of property and enterprise.
> However much at odds on specific issues, the major political
> traditions have shared a belief in the rights of property, the
> philosophy of economic individualism, the values of compe-
> tition; they have accepted the economic virtues of capitalist
> culture as necessary qualities of man ... American traditions
> also show a strong bias in favor of egalitarian democracy, but

it has been a democracy in cupidity rather than a democracy in fraternity.[3]

Although Rossiter, a conservative, was attempting to explain the absence of a strong conservative tradition in America, and Hofstadter, writing from a "somewhat . . . left" perspective, was seeking to explain the absence of a strong radical left tradition in America, both believe that the values of democracy and capitalism lie at the heart of the American ethos. Reflecting the importance of traditional values to American politics, Samuel Huntington has observed that "for most peoples, national identity is the product of a long process of historical evolution involving common ancestors, common experiences, common ethnic background, common language, common culture, and usually common religion. National identity is thus organic in character. Such, however, is not the case in the United States. American nationalism has been defined in political rather than organic terms. The political ideas of the American Creed have been the basis of national identity."[4]

We are not suggesting, of course, that the United States has been free of ideological disagreement. Yet, to a striking degree, ideological conflicts have taken place within the boundaries of the democratic and capitalist traditions. Among liberals and the left, many of whom are unenthusiastic about capitalism, only a handful have actually favored its abolition; while conservatives, though often worried about the danger of "too much democracy," have nonetheless accepted the principal values of the democratic tradition. Thus capitalism and democracy have always commanded broad support as the authoritative values of the nation's political culture. They determine in large measure what kinds of arguments about public affairs Americans find fair, reasonable, and attractive, what kinds they do not, and hence what kinds of arguments one dares to make (or is better advised not to make). The values of the two traditions serve, in effect, to legitimate some issues and to delegitimate others. They may mute or soften conflicts reflecting deep-seated differences by denying credibility to their respective spokesmen, or they may create and perpetuate conflicts that might not otherwise exist. And in the long run, they can nourish some kinds of political change and impede others.

Witness the influence of traditional American values on the turbulent politics of the 1960s. Social and political protests that sought to alter or (in some cases) sweep away important institutions and practices in American life were commonplace in that period. In retrospect, however, it appears that the protesters were successful only to the extent that their challenges could be buttressed by—or at least made consistent with—traditional American values. Their demands for the popular control of large corporations, for example, made little headway in the face of the traditional American attachment to capitalism. Their unruly modes of protest—mass confrontation, urban guerrilla tactics, and occasional violence—were often counterproductive in a society accustomed to the democratic principles of free elections, peaceful debate, and orderly opposition. To the extent, however, that the causes championed by the protesters of the 1960s and 1970s were consonant with the values of the ethos, they helped to bring about important changes. One can argue, in fact, that some of the "new issues" of the 1960s represented, in reality, efforts to extend certain values of the traditional ethos to new groups and new contexts. These issues included a concern for greater equality (women's rights and racial discrimination), political dissent (protests against the nation's participation in war), personal freedom (abortion, homosexual rights), and opposition to traditional forms of social control (the counterculture). Long after the atmosphere of confrontation had dissipated and the era of militancy had subsided, concern for these issues—a concern anchored in the values of the ethos—remained strong.

This argument suggests that values such as liberty and equality, although deeply rooted in the American tradition, are nevertheless able to stimulate intense assaults on conventional practice. Indeed, Samuel Huntington, among others, has argued that over the past 200 years traditional values have often inspired attacks on the status quo:

> Prevailing ideas of the American creed have included liberalism, individualism, equality, constitutionalism, rights against the state. They have been opposed to hierarchy, discipline, government, organization, and specialization. The major periods of fundamental change in American history have occurred when social forces have emerged to reinvigorate the creed and hence stimulate new attacks on estab-

lished authority. Such a confrontation took place during the Jacksonian period with the attack on the undemocratic elements of the constitutional system, at the time of the Civil War with the opposition to the extension of slavery and the slave system in the southern states, and in the 1890's with the populist and progressive responses to the rise of industrial corporations. The confrontation between ideology and institutions in postindustrial society thus fits into a well-established American pattern.[5]

It is true, of course, that the United States has never fully lived up to the ideals of its democratic and capitalist creeds. Yet one should not infer from this, as some do, that traditional ideals have a negligible influence on American politics. Failure to live up to the values of the ethos is likely to engender guilt, discomfort, and dissatisfaction.

In the treatment of blacks, for example, the nation has obviously violated almost every principle of its democratic tradition. Yet democratic values have never lost their capacity to induce guilt among whites and to evoke criticism of the status quo. Jefferson's well-known qualms about his dual status as slave owner and champion of human equality eloquently typify the conflicts experienced by many less prominent Americans when the values of the ethos have been violated. As Jefferson wrote: "I tremble for my country when I realize that God is just; that his justice cannot sleep forever; that considering numbers, nature, and the natural means only, a revolution of the wheel of fortune, an exchange of situation, is among possible events ... The Almighty has no attribute which can side with us in such a contest."[6]

Throughout American history, thoughtful Americans have always known that their treatment of blacks was indefensible, a fact that has made them more susceptible to appeals for reform than they might otherwise have been. When Gunnar Myrdal conducted his classic study of American race relations in the 1940s, he concluded that the black man's greatest ally in the struggle for equality was the white man's bad conscience over the nation's failure to live up to the ideals of the American creed.[7]

One can detect the powerful subterranean pull of traditional values in many other instances in which they are violated. For example, it is striking that although the United States has lapsed into episodes of political intolerance at several points in its history—the "McCarthyism" of the 1950s is one of the more recent examples—it has almost always rebounded from them by repudiating the people responsible for the intolerance and proclaiming anew its dedication to liberty.

However vital the roles of democracy and capitalism have been in American life, not all of the values incorporated into the ethos are mutually consistent and harmonious. Value conflicts, after all, are endemic to all complex societies, including the United States. Among the most important of these, as we have suggested, are the conflicts that arise from the differing perspectives of the two traditions. Capitalism is primarily concerned with maximizing private profit, while democracy aims at maximizing freedom, equality, and the public good. From this difference, others follow. Capitalism tends to value each individual according to the scarcity of his talents and his contribution to production; democracy attributes unique but roughly equivalent value to *all* people. Capitalism stresses the need for a reward system that encourages the most talented and industrious individuals to earn and amass as much wealth as possible; democracy tries to ensure that all people, even those who lack outstanding talents and initiative, can at least gain a decent livelihood. Capitalism holds that the free market is not only the most efficient but also the fairest mechanism for distributing goods and services; democracy upholds the rights of popular majorities to override market mechanisms when necessary to alleviate social and economic distress.

These differences are not easily reconciled. As Arthur Okun, an economist and former chairman of President Johnson's Council of Economic Advisers, has written:

> American society proclaims the worth of every human being. All citizens are guaranteed equal justice and equal political rights. . . . As American citizens, we are all members of the same club.
>
> Yet at the same time, our institutions say "find a job or go hungry," "succeed or suffer." They prod us to get ahead of our neighbors economically after telling us to stay in line socially. They award prizes that allow the big winners to feed their pets better than the losers can feed their children.
>
> Such is the double standard of a capitalist democracy, pro-

fessing and pursuing an egalitarian political and social system and simultaneously generating gaping disparities in economic well-being.[8]

Some readers will surely take issue with Okun's argument. For example, some 87 percent of the "opinion leaders" (politically active or influential respondents) in one of our surveys asserted that "our freedom depends on the free enterprise system."[9] Milton Friedman, one of the most renowned advocates of this point of view, argues that if government ever abolished the right to own property, to manufacture and sell goods in the free market, and to determine the course of one's own economic life, citizens would become so dependent upon the state for their livelihood that they would soon lose their democratic right to self-government as well.[10]

Although views similar to Friedman's are expressed by many proponents of capitalism, the historical record shows that aspects of the two traditions are frequently incompatible with each other. Modern industrial capitalism, on the one side, has spawned powerful private interests and concentrations of wealth and capital that have sometimes threatened the integrity of the democratic process. Popular majorities, on the other side, have demanded a variety of government regulations—on the uses of property, the protection of the environment, the distribution of income, standards of product safety, among many others—that greatly impinge on the workings of the free market and the private enterprise system.

One of the principal concerns of this book is the documentation and analysis of such value conflicts. A second important concern, but one that is often neglected by analysts of American political culture, is the vital role played by opinion elites in articulating and promoting the values of the ethos. Pondering the importance of elites in helping to maintain a democratic system, V. O. Key, Jr., speculated that "perhaps a healthy democratic system must contain within itself a suitable strain of political aristocracy":

The strain of "aristocracy" within an operating democracy consists of diverse sorts of people, not of a social or an economic upper crust. Broadly, it includes the political influentials and the political activists ... the journalists, the publicists, and others concerned with public information and education . . . [as well as] those individuals who seem to be sprinkled throughout the social hierarchy who pay heed to public affairs, who have opinions, and who in turn shape the opinions of others. All these sorts of persons, who constitute a small proportion of the population, perform an important role in the formation of public opinion, in the creation of support for public policy, and in the maintenance of the morale of the citizenry. I do not mean to intimate that those I have labeled the political activists constitute a cohesive ruling class. They are by no means unified and they hold disparate views. They are of many types, some of them unsavory. But by their attention to public affairs and by their activities, they perform, as a class, a special role in the politics of a democracy. In the division of political labor others fill a far more passive role.[11]

Although our data underscore Key's observation that elites are "diverse sorts of people" with diverse political views, they also show that elites share certain characteristics and perspectives that distinguish them from the more "passive" members of the citizenry. While most members of the general public are preoccupied with the problems of daily life—earning a living, raising a family, recreation, and so forth—the political elite are characterized by a more intense and continuing concern with the affairs of the larger community. Hence they exert a disproportionate influence on the operation of the political system. By reason of their greater involvement in the public life of the nation, the elites also have a better grasp of how the system works and exhibit higher overall levels of support for its values than do members of the mass public. (These observations can be inferred from previous research and will be further borne out by the data we shall present.) Thus opinion leaders (or elites) become for most purposes the principal carriers and expositors of the nation's political creed.

To suggest, however, that opinion leaders are the major repositories of the traditional value system is not to say that they are custodians of a fixed and determinate body of cultural influences. The values of the American ethos are, after all, somewhat general and open-ended and do not always offer guidance on the details of public policy. Moreover, as we have observed, those values

sometimes conflict with one another, and therefore it may be unclear in any given case which of two competing values ought to be
pursued. Thus, despite the vital role of the ethos in American life,
it leaves many specific issues and problems unresolved. For example, how much freedom, equality, or concern for the rights of the
accused is practical if one hopes to retain a well-ordered and
thriving democracy? When, if ever, does an unregulated market
become so costly to an economy that its effect on the general welfare is largely adverse?

Such questions require specific answers, and it is the people
who are most intensely involved in the nation's decision-making
processes who play the major role in answering them. In doing so,
they help to set the norms or standards of belief that other, less active members of the general public tend to learn and adopt as
their own.

Consider the notion of freedom of expression. This value, of
course, is a vital part of the American ethos, guaranteed by the
First Amendment's prohibitions against the abridgement of free
speech, press, assembly, and religion. Yet the exact meaning of a
right like "freedom of speech" is by no means obvious. As the history of the term shows, it sanctions some forms of speech but not
others. It authorizes, for example, debate over political issues, but
not slander of private citizens, incitement to violence, or, for that
matter, public use of obscene language.

The task of interpreting the First Amendment has fallen not to
the mass of ordinary citizens but to leading members of the legal
and political communities—to legislators, civil servants and political appointees, participants in civic organizations, academics,
journalists, and other commentators on public affairs. Such individuals have discussed the meaning of that amendment in law
journals, legal briefs, court opinions, political tracts, newspaper
columns, public speeches, congressional debates, and administrative memoranda. Most of these discussions, of course, have been
open to the public; however, the vast majority of the public (and,
for that matter, many members of the opinion elite) are too preoccupied with other affairs and are, in any event, too little trained
in the fine points of legal and political discourse to attend closely
to debates on the First Amendment, much less to participate actively in them. As a result, the meaning of a right like "free

speech"—by its very nature an abstract notion—comes to depend heavily on the reasoning and interpretation it receives from relevant segments of the opinion elite.

Although members of the public, of course, are capable of grasping the basic meaning of such rights as freedom of speech and press without the explicit guidance of legal and political elites, the right of free expression (or any other right) is never unencumbered but invariably comes into conflict with other cherished values, such as law and order, property, religious freedom, privacy, or community standards of "decency." Such conflicts cannot effectively be resolved without the most careful examination—the sort of scrutiny one can scarcely expect from individuals who have given these matters little or no thought.

Opinion leaders, of course, often disagree among themselves about the "correct" interpretation of the values of the ethos. Such disagreements are typically argued out in the context of overarching principles or ideologies. In the early years of the Republic, for example, men like Jefferson and Madison, on the one side, and Adams and Hamilton, on the other, developed conflicting views about issues such as equality, civil liberties, states' rights, and the proper role of government in human affairs. Their divergent outlooks hardened into ideologies that became the basis for important divisions on many public questions. Then as now, the great mass of citizens could choose between competing ideologies, but they could scarcely be considered their creators.

As these observations suggest, opinion leaders play a critical role in the process by which ordinary citizens learn political norms. Citizens, however, differ in their capacity for this kind of social learning. Those who are more interested in political events and closer to the mainstreams of opinion are more likely to encounter, and hence to understand, the principles on which the system operates and the values espoused by the elites. Others, more circumscribed in their social roles and experiences, more parochial in their perspectives, or perhaps less discerning in their powers of observation, are less familiar with the workings of the system and its norms. Their interest in public affairs is narrowly limited and, at best, intermittent. Unless their own interests are concretely engaged, their participation in the political system is limited to the act of voting—and approximately half of them do not even do that. Many of them find public life profoundly mysterious, a confusion of remote and inscrutable events that make it difficult for them to learn the norms embodied in the political culture.

By "learning," in this context, we have in mind not formal education or classroom instruction (although these may also play a role), but a more informal process by which individuals acquire their beliefs through interaction with their political environments. This kind of learning, which may be described as "social learning," involves *exposure* to a variety of social, psychological, and cognitive influences. For effective social learning to occur, one must be aware of the values and behavior transmitted from one generation to the next and endorsed by the political culture. This type of learning further requires that one be able to *comprehend* in some measure what is implicit in sophisticated political and economic discourse. It also requires that one be able to sort out the countless fragments of political thought and opinion encountered in the course of everyday life, discriminating between those that help to define the political culture and those the culture rejects or finds irrelevant. Finally, social learning involves a willingness and ability to *accept* or internalize the norms intrinsic to the prevailing political culture.

We can now summarize these observations as follows. The values of capitalism and democracy are the principal components of the American political culture. They guide American political policies and practices in certain directions by influencing most Americans—opinion leaders as well as members of the general public—to be favorably disposed toward certain objectives and negatively disposed toward others. The values of the ethos, however, are not in themselves sufficient to determine policy. The values of capitalism and democracy, as usually stated, are too general and abstract, and too often in conflict with one another, to provide more than general guidance on specific issues. Elites perform the vital task of interpreting traditional values, resolving conflicts among them, and translating them into concrete norms and public policies. To the extent that members of the general public pay attention to politics, they will tend to espouse the same interpretations of traditional values that opinion leaders do.

These observations about our political process constitute the organizing principles for the research and analysis presented in this book and inspire several of the hypotheses we attempt to test. Before proceeding to the findings of our research, however, we need to clarify several matters of definition and research methodology.

Opinion Leaders and the Mass Public

Our use of the terms *opinion leaders, influentials,* and *political elites* in the present study has little to do with traditional European notions of a "ruling class," a political oligarchy that monopolizes power, an upper economic stratum that controls the nation's wealth, a "privileged class" stratified by birth or caste, or even a so-called military-industrial complex. We consider someone to be a member of the political elite or an opinion leader if he or she exerts disproportionate influence on public opinion by virtue of greater political activity or knowledge. Such influence may arise from participation in government or the political parties, from activity in the dissemination of political ideas, or from other positions of prestige and visibility in the political or social structure. Our definition of the elite would therefore include citizens who join political organizations, work for the adoption of legislation and other public policies, or participate in campaigns for the election of candidates. It would include judges, lawmakers, local officials, newspaper editors, party activists, and leaders of civic organizations who, though they may not participate in party politics, nonetheless make decisions and articulate views that influence the public opinions of large numbers of people. It would also include leaders in the fields of education, business, labor, law enforcement, civil rights, political and social reform, fraternal organizations, and others who help to formulate and decide public policies. The American elite, in sum, is a highly open and permeable body of people active in roles that influence public opinion and shape public affairs.

Given this understanding of what it means to be an opinion leader, an "influential," or a member of the political elite, how does one go about locating such individuals for the purpose of studying them? Unfortunately for the "neatness" of a research design that includes elites as well as the mass public, only a small number who qualify as members of the political elite will turn up in a cross-section survey of the general population. Although many Americans may vote in elections or seek to influence the votes of their neighbors, relatively few engage in the more demanding forms of participation or fulfill roles that would warrant their classification as opinion leaders.

Nor do we know of an economical way of identifying the members of the political elite with enough precision to permit the selection of a statistically random sample of them (or of their opinions). This difficulty arises partly from the vagueness inherent in any operational definition of the political elite (since one cannot always be certain about who exerts "disproportionate influence" on public affairs) and partly from the extreme dispersion of elites within a society as large and complex as ours. Unlike the general population, whose members can be randomly drawn from a known universe and whose characteristics can, if necessary, be checked against census data, there is no known, agreed-upon universe of elite members from which a genuine random sample can be drawn. Strategies for sampling elite opinion do, however, exist. One can, for example, first identify associational and vocational groups whose members are unusually active in public life. By sampling as randomly as possible from the membership of a large number of such groups, one may obtain a rough catalogue of the views held by the nation's opinion elites.

With this possibility in mind, we have collected data by surveying a variety of elite populations (along with mass opinion data from parallel surveys of the general public). Among these surveys is a 1958 study of Political Affiliations and Beliefs (PAB), conducted by Herbert McClosky, which included some 3,020 delegates to the 1956 Democratic and Republican conventions. Since attendance at party conventions was at that time a reward for high standing or long service in the party, we believe that nearly all of the respondents in this survey qualify as opinion leaders or members of the political elite. (With minor modifications, the same questionnaire was used to survey the views of a national cross-section sample of the general public.)

Much of the data we shall present in this volume are drawn from a series of surveys conducted between 1975 and 1977 on the Opinions and Values of Americans (OVS). In addition to a national cross-section sample of 938 respondents in the general population (to whom our questionnaires were distributed by Gallup interviewers), the OVS study included 2,142 members of the political elite drawn randomly from twenty organizations and groups widely known for their ideological commitment and activity (their political views ranged across the spectrum from the liberal left to the conservative right). A second set of 845 elite respondents was chosen randomly from the membership lists of five different nonpartisan elite subgroups—*Who's Who in America, Black Who's Who in America,* the Conference of Editorial Writers, the League of Women Voters, and Common Cause. Since the members of the last three groups are directly concerned with public affairs, we feel little hesitancy about including them among our sample of political opinion leaders. Membership in *Who's Who,* of course, signifies outstanding achievement in some field of endeavor—science, literature, medicine, entertainment, and so forth—rather than in public affairs per se. People who achieve extraordinary status in any professional field, nevertheless, can (and often do) exert above-average influence in politics—when they wish to do so. To ensure that this criterion was met, we screened the two *Who's Who* samples to exclude individuals engaged in activities remote from public affairs (for example, athletics or entertainment). The remainder, we believe, can be fairly considered members of the political elite.

The third major national survey from which we will present data, the Civil Liberties study, was conducted in 1978–1979 with the cooperation of the Gallup Organization. This survey also included a large national cross-section sample of 1,993 respondents in the general population and an additional sample of 1,891 community leaders selected according to our instructions by Gallup interviewers from the same 300 sampling units used for our national general population sample. Included in the community elite sample were leading members of local government, the press, the courts, the professions, education, business, labor, and civic associations. Since all were chosen because of their prominence or their public activities, or both, the vast majority of the respondents in the community leader samples would clearly qualify as members of the opinion elite.[12]

Although we cannot be certain that the opinion leaders surveyed in these studies are, in a strictly statistical sense, representative of the entire universe of political elites, we have nevertheless sampled from a wide range of elite subpopulations. It will become clear that the opinions and attitudes of elite respondents (though selected by different procedures) tend to differ from those of the general public in essentially the same ways for each of the four sets of elites surveyed. This fact encourages us to believe that the views expressed by our elite samples broadly reflect the views held by the opinion leaders of this country.

As noted, the principal source of data for this book is our survey of the Opinions and Values of Americans, which utilized a 24-page mailback questionnaire. In addition to the usual demographic and "face-sheet" questions, the OVS questionnaire contained 267 items that were presented in random order and covered a wide variety of opinions and attitudes on matters of public interest. Particular emphasis was given to ideological and other major political, social, and economic outlooks, although questions were also included that assess key personality dispositions as well as political participation, knowledge, and sophistication. While each item in the OVS questionnaire is self-contained and can be analyzed in its own right, it is also part of a cluster of items that permits us to form scales and assign scale scores to each respondent by cumulating his answers to the questions in a given cluster. The democracy scale employed in this study, for example, has 44 items, the capitalism scale, 28. Each set of items in turn can be broken down into several subscales. (For additional information on empirical methods, see Appendix I.)

Political Culture

This book is, in a sense, a study of the political culture of the United States—its principal values, their sources and historical development, and the extent of popular support they enjoy. The notion of political culture has been used to account for the stability of political regimes,[13] for differences between political systems,[14] and variations among preindustrial societies.[15] So far, however, social scientists have not been able to agree on a common definition of the concept.[16] In the absence of such agreement, we shall adhere to a relatively straightforward use of the term. In this study, political culture will be viewed as a set of widely shared beliefs, values, and norms concerning the relationship of citizens to their government and to one another in matters affecting public affairs.

In arguing that the traditions of capitalism and democracy are the principal components of the American ethos, we do not mean to imply that they are the only elements of the country's political culture. Beliefs about progress and the perfectibility of man, patriotism, faith in rationalism, compassion for the needy, and religion are examples of other values with important political ramifications—some of which we shall discuss as the occasion arises. We believe, however, that the ideas associated with capitalism and democracy constitute the principal components of American political culture.

Nor, by emphasizing the role of political values, do we mean to deny that material interests play a vital role in influencing political decisions, or that such interests may have a considerable impact on the formulation and tenacity of certain political values and traditions. Obviously, a society's material conditions, its levels of technology, and its distribution of wealth strongly affect the operation of its political system. But a society's ideas are also vital to its development. As Max Weber so convincingly argued, even ideas about religion can help to shape business practices and the forms of economic life. It clearly matters greatly to the political life of a nation whether its prevailing ideas favor democracy or authoritarianism, laissez-faire or socialism, civil rights or segregation. Cultural traditions, once formed, take on a life of their own and can influence events in countless ways. In this book we focus primarily on beliefs and values, not because they are the entire story but because without them the story could not be understood at all.[17]

2 The Libertarian Tradition

No value in the American ethos is more revered than freedom. The rights of individuals to speak, write, assemble, and worship freely, to engage in occupations and pastimes of their own choosing, and to be secure from arbitrary restraints on their conduct are central to the nation's democratic tradition. Equality and popular sovereignty, of course, are given their due, but liberty is more deeply embedded in the nation's system of values than any of the others. As Clinton Rossiter has observed: "We have always been a nation obsessed with liberty. Liberty over authority, freedom over responsibility, rights over duties—these are our historic preferences. From the days of Williams and Wise to those of Eisenhower and Kennedy, Americans have talked about practically nothing else but liberty. Not the good man, but the free man has been the measure of all things in this 'sweet land of liberty'; not national glory but individual liberty has been the object of political authority and the test of its worth."[1]

A recent Gallup survey not only provides evidence of the American preference for liberty but enables us to compare American attitudes with those prevailing in other nations. When asked whether personal freedom or equality was more important, Americans preferred freedom over equality by a margin of 72 percent to 20 percent. In Western Europe, by comparison, only 49 percent chose freedom while 35 percent chose equality.[2]

The American attachment to liberty can be traced, in part, to the political and intellectual tradition inherited from Great Britain, which emphasized the need to limit the power of the British monarchy through the rule of law. The bearers of this tradition—originally the British nobility, and later Protestant nonconformists and the rising middle classes—had little use for radical egalitarianism but found the notion of individual freedom to their advantage. The British concern for freedom made its way across the Atlantic, where it gained influence in the eighteenth century and was increasingly invoked in the growing conflicts between the British government and the colonists.[3] The generation of leaders who led the struggle for independence prized freedom not only as a political value but also as a value that reflected the dignity and worth of human beings and made possible the democratic process by which citizens choose their leaders and hold them accountable through free elections. The libertarian convictions of the Founders were clearly reflected in the structure of the national government they established in 1787—a relatively small, internally partitioned federal authority with carefully delimited powers. Their libertarianism could above all be discerned in the Bill of Rights, which severely restricted the power of the federal government to infringe individual liberties in such matters as speech, press, religion, and assembly.

Another reason for the extraordinary American emphasis on freedom arises (contrary to widespread opinion) from the country's attachment to capitalism. Although capitalism is obviously incompatible with the more radical forms of equality, such as equality of economic rewards, it is quite compatible with most forms of individual freedom. Indeed, some kinds of freedom are integral features of capitalism as ideally conceived. Capitalism presupposes, for example, freedom of competition, freedom of exchange between producers and consumers, buyers and sellers. It emphasizes freedom to choose one's vocation, to engage in the production and sale of such goods and services as one sees fit, and to acquire as much wealth as the free market makes possible.

Thus the American celebration of freedom emphasizes several forms of liberty—political, religious, moral, and economic. We shall concentrate at this point, however, on the noneconomic dimensions of freedom. We begin by asking whether one can conclude from the importance of freedom in the American system of values that Americans are actually free to think as they wish and to behave as they choose. Can they in fact advocate revolution, criticize the government, express unconventional ideas, hold unpopular parades and assemblies, and worship (or refuse to worship) God in any fashion they like—all with complete immunity from formal or informal sanctions?

The answer would seem to be "Yes, but . . ." When pressed, most Americans will admit that their society, like every other, tries to impose on its members its own conception of morality and its own standards of conduct. Most, moreover, would agree with the need for doing so. "Liberty is not license" is a refrain that has been familiar throughout the nation's history. But when does liberty become license? J. R. Pennock has outlined an approach which, in one form or another, recurs in many efforts to reconcile the idea of individual liberty with the need to constrain "license." If thieves were free to steal, he argues, the freedom of others to own property would be jeopardized. In prohibiting theft, therefore, society actually enhances the freedom of the majority of its members who are not thieves.[4] The principle here is that every person is free to act as he pleases, so long as his exercise of freedom does not violate the equal rights of others.

This standard, however, has often been violated as well. Throughout American history, individuals who have ignored or attacked society's values have suffered the wrath of their fellow citizens, even when infringements on the rights of others were not really at issue. Consider, for example, the public reaction to flag burning as a form of political protest. Although this was one of the more harmless tactics used by the antiwar radicals of the 1960s, 72 percent of the American public and 61 percent of the community leaders surveyed by us said as late as 1978 that someone "who publicly burns or spits on the flag" should be "fined or punished in some way." (See Table 2-17 later in the chapter.) Many Americans, clearly, are unwilling to permit the symbols and values of their society to be openly attacked or ridiculed—even when no one is actually injured by such "symbolic speech."

Why this reaction in a country that professes to venerate freedom? One explanation, accepted by many social scientists and supported by an impressive body of research, is that intolerance is a product of institutionalized prejudice, and of such psychological difficulties as rigidity, fear of out-groups, and hostility. Although our own data provide additional evidence for this point of view,[5] we do not believe that all feelings of outrage toward those who flout basic social values stem from social and psychological maladjustments. Such responses to nonconformity are, to some extent, products of forces that operate in every society to maintain it on a familiar, steady course. The point is so obvious it may easily be overlooked: all societies have certain tasks to perform, such as the coordination of productive efforts, the maintenance of order and stability, and the enforcement of rules governing the uses of power, property, rewards, and punishments. Every society, therefore, attempts to channel and control individual behavior. Except in extreme cases, physical coercion is a clumsy and inefficient method for accomplishing this. Far more effective are the informal pressures arising from widely shared feelings of right and wrong. These pressures, often reinforced by political and religious authorities, sometimes take the form of popular intolerance of nonconformity.

America's traditional attachment to liberty must, then, be evaluated in light of the elementary fact that no society is, or can be, absolutely free. A society professing special reverence for liberty is thus bound to experience a profound tension between the forces of social cohesion and the ideal of unfettered individual freedom.

In this chapter we examine this tension as it manifests itself in three domains: religious freedom, freedom of speech, press, and assembly, and individual freedom in matters pertaining to sex and morals. In each domain we shall see that the scope of liberty has increased dramatically over the course of the nation's history. Although various influences have undoubtedly contributed to the increase in freedom, we shall pay particular attention to two of them. The first is the decline of a theocratic attitude toward society and its replacement by a more secular view. This development has made new ideas seem less dangerous and shocking, and hence easier to tolerate. The second influence has been the nation's libertarian tradition as embodied in the Constitution, legislation, court decisions, and political discourse. This tradition has induced many Americans to tolerate ideas and practices they nevertheless dislike intensely.[6]

The Expansion of Religious Freedom

Although the first Puritan colonists were refugees from religious persecution, they scarcely intended their new home to be a haven for moral or religious diversity. They sought, on the contrary, to make New England an exemplar of religious orthodoxy—a "city upon a hill," which would be known throughout the world for its pious devotion to the one true faith. Religious freedom obviously had no place in this plan. As Perry Miller has written:

> The government of Massachusetts, and of Connecticut as well, was a dictatorship, not of a single tyrant, or of an economic class, or of a political faction, but of the holy and regenerate. Those who did not hold with the ideals entertained by the righteous, or who believed God had preached other principles, or who desired that in religious belief, morality, and ecclesiastical preferences all men should be left at liberty to do as they wished—such persons had every liberty, as Nathaniel Ward said, to stay away from New England. If they did come, they were expected to keep their opinions to themselves; if they discussed them in public or attempted to act upon them they were exiled; if they came back, they were cast out again; if they still came back, as did four Quakers, they were hanged on Boston Common. And from a Puritan point of view, it was good riddance.[7]

The New England Puritans believed they had formed a covenant with God whereby they pledged their total obedience to His will, in return for which He would care for their needs. Anyone who violated this covenant stirred God's anger, thereby risking not only personal damnation but calamity for the entire community.

The Puritans, to be sure, were not entirely typical of early American settlers. Yet the differences between them and their contemporaries were often smaller than one might suppose. Blasphemy and the breaking of the Sabbath, for example, were civil offenses not only in Massachusetts and Connecticut but in all the early colonies. Nor, except in a few settlements such as Maryland, was religious diversity tolerated. Typically, the members of a religious sect would establish their own colony and then prohibit members of other churches from settling there.

Given these beginnings, how can one account for the development of America into a nation which accepts moral and religious freedom as the established—even the celebrated—norm?

Perhaps the most widely cited factor in the growth of religious freedom has been the multiplication of diverse sects and creeds. In a country lacking a powerful central authority, which accepted refugees of diverse religions and nationalities and which rapidly established settlements across a vast continent, it proved impossible to impose a single religious orthodoxy. Where numerous sects were forced to live side by side, a measure of toleration between groups became a practical necessity. Pressure toward religious toleration also came from overseas. After the Glorious Revolution of 1688, the British government instituted a policy of religious toleration at home, and it soon pressed for similar policies in its American colonies. But perhaps the most important influence in the long run was the increasingly secular and commercial nature of American society. A subtle turning point had already been reached in the early eighteenth century when, as Perry Miller has observed, Calvinist ministers began recommending piety not only because it was pleasing to God, but because it promoted economic order and prosperity. These trends toward secular preoccupations have continued down to the present. Most Americans still regard themselves as in some sense religious, but few still believe that they live under a special covenant with God. Even those who consider themselves religious rely primarily on scientific or secular modes of reasoning to explain human affairs. Most people now relate to one another not primarily as Congregationalists or Catholics, but as businessmen, lawyers, farmers, and workers, as rich or poor, educated or uneducated.

Survey data we have collected in recent decades clearly bear out the predominantly secular nature of American concerns. In the PAB survey conducted in 1958, for example, 58 percent of the general public and 67 percent of the political influentials said that "it doesn't matter to me what church a man belongs to, or whether or not he belongs to a church at all" (see Table 2-1). In contrast to the once-existing emphasis on religious homogeneity, a large majority of Americans now feel that uniformity of religious belief is undesirable. Seventy-three percent of the general public and 85 percent of the influentials in the OVS study said in 1976 that "the United States was meant to be . . . a country made up of many races, religions, and nationalities." Only a small minority thought that America was meant to be "a Christian nation."

Our data further suggest that even within the short span of the last fifteen years, there has been a perceptible drift toward greater acceptance of religious skepticism and diversity. The number of

Table 2-1   Attitudes toward religious diversity[a]

	General public	Influentials
1. It doesn't matter to me what church a man belongs to, or whether or not he belongs to a church at all.		
—Agree	58	67
—Disagree	42	33
	(N = 1,484)	(N = 3,020)
2. The United States was meant to be:		
—a Christian nation	20	8
—a country made up of many races, religions, and nationalities	73	85
—Decline to choose[b]	7	8
	(N = 938)	(N = 845)

Sources: question 1, Political Affiliations and Beliefs study, 1958; question 2, Opinions and Values of Americans survey, 1975–77.

a. In this and subsequent tables in this book, all figures are percentages. As a result of rounding, these percentages may not always sum to 100 percent.

b. In this and subsequent tables throughout this book, we have grouped within the "decline to choose" category all respondents who gave a "neither" or "undecided" answer to the question asked. Also included in the "decline to choose" category are the small number of respondents (usually fewer than 1 percent) who failed to answer the question.

Americans who believe that atheists are harmful to American life fell from 72 percent to 46 percent in the eight-year period ending in 1973.[8] One of our own more recent surveys found that hostility toward atheists may have declined even further: in 1978–1979, only 41 percent of the general public and 26 percent of the community influentials said that atheists are harmful to society.

Since, as these findings suggest, only a small minority continues to care deeply about purely theological differences, it is scarcely surprising that freedom of worship is largely taken for granted in modern America. The issue, in fact, is so widely considered to be settled that few poll takers now bother to ask questions about it. In our surveys we tried to test religious toleration at the margins by asking whether such unorthodox cultists as the followers of Hare Krishna and the so-called Moonies ought to be able to practice their religions freely. Even in these cases, however, only 18 percent of the general public and 11 percent of the community influentials would deny freedom of worship to "religious cults that the majority of people consider 'strange,' 'fanatical,' or 'weird.' " The great majority believes instead that the right to worship freely "applies to all religious groups, regardless of how extreme their beliefs are."

We are not claiming, of course, that freedom of religious conscience is universally accepted in the United States today. Many people, for example, still find atheism so deeply offensive that they are disposed to deny atheists rights that they readily grant to others. In a recent survey, we asked respondents whether several controversial groups—including atheists and Protestant revivalists—should be permitted to use a local civic auditorium for their meetings. Table 2–2 shows that far more respondents (68 percent) were willing to let Protestants use the hall than were willing to permit atheists to do so (17 percent). This difference of 51 percentage points suggests that, despite the widespread endorsement of religious freedom, intolerance may still flare up in American society when people's religious sensibilities are deeply offended.

To investigate this possibility, we have created a summary index that assesses each individual's degree of commitment to secular as opposed to religious values. The individual items included in this "religiosity index" are shown in Table 2–3, as scored by respondents at different levels of political sophistication. We note in passing that although the opinion leaders are almost as likely as the general public to describe themselves as "deeply" or "fairly" religious, they are less inclined than the general public to believe that God and religion are important for understanding and controlling everyday events. In this respect, the opinion leaders hold a more secular view of the world than do members of the general

Table 2–2   Differences in public support for the rights of atheists and Protestant revivalists (N = 1,993)

	Yes	No	Depends
Should a community allow its civic auditorium to be used by the following groups for the following purposes?			
—Atheists who want to preach against God and religion	17	70	13
—Protestant groups who want to hold a revival meeting	68	15	16

Source: Civil Liberties study, 1978–79.

Table 2-3   Effect of political sophistication on attitudes toward God and religion

	General public			Total general public (N = 929)	Total opinion leaders (N = 845)
	Low soph. (N = 309)	Middle soph. (N = 310)	High soph. (N = 310)		
1. How religious are you?					
—Deeply	17	17	17	17	16
—Fairly	56	50	48	50	37
—Not very religious	16	19	17	17	21
—Not at all religious	11	14	18	14	24
2. The best hope for the future of mankind lies in:					
—science and human reason	19	33	43	30	49
—faith in God	69	52	39	51	23
—Decline to choose	12	15	18	17	28
3. What happens to a man will mostly depend on:					
—mankind's own efforts	41	59	69	55	73
—the will of God	44	33	20	31	10
—Decline to choose	15	8	11	13	14
4. I believe that religion:					
—is largely old-fashioned and out of date	8	11	15	11	17
—can still answer most of today's problems	64	56	47	55	27
—Decline to choose	28	32	38	33	56

Source: Opinions and Values of Americans survey, 1975–77.

public. Similar differences turn up if we compare the most politically sophisticated members of the general public with the least sophisticated. (For a description of our measure of political sophistication, see Appendix I.) Although the sophisticated are almost as likely as the unsophisticated to consider themselves religious, they are much less inclined to believe that religion is important in determining the course of human affairs. This attitude may reflect, among other things, the greater exposure of sophisticated respondents to the thought and writings of the philosophers, social scientists, and other intellectuals who have played so important a role in developing and disseminating secular modes of thought.

After combining the items shown in Table 2–3 into a single index of religiosity, we divided our respondents into three groups:

those scoring in the top third of the mass distribution on the religiosity measure, those in the middle third, and those in the lowest third. As shown in Table 2–4, where we compare those who score high and low on this measure, such vestiges of religious intolerance as still exist in the United States are found disproportionately among those who remain most strongly committed to a religious view of the world.[9] The more emphasis people place on religion, the more likely they are to deny religious freedom to unorthodox sects and cults and to uphold the right of parents to remove their children forcibly from such cults. They are also more inclined to restrict the right of atheists to disseminate their views. The rights of Protestant revivalists, by contrast, were supported as strongly by highly religious respondents as by those with predominantly secular views of the world.

Our argument so far has focused on the growth of secular modes of thought. Yet this development is scarcely the only reason for the expansion of religious and moral freedom in America. One must also take into account the nation's tradition of libertarian values and, in particular, the embodiment of those values in the Bill of Rights. From its adoption in 1791 to the present, the Bill of Rights has remained the primary legal bulwark of individual liberty in the United States.

The Bill of Rights reflected the colonists' suspicion of government. Having recently fought a war to preserve certain rights from encroachment by the central government in London, many feared that in setting up a national government of their own, they might be imposing upon themselves a new, oppressive oligarchy. At the insistence of some of the state legislatures, they adopted a set of constitutional amendments (namely, the Bill of Rights) which guaranteed a number of individual rights and liberties and expressly prohibited the national government from infringing upon them.

Not all the Founders who opposed a strong central government, however, were equally concerned with maximizing individual liberty. Consider, in this regard, the First Amendment's provision that "Congress shall make no law respecting an establishment of religion, or prohibiting the free exercise thereof." Some members of the Congress who voted for this guarantee belonged to religious sects that not only used public tax monies to help finance their

Table 2–4 Effect of religiosity on support for freedom of conscience

	General public		Community influentials	
	Low relig. (N = 182)	High relig. (N = 467)	Low relig. (N = 130)	High relig. (N = 235)
1. The freedom of atheists to make fun of God and religion:				
—should be legally protected no matter who might be offended	50	15	73	41
—should not be allowed in a public place where religious groups gather	29	68	15	42
—Decline to choose	22	18	12	16
2. Freedom to worship as one pleases:				
—applies to all religious groups, regardless of how extreme their beliefs are	75	65	90	77
—was never meant to apply to religious cults that the majority of people consider "strange," fanatical, or "weird"	14	22	5	15
—Decline to choose	10	14	5	8
3. When a young woman joins an "offbeat" cult like the Moonies or Hare Krishnas, should her parents have the legal right to force her to leave the group and be "deprogrammed"?				
—No, because that would take away her individual freedom to practice any religion she chooses	23	10	46	21
—Yes, because parents have the right and duty to protect their children from influences they consider harmful	53	73	31	59
—Decline to choose	24	17	23	20
4. Should a community allow its civic auditorium to be used by atheists who want to preach against God and religion?				
—Yes	34	7	67	29
—No	49	87	25	57
—Decline to choose	17	6	8	14
5. Should a community allow its civic auditorium to be used by Protestant groups who want to hold a revival meeting?				
—Yes	70	70	71	72
—No	17	17	19	13
—Decline to choose	13	13	10	15

Source: Civil Liberties study, 1978–79.

operations but also favored state laws to punish blasphemy, compel church attendance, and otherwise help assure the moral rectitude of the citizenry. While the members of these sects wanted *state* support for religious activities at the local level, they feared that the *federal* government might try to set up an established church of its own. Their support for the "establishment" clause of the First Amendment, therefore, was motivated in part by their desire to keep the federal government from interfering with "established" religion at the local level.

Others of the Founders, however, including Jefferson, Madison, and Franklin, embraced freedom of religion partly because they had been deeply influenced by the libertarian philosophies of such European writers as Locke, Voltaire, and the French Encyclopedists. Most of these philosophers had argued that *no* government had the rightful authority to control the religious and political beliefs of its subjects, and that it was, in any event, impossible for government to do so without arousing resistance. Madison, the most influential member of the congressional committee that drafted the Bill of Rights, tried to write these libertarian convictions into the First Amendment. He met with only partial success, however. Language that would have forbidden the individual states (as well as the federal government) from involving themselves in religious affairs had to be abandoned. Also dropped was the phrase "equal right of conscience," which would have given agnostics and other nonbelievers rights equal to those of the conventionally religious. Neither defeat is surprising in light of the strong religious sentiments that still dominated the age.[10]

Thus, in its origins, the American tradition of religious liberty was nourished from two quite different sources. Some of the Founders wanted complete freedom of conscience and complete individual independence in matters of religion, from both state and federal government; others, however, were motivated in part by fear that the federal government might try to establish a national church that would undermine the states' involvement with religion. Yet, despite these differences in the motives that led to the adoption of the religion clauses of the First Amendment, the idea of religious liberty grew stronger as the Constitution gained esteem. Then, too, as social conditions changed, the privileged status of the locally established churches grew weaker and eventually disappeared, as did the arguments favoring the unity of church and state. By the second quarter of the nineteenth century, freedom of conscience and the separation of church and state had emerged as virtually uncontested constitutional principles.

Very likely the long-term growth of secular values would have led to greater religious freedom in America even if the First Amendment had never existed. But the emergence of religious liberty as a constitutional principle has doubtless led to a more rapid and thorough separation of church and state than would have occurred in its absence. Consider, for example, the issue of prayer in the public schools. Every public opinion survey of which we are aware has shown strong popular majorities favoring some form of school prayer (see Table 2–5). Yet, since the Supreme Court ruling in *Engel v. Vitale* in 1962, such prayers have been illegal. In the opinion of the Court, the recitation of prayers in public schools—even when the prayers have been designed by officials to be as nonsectarian and inoffensive as possible—violates the principle of separation of church and state. As Justice Black wrote for the Court: "We think the constitutional prohibition against laws respecting the establishment of religion must at least mean that in this country it is no part of the business of government to compose official prayers for any group of the American people to recite as part of a religious program carried on by the government."[11]

Such Supreme Court decisions are important, of course, in deciding what policies the government is free to carry out. They also help, however, to determine which of the nation's values are most critical and how they should be interpreted. The Court does not, of course, act in a political vacuum; in many cases its decisions tend to reflect a consensus that has already begun to develop among other legal and political elites. Nevertheless, both for elites and for the more politically sophisticated members of the public, the Court's decisions serve to legitimate moral and political norms.

These observations would lead one to expect that support for religious liberty would be strongest among people most likely to be knowledgeable about Supreme Court decisions. Such is in fact the case. Our surveys show that education, participation in poli-

Table 2-5 Attitudes toward prayer in public schools

	General public	Opinion leaders
1. Prayers in the public schools should be:		
—forbidden	10	33
—permitted	79	47
—Decline to choose	11	20
	(N = 938)	(N = 845)
2. Do you approve or disapprove of religious observances in public schools?		
—Approve	79	—
—Disapprove	14	—
—No opinion	7	—
	(N = 1,779)	
3. The U.S. Supreme Court has ruled that no state or local government may require the reading of the Lord's Prayer or Bible verses in public schools. What are your views on this?		
—Approve	24	—
—Disapprove	70	—
—No opinion	6	—
	(N = 1,837)	
4. Some people think it is all right for the public schools to start each day with a prayer. Others feel that religion does not belong in the public schools and should be taken care of by the family and the church. Have you been interested enough to take one side or the other? Which do you think?		
—Favor school prayer	75	—
—Oppose school prayer	15	—
—No interest, unsure	10	

Sources: question 1, Opinions and Values of Americans survey, 1975–77; question 2, *The Gallup Poll, 1935–1971* (New York: Random House, 1972), p. 1779; question 3, *Gallup Poll,* p. 1837; question 4, University of Michigan, National Election Study, 1964.

tics, and knowledge about political and legal affairs are all associated with support for freedom of religion as an abstract value. As Table 2-6 shows, those who rank as politically knowledgeable are significantly more likely than the politically uninformed to say that "religious toleration for any and all religions" is an "extremely important" value. Among our sample of community influentials, who are more exposed to the norms of the political culture than are the mass public, support for religious liberty as

Table 2-6 Attitudes toward religious toleration as an abstract value

| | General public | | | Community influentials (N = 1,157) | Legal elite[a] (N = 510) |
	Low soph. (N = 657)	Middle soph. (N = 658)	High soph. (N = 659)		
How would you rate toleration for any and all religions?					
—Extremely important	45	52	59	64	74
—Fairly/somewhat important	43	41	37	33	25
—Less important/unsure	12	7	4	3	1

Source: Civil Liberties study, 1978–79.
a. Legal elite consists mainly of lawyers and judges.

an abstract value is even higher. It is higher still among members of the legal profession, who are most informed about the opinions of the higher courts and most inclined to adopt them.

Political sophistication is associated with support for religious liberty not only in the abstract but in concrete situations as well. Table 2–7 demonstrates that both the community influentials and the most politically aware members of the general public are substantially more likely to uphold the rights of atheists and cultists than are the least sophisticated of our respondents.

As we saw in Table 2–5, which concerned the issue of prayers in the public schools, a plurality of the opinion leaders reject the Supreme Court's conclusion in *Engel v. Vitale.* For these Americans, the right of local majorities to promote religious beliefs through use of the public schools is apparently taken as an aspect of freedom of worship—an interpretation in direct conflict with that of the Court. Still, it is worth noting that support for the separation of church and state is strongest, relatively speaking, among elites and the politically sophisticated.

These data lend support to the claim that popular approval of religious liberty in the United States can partially be attributed to the influence of libertarian values as embodied in the Bill of Rights, interpreted by the Supreme Court, learned by elites, and transmitted by various means to the general public, and especially its more politically attentive members. Is it possible, however, that sophisticated respondents, and others who profess a

Table 2-7   Effect of political sophistication on support for freedom of conscience

	General public			Community influentials (N = 1,157)	Legal elite (N = 487)
	Low soph. (N = 763)	Middle soph. (N = 753)	High soph. (N = 456)		
1. The freedom of atheists to make fun of God and religion:					
—should be legally protected no matter who might be offended	12	29	45	53	75
—should not be allowed in a public place where religious groups gather	66	48	39	30	15
—Decline to choose	23	23	16	17	10
2. Freedom to worship as one pleases:					
—applies to all religious groups, regardless of how extreme their beliefs are	63	70	80	80	85
—was never meant to apply to religious cults that the majority of people consider "strange," fanatical, or "weird"	21	19	11	11	4
—Decline to choose	16	11	9	9	11

Source: Civil Liberties study, 1978–79.

high regard for religious and moral liberty, are not so much "tolerant" of religious differences as indifferent to religion as a whole, and that what they are registering is not tolerance but indifference?

Our data, as shown in Table 2–8, indicate that even among respondents who are worried about the danger posed by atheists and cultists, the opinion leaders and the more sophisticated remain substantially more tolerant than the unsophisticated. Beyond the fact that they are more secular in their outlook, the more knowledgeable are more willing to put up with groups they find obnoxious or distasteful—or for that matter, harmful. Being more informed about public affairs, they have absorbed more fully the libertarian norms of the political culture.

We have tried to show how changes in religious views and libertarian values (particularly as interpreted by political elites) have

Table 2–8 Joint effects of political sophistication and perception of danger on support for religious freedom

	Respondents who consider atheist groups harmful to the nation					Respondents who consider atheist groups obnoxious but not harmful				
	General public			Community influentials (N=302)	Legal elites (N=63)	General public			Community influentials (N=547)	Legal elites (N=241)
	Low soph. (N=310)	Middle soph. (N=310)	High soph. (N=187)			Low soph. (N=146)	Middle soph. (N=228)	High soph. (N=289)		
1. The freedom of atheists to make fun of God and religion:										
—should be legally protected no matter who might be offended	8	15	16	24	37	11	25	53	60	76
—should not be allowed in a public place where religious groups gather	79	67	63	57	49	63	43	27	24	12
—Decline to choose	12	18	21	19	14	36	32	20	16	12

	Respondents who consider "Moonies" harmful to the nation					Respondents who consider "Moonies" obnoxious but not harmful				
	Low soph. (N=314)	Middle soph. (N=415)	High soph. (N=401)	Community influentials (N=632)	Legal elites (N=201)	Low soph. (N=104)	Middle soph. (N=146)	High soph. (N=181)	Community influentials (N=381)	Legal elites (N=211)
2. The freedom to worship as one pleases:										
—applies to all religious groups, regardless of how extreme their beliefs are	57	62	76	76	76	68	71	86	87	92
—was never meant to apply to religious cults that the majority of people consider "strange," fanatical, or "weird"	29	25	13	15	8	22	17	8	5	2
—Decline to choose	14	13	11	9	18	10	12	6	8	6

Source: Civil Liberties study, 1978–79.

influenced the growth of popular support for religious freedom. Similar developments have played a vital role in promoting support for freedom of speech, press, and assembly.

Freedom of Speech, Press, and Assembly

No feature of democracy is more essential than the freedom of citizens to debate political issues and criticize the policies of their elected leaders. Yet, even in the United States, freedom of expression has never been completely secure. Whenever fundamental values or institutions have appeared to be endangered, many Americans have attempted to suppress political criticism and debate. In 1798, for example, a Federalist-dominated Congress, fearing the subversion of American institutions by the French, enacted the Sedition Act, which in effect made it a crime to criticize the government and was used to prosecute the editors of leading opposition journals. In the 1830s abolitionists, denounced as radicals, were frequently harassed by mobs. In 1917 and 1918 people who spoke out against American involvement in World War I ran a serious risk of being arrested for obstructing the war effort. As recently as the 1950s American citizens were seriously harassed, fired from their jobs, or in some cases even sent to prison for joining radical organizations or expressing opinions thought to be sympathetic to communism.

Although the American record of support for freedom of expression has been somewhat uneven, popular support for freedom of speech *in the abstract* is overwhelming. Nearly nine out of ten Americans claim to "believe in free speech for all, no matter what their views might be," while almost as many assert that "people who hate our way of life should still have a chance to be heard" (see Table 2–9). Substantial majorities of both the elites and the general public say they would be unwilling to allow any person or group to decide which opinions may or may not be expressed. Even children, the majority maintains, "should be free to discuss all ideas and subjects."

Notwithstanding these seemingly unequivocal attitudes, many Americans—and in some cases a majority—refuse to tolerate groups or ideas that they find threatening, offensive, or otherwise objectionable. For example, 97 percent of the respondents in a

Table 2-9 Attitudes toward freedom of speech among influentials and the general public

	General public	Influentials
1. I believe in free speech for all no matter what their views might be.		
—Agree	89	90
—Disagree	11	10
	(N = 1,484)	(N = 3,020)
2. People who hate our way of life should still have a chance to be heard.		
—Agree	82	87
—Disagree	18	13
	(N = 1,484)	(N = 3,020)
3. I would not trust any person or group to decide what opinions can be freely expressed and what must be silenced.		
—Agree	65	80
—Disagree	35	20
	(N = 1,484)	(N = 3,020)
4. For children to be properly educated:		
—they should be free to discuss all ideas and subjects, no matter what	70	84
—they should be protected against ideas the community considers wrong or dangerous	15	3
—Decline to choose	16	13
	(N = 938)	(N = 845)

Sources: questions 1–3, Political Affiliations and Beliefs study, 1958; question 4, Opinions and Values of Americans survey, 1975–77.

1940 national survey professed to believe in freedom of speech, yet only 22 percent of these respondents would permit fascists or communists to speak in their community. Similarly, more than 80 percent of Americans said in one of our surveys that "nobody has a right to tell another person what he should or should not read"; yet in a later survey, a majority of the general public (though only 13 percent of the opinion leaders) said that books preaching the overthrow of the government should be banned from the library (see Table 2–10).

In both these examples, a majority of Americans upheld the value of free expression in the abstract while denying it in practice. One can, however, also find cases in which popular majorities want to limit freedom of expression even at the level of

Table 2-10   Conflicting attitudes toward political freedom

	General public	Influentials
1. Nobody has a right to tell another person what he should and should not read.		
—Agree	81	82
—Disagree	19	18
	(N = 1,484)	(N = 3,020)
2. Books that preach the overthrow of the government should be:		
—made available by the library, just like any other book	32	72
—banned from the library	50	13
—Decline to choose	17	14
	(N = 938)	(N = 845)
3. Do you believe in freedom of speech?		
—Yes	97	—
—No; other	3	—
4. (If yes) Do you believe in it to the extent of allowing fascists and communists to hold meetings and express their views in the community?		
—Yes	22	—
—No	76	—
—No opinion	2	—

Sources: question 1, Political Affiliations and Beliefs study, 1958; question 2, Opinions and Values of Americans survey, 1975–77; questions 3 and 4, Gallup Poll, 1940; Hazel Erskine, "The Polls: Freedom of Speech," *Public Opinion Quarterly*, 36 (Fall 1970), p. 486.

abstract principle. Table 2–11, for example, indicates that a majority of both the general public and the opinion leaders want to deny citizens the right to live by any standards they choose. A majority of the general public (though only a minority of opinion leaders) also believe that "to protect its moral values, a society sometimes has to forbid certain things from being published."

Data like these are often cited as evidence that Americans are confused about the meaning of freedom of expression. On some occasions the vast majority endorses freedom of speech and press in seemingly unqualified terms, while at other times its members either deny such freedom to some unpopular group or uphold views that are clearly hostile to libertarian values. Although such

Table 2-11   Opposition to libertarian values among opinion leaders and the general public

	General public (N = 938)	Opinion leaders (N = 845)
1. Our laws should aim to:		
—protect a citizen's right to live by any moral standards he chooses	23	33
—enforce the community's standards of right and wrong	55	34
—Decline to choose	23	33
2. Which of these comes closer to your own view?		
—Nobody has the right to decide what should or should not be published	29	51
—To protect its moral values, a society sometimes has to forbid certain things from being published	54	33
—Decline to choose	17	16
3. A newspaper has a right to publish its opinions:		
—no matter how false and twisted its opinions are	9	31
—only if it doesn't twist the facts and tell lies	81	57
—Decline to choose	10	12

Source: Opinions and Values of Americans survey, 1975–77.

vacillation is most common among the less sophisticated members of the general public, it can be found to some extent at all levels of the population.

Such apparent inconsistencies may be inherent in the nature of open societies. For such societies, although they may esteem freedom in the most honorific terms, must also consider the practical problem of maintaining social cohesion. The degree of freedom an open society permits is bound to vary somewhat from one group or occasion to another, and from one period to another, depending on the estimates made by the authorities, the elites, and the general public about the degree of danger they face.

Yet, despite the uncertainties relating to freedom of speech and press, the dominant trend in the United States has been toward greater freedom of political expression. Compare, for example, the rights of dissenters during World War I and the Vietnam War. Government policy toward dissent in the earlier war was reflected in the remark made by Attorney General Thomas Gregory: "May God have mercy on them [the protesters]," he said, "since they need expect none from an outraged people and an avenging government." In an effort to locate draft resisters, the attorney general asked the American Protective League, a nationwide organization of superpatriotic citizens, to conduct a series of "slacker raids." In response, the members of the league descended en masse on union halls, pool rooms, inner-city hotels, and other locations where they thought resisters might congregate. Over the course of the war, they made 40,000 citizens' arrests of suspected slackers and also carried out an estimated 3 million "investigations" of suspected subversives.[12]

The Post Office decided early in the war on a policy of destroying any pamphlet, magazine, or newspaper that carried articles opposing the war. Anyone who spoke or wrote against the war ran a serious risk of being convicted for subversive activity under the Espionage Act. In a typical example, "D. T. Blodgett was sentenced to twenty years in prison for circulating a pamphlet urging the voters of Iowa not to re-elect a congressman who had voted for conscription."[13]

The handful of judges who tried to resist the patriotic fervor of jurors often failed in this effort. As a federal judge recalled after the war had ended: "[I] tried cases before jurymen [who] under ordinary circumstances would have had the highest respect for my declarations of law, but during that period they looked back into my eyes with the savagery of wild animals, saying by their manner, 'Away with the twiddling, let us get at him.' Men believed during that period that the only verdict in a war case, which could show loyalty, was a verdict of guilty."[14]

Efforts to discourage opposition to the Vietnam War were, by comparison, mild. No attempts were made to prevent political dissidents from using the mails to disseminate their literature; no calls were issued to private patriotic groups to search out subversives; and no policies were enacted to punish those who spoke or wrote against the war. Even those who engaged in civil disobedience, such as blocking entrances to induction centers or occupying public buildings, were usually given mild punishments or none at all. On several occasions, to be sure, federal prosecutors charged war protesters with "conspiracy" to interfere with the Vietnam War effort or to commit other crimes related to the war. Yet in sharp contrast with the success of prosecutors during World War I, prosecutors during the Vietnam era were consistently unable to persuade juries to vote for convictions. Anthony Lewis, reviewing government efforts to prosecute antiwar radicals during the Vietnam War, observed that "conspiracy was the charge the government used most often, but it never succeeded in proving one. Juries or appellate courts almost always found the evidence wanting. Not a single defendant went to prison as a result of conviction in the great conspiracy prosecutions."[15]

This is not to say that dissenters enjoyed perfect freedom to express opposition to the war in Vietnam. Clear abuses of civil liberties occurred, for example, when the FBI monitored, infiltrated, or otherwise harassed certain radical or antiwar political organizations. But the attempts to suppress dissent during the Vietnam period were far weaker than the efforts made during earlier wars.

For the past few decades we have had available a more direct form of evidence about trends in popular attitudes toward nonconformists—namely, public opinion polls. In 1954 and 1973, cross sections of the American public were asked whether it was more important to uncover "all the Communists even if some innocent people should be hurt," or to "protect the rights of innocent people even if some Communists are not found out." In 1954 Stouffer found that 58 percent felt it was more important to flush out all the communists, while only 32 percent were concerned with protecting the rights of the innocent.[16] Two decades later, however, only 23 percent were primarily concerned about ferreting out communists, while 70 percent were more concerned about the rights of the innocent.[17]

Since Stouffer conducted his 1954 survey at the height of the McCarthyite campaign against communism, it may have registered an abnormally high level of disregard for the libertarian rights of radicals; this, in turn, may have produced an exaggerated impression of the change that occurred between 1954 and 1973. However, Table 2–12 demonstrates that the shifts in public

Table 2-12   Changing attitudes toward freedom of expression

	1954 (N = 4,933)	1973 (N = 3,538)
Percentage willing to grant freedom of speech to:		
—admitted communists	27	53
—persons against religion and churches	37	62
—persons who favor government ownership of all the railroads and big industry	58	72

Source: Adapted from Clyde A. Nunn, Harry J. Crockett, and J. Allen Williams, *Tolerance for Non-Conformity* (San Francisco: Jossey-Bass, 1978), chap. 3.

opinion toward greater tolerance of free speech turn up not only for communists but for persons who are "against religion and churches" or who favor "government ownership of all the railroads and big industry." It seems clear from these findings that the shift in popular support for freedom of expression in the two decades following 1954 represented more than just a reduction in the fear of communism and the relaxation of the cold war.[18]

What are the reasons for this change? Several influences seem important to us and are consistent with the data we have collected. One possible explanation concerns the increasing secularization we discussed earlier in the context of religious freedom. Although a causal connection between the growth of secularism and increasing tolerance toward dissenters and nonconformists cannot be conclusively demonstrated, the two have obviously developed simultaneously, and the correlation between them today remains very strong. We see in Table 2–13 that respondents who retain a highly religious view of the world are far less likely to tolerate unconventional political groups and ideas than are those who embrace a more secular view. This finding holds for a wide range of target groups and issues—left-wing groups (for example, radicals), right-wing groups (for example, Nazis), and ideologically neutral groups (for example, "crackpots"). Intense feelings of religiosity, as these data suggest, are associated with the desire for orthodoxy in political and social as well as religious affairs. The negative correlation between religiosity and support for freedom of expression remains significant even after statistical controls are introduced for respondents' age, education, and place of residence.

Table 2-13 Influence of secular attitudes on tolerance of different ideological
groups and ideas

	General public		Opinion leaders	
	Highly secular (N = 238)	Highly religious (N = 321)	Highly secular (N = 449)	Highly religious (N = 126)
1. "Crackpot" ideas:				
—have as much right to be heard as sensible ideas	72	34	86	74
—sometimes have to be censored for the public good	17	43	6	19
—Decline to choose	11	23	8	7
2. Books that preach the overthrow of the government should be:				
—made available by the library, just like any other book	58	15	82	59
—banned from the library	25	70	7	27
—Decline to choose	17	15	11	16
3. Should a community allow the American Nazi Party to use its town hall to hold a public meeting?				
—Yes	32	8	46	34
—No	48	80	37	46
—Decline to choose	20	12	17	20
4. When it comes to free speech, extremists:				
—should have the same rights as everyone else	82	44	90	82
—should not be allowed to spread their propaganda	5	29	2	6
—Decline to choose	13	27	8	12

Source: Opinions and Values of Americans survey, 1975–77.

These data are consistent with our belief that the growth of political tolerance in the United States is related to the development of a secular perspective toward social affairs. In a society dominated by religious modes of thought, many institutions and customs are considered divinely ordained and hence sacred; anyone who criticizes or seeks to change them is open to the charge of opposing God's will. In modern secular societies, by contrast, institutions are predominantly viewed as man-made and can more easily be discussed or rationally criticized without giving offense.

In the one case, certain fundamental questions tend to be excluded from discussion; in the other, they are more likely to be open to debate and to empirical proof of refutation.

Secularization, however, is only one of several social and cultural developments that appear to have contributed to greater support for freedom of expression in America. The transformation of the country from a predominantly rural to a predominantly urban, industrialized society had an equally profound effect. The Republic in its early years was largely a nation of small farmers, some of whom functioned largely outside the market system and subsisted on only a few crops. Many were isolated from their neighbors, illiterate, and far from the mainstreams of thought and culture. In 1833 an itinerant missionary to the then-remote region of rural Indiana deplored the universal ignorance he discovered, and lamented its results in the strongest terms: "Ignorance and her squalid brood. A universal dearth of intellect. Total abstinence from literature is very generally practiced . . . there is not a scholar in grammar or geography or a *teacher capable of instructing* them to my knowledge. There are some neighborhoods in which there *has never been a school of any kind.* Parents and children are one dead level of ignorance."[19]

The industrial slums of the late nineteenth and early twentieth centuries may have represented little immediate improvement in the cultural development of the nation. Nevertheless, by the second and third quarters of the twentieth century, urban life had produced cultural changes of great significance for tolerance and civil liberties. Henceforth, the typical urban resident was likely to be literate and to have attended school for a few years at least; he was exposed to a steady stream of novel ideas in the media; and he also encountered and mingled with—to some degree at least—people of different religious, ethnic, and cultural backgrounds. Under these conditions, novel or "deviant" ideas are less likely to appear threatening or morally offensive. As Samuel Stouffer observed in 1955: "Great social, economic, and technological forces are working on the side of exposing ever larger proportions of our population to the idea that 'people are different from me, with different systems of values, and they can be good people, too.'"[20]

The forces to which Stouffer alludes have had a profound impact on American life everywhere, but they have particularly in-

Table 2–14   Influence of place of residence on support for libertarian values

Scores on civil libertarian scale	Rural (N = 359)	Town or small city (N = 587)	Medium city or suburb (N = 704)	Large city (N = 333)
Low	50	33	31	28
Middle	31	36	31	28
High	19	31	38	45

Source: Civil Liberties study, 1978–79.

fluenced life in the metropolitan areas. As one moves away from the great population centers into the farm and mountain regions, conditions more closely resembling those typical of American life in earlier centuries can be found. Given that these differences between rural and metropolitan life still exist, we expected to find that people living in the countryside are less tolerant than those residing in and around the cities.

Table 2–14 confirms this expectation. Nineteen percent of those living in rural areas and small towns scored as highly tolerant on our omnibus civil-liberties scale, compared with 45 percent of those living in metropolitan areas.[21] Residents of the countryside, to be sure, tend to be less well educated and more religiously oriented than their urban counterparts characteristics that in some degree contribute to their lower tolerance scores. However, the differences shown in Table 2–14 remain significant even after taking account of such social influences as education and religiosity. Thus urbanization joins secularism in promoting the growth of popular support for freedom of expression.

An entirely different source of increased support for freedom of expression is the influence of civil libertarian values as such in leading people to tolerate ideas that frighten or repel them.

The Influence of Libertarian Ideals

One of the most striking features of political intolerance in American history is its chronic, episodic nature. Periods of political intolerance, such as the Red Scare following World War I or McCarthyism in the early 1950s, recur at irregular intervals but usually do not last long. After such periods the country eventually regains its composure, relaxes the extraordinary restrictions on freedom of expression that have been introduced, and—more often than not—repudiates the people responsible for the restrictions in the first place. Senator McCarthy, for example, was censured by the Senate and ended his career in disgrace. The word *McCarthyism* became synonymous with repression, ruthlessness, and high-handedness in government. Even now, some thirty years after the McCarthy era, its memory is still invoked as a forceful warning of the evils that can occur when the country ignores its commitment to civil liberties.

If the intolerance of the McCarthy period is evidence of the fragile nature of freedom, the *reaction* to McCarthyism is evidence of the strength and resilience of the American libertarian tradition. In the long run, the abuses of individual rights associated with McCarthyism appear to have heightened popular awareness of the importance of civil liberties and served to strengthen rather than weaken the libertarian tradition.

An essentially similar conclusion can be drawn from the reaction that followed the enforcement of the Alien and Sedition laws of 1798. In the election of 1800, Thomas Jefferson and the Democratic-Republicans won handily by making the Sedition Act (which had been passed by their Federalist opponents) a primary campaign issue. Once in office, Jefferson pardoned all those still in jail under the Sedition Act, while Congress not only refused to renew the act but appropriated money to repay those who had been fined for violating it during the two years it had been in force. In thus repudiating the Sedition Act, Jefferson and his party pronounced a verdict on government efforts to limit political criticism, which, as the Supreme Court observed more than 150 years later, "has carried the day in the court of history."[22] Similar reactions against the denial of liberty have followed the attempts to muzzle the abolitionist press, the repression associated with the Red Scare following World War I, and the internment of Japanese-Americans during World War II.

The intermittent eruptions of intolerance in American history can readily be understood as responses by some Americans and their leaders to perceived threats to order or national security. But the reactions that have followed these periods of heightened intolerance are more puzzling. Why does the nation seem not only to relax constraints on freedom of expression, but even to repudiate them? Why not simply leave repressive policies in place to guard against future threats of disorder or subversion?

The answer, we believe, is that severe restraints on political freedom are manifestly incompatible with the American libertarian tradition. Among many Americans, such violations of freedom evoke feelings of guilt and discomfort. Thus, although even sober-minded Americans may countenance restraints on freedom of expression in times of crisis, they usually cast them off when the crises and the fears arising from them have passed. It appears, moreover, that the nation's political elites play an especially vital role in the reactions that typically follow periods of political intolerance. As we show more fully in Chapters 7 and 8, most elites— and especially liberal elites—tend to be strongly committed to democratic values and highly sensitive to actions that violate them. If these elites are sometimes induced to acquiesce to repression during periods of great public stress, they are all the more outspoken in denouncing such intolerance once the appearance of danger subsides. These denunciations, in turn, help to shape popular opinion. The view articulated by Justice Brandeis in the aftermath of the Red Scare expresses sentiments that Americans have traditionally found highly persuasive:

> Those who won our independence   valued liberty both as an end and as a means. They believed liberty to be the secret of happiness and courage to be the secret of liberty. They believed that freedom to think as you will and to speak as you think are means indispensable to the discovery and spread of political truth; that without free speech and assembly discussion would be futile; that with them, discussion affords ordinarily adequate protection against the dissemination of noxious doctrine; that the greatest menace to freedom is an inert people; that public discussion is a political duty; and that this should be a fundamental principle of the American government. They recognized the risks to which all human institutions are subject. But . . . those who won our independence by revolution were not cowards. They did not fear political change. They did not exalt order at the cost of liberty . . . If there be time to expose through discussion the falsehood and fallacies, to avert the evil by the processes of education, the remedy to be applied is more speech, not enforced silence.[23]

No one has yet discovered how to measure the influence of this kind of rhetoric on public opinion, but it is nonetheless clear that such appeals to traditional principles and values can be formidable weapons of political debate.

Appeals to libertarian values do not affect all Americans equally, of course. One would expect them to have the greatest influence on the elite audiences most likely to encounter them—legislators, administrative officials, judges, academics, intellectuals, political activists, journalists, lawyers, and others who pay particular attention to the political process. These are also the people who tend to react most strongly against the intolerance we have described. Although the great mass of Americans also encounter appeals to civil libertarian norms, they do so less often, pay less attention to their implications, and are less likely to assimilate them.

These are, of course, some of the same considerations that led us in our earlier discussion of freedom of religion to expect a strong positive correlation between political sophistication and support for certain libertarian values. In Tables 2–15 and 2–16, this expectation is again confirmed. The sophisticated respon-

Table 2-15   Influence of sophistication on support for political freedom as an abstract value[a]

	General public		Community influentials (N = 1,166)	Legal elite (N = 510)
Low soph. (N = 657)	Middle soph. (N = 667)	High soph. (N = 664)		

1. Freedom to express unpopular and even "dangerous" opinions is "extremely important."

| 24 | 30 | 39 | 45 | 58 |

2. The right of newspapers to publish freely without censorship of any kind is "extremely important."

| 38 | 39 | 45 | 51 | 54 |

3. The right to hold peaceful protest meetings is "extremely important."

| 22 | 33 | 45 | 51 | 67 |

Source: Civil Liberties study, 1978–79.

a. Cell entries are percentages of each sophistication subgroup who say that a given value is "extremely important."

Table 2-16   Influence of sophistication on tolerance of different ideological groups and ideas[a]

	General public			Opinion leaders (N = 845)
	Low soph. (N = 309)	Middle soph. (N = 310)	High soph. (N = 310)	
Percentage highly tolerant of ideologically neutral groups (e.g., "crackpots")	20	35	49	70
Percentage highly tolerant of left-wing groups (e.g., radicals)	27	37	47	77
Percentage highly tolerant of right-wing groups (e.g., Nazis)	29	40	59	55

Source: Opinions and Values of Americans survey, 1975–77.

a. For examples of items in each of the tolerance subscales used in this table, see Table 2–13.

dents are not only more inclined to say that freedom of expression is, in the abstract, an "extremely important" value, but they are also more likely (as shown by their scale scores) to support specific civil liberties for deviant groups. Partly because of their greater sophistication and involvement in public affairs, community influentials tend to uphold libertarian norms even more strongly than do the sophisticated members of the general public. Also worth noting in Table 2–16 is that the opinion leaders and the politically sophisticated are substantially more tolerant than the other members of the public regardless of the ideological character (left, right, or neutral) of the target groups involved.

In this connection we might observe that one group of investigators has argued that political sophistication is only weakly associated with tolerance for controversial groups, once a respondent's attitude toward the groups is taken into account.[24] Our data do not support this conclusion. Even when we control for affect toward extreme ideological groups, elites and the more sophisticated remain more tolerant than the unsophisticated (see Table 2–17 and also Table 2–8).

Table 2-17 Joint effects of sophistication and perception of danger on support for political liberty

	Respondents who consider extreme left-wing groups harmful to the nation					Respondents who consider extreme left-wing groups obnoxious but not harmful				
	General public			Community influentials (N=839)	Legal elites (N=305)	General public			Community influentials (N=235)	Legal elites (N=142)
	Low soph. (N=491)	Middle soph. (N=555)	High soph. (N=477)			Low soph. (N=29)	Middle soph. (N=57)	High soph. (N=116)		
1. A person who publicly burns or spits on the flag:										
—may be behaving badly but should not be punished for it by law	9	12	21	19	27	28	30	50	57	66
—should be fined or punished in some way	83	80	72	72	65	55	58	35	30	30
—Decline to choose	8	8	7	9	8	17	12	15	13	4

2. Should groups like the Nazis and Ku Klux Klan be allowed to appear on public television to state their views?

	Respondents who consider extreme right-wing groups harmful to the nation					Respondents who consider extreme right-wing groups obnoxious but not harmful				
	Low soph. (N=199)	Middle soph. (N=262)	High soph. (N=306)	Community influentials (N=588)	Legal elites (N=229)	Low soph. (N=100)	Middle soph. (N=167)	High soph. (N=207)	Community influentials (N=414)	Legal elites (N=217)
—Yes, they should be allowed no matter who is offended	16	27	48	54	69	19	35	51	57	81
—No, because they offend certain racial or religious groups	60	42	28	22	11	52	39	26	19	9
—Decline to choose	21	31	24	24	20	19	26	23	24	10

Source: Civil Liberties study, 1978–79.

Our discussion so far has emphasized the role of the higher courts and other political elites in upholding freedom of expression. We should bear in mind, however, that although the courts have set forth clear libertarian standards on *most* issues involving expression, they have not done so in all cases. For example, the use of "fighting words" that may incite violence is still punishable under the Constitution. The courts have also refused to protect the freedom of protesters who attempt to dramatize their dissent by breaking the law—by engaging, in effect, in civil disobedience. In such cases, the courts have held that the maintenance of social order takes precedence over the freedom of expression. The courts have also shown great respect for the value of national security, holding, for example, that the government may under certain circumstances conduct covert surveillance of radical or other "dangerous" groups.

If, as we have been arguing, the courts function for many citizens as a source of opinion leadership, the association between political sophistication and support for free expression should be strongest for issues on which the courts have set a clear and uncontested libertarian standard, and relatively weak for issues on which the courts have not set such a standard. This is indeed the case. In the first part of Table 2–18, the politically sophisticated indicate far more willingness than the unsophisticated to uphold the rights of free expression for such groups as Nazi marchers or foreign visitors who criticize our government, groups whose rights the courts have upheld in the past. Yet, on issues for which the courts have set no clear libertarian standard—for example, police surveillance of political extremists or the obligation of television stations to present a balanced editorial view—the sophisticated and the unsophisticated differ scarcely at all. These findings—illustrated in the second part of Table 2–18—point up the importance of political elites, and especially of the higher courts, as opinion leaders who establish the libertarian standards acquired by the politically attentive public.

The Emerging Issues of Moral Freedom and Unconventional Lifestyles

Although Americans have sometimes violated the precepts of their libertarian creed, most of them, as we have seen, would nonetheless have agreed with the abstract principle that everyone ought to be free to speak, publish, and worship as he pleases—liberties that are obviously central to the democratic creed.

Popular attitudes toward moral and sexual freedom, however, are less clear-cut. In the opinion of many Americans, past and present, the democratic creed affords no license to violate the conventional standards of moral conduct. Thus when the Frenchman Michel Chevalier visited the United States in the early nineteenth century, he described "Yankee liberty" in these terms: "Their liberty is not the liberty to outrage all that is sacred on earth, to set religion at defiance, to laugh morals to scorn, to un-

Table 2–18 How legal norms affect popular support for civil liberties

	General public			Community influentials (N = 1,157)	Legal elite (N = 487)
	Low soph. (N = 772)	Middle soph. (N = 755)	High soph. (N = 458)		
Issues on which the courts have set a clear libertarian norm					
1. Protestors who mock the president by wearing death masks at one of his public speeches:					
—should have the right to appear in any kind of costume they want	18	34	52	53	70
—should be removed from the audience by the police	63	49	34	30	15
—Decline to choose	19	17	14	17	15
2. When groups like the Nazis or other extreme groups require police protection at their rallies and marches, the community should:					
—supply and pay for whatever police protection is needed	7	20	34	44	66
—prohibit such groups from holding rallies because of the costs and dangers involved	69	55	41	31	14
—Decline to choose	24	25	25	25	20
3. Should foreigners who dislike our government and criticize it be allowed to visit or study here?					
—Yes	23	39	59	69	69
—No	59	50	35	24	24
—Decline to choose	19	11	6	7	7

Table 2-18   (continued)

	General public			Community influentials (N = 1,157)	Legal elite (N = 487)
	Low soph. (N = 772)	Middle soph. (N = 755)	High soph. (N = 458)		

Issues on which the courts have failed to set a clear libertarian norm

1. When undercover police agents secretly join far-right or far-left political groups to keep an eye on them:

	Low soph.	Middle soph.	High soph.	Community influentials	Legal elite
—they are violating the rights of the group's members	6	8	10	11	13
—they are only doing what is necessary to protect our society	70	79	80	75	70
—Decline to choose	24	13	10	14	17

2. A radio or television station that always speaks for one political group and against others:

	Low soph.	Middle soph.	High soph.	Community influentials	Legal elite
—should have the right to support or oppose any groups it chooses	26	27	26	28	29
—should be required by law to present a more balanced view	54	60	65	61	60
—Decline to choose	20	13	9	11	11

3. When a law goes against a person's conscience, he should:

	Low soph.	Middle soph.	High soph.	Community influentials	Legal elite
—be allowed to disobey it as long as he has good reason and doesn't hurt anyone else	17	17	22	23	21
—be required nevertheless to obey it, or else all law will lose its meaning	58	64	59	57	63
—Decline to choose	25	19	19	20	16

Source: Civil Liberties study, 1978–79.

dermine the foundations of social order, to mock at all traditions and all received opinions; it is neither the liberty of being a monarchist in a republican country, nor that of sacrificing the honour of the poor man's wife or daughter to one's base passions . . . nor even that of living in private different from the rest of the world. The liberty of the Yankee is essentially limited and special like the nature of the race."[25]

Contemporary survey data suggest that a majority of Americans continue to hold views similar to those encountered by Chevalier. As we saw in Table 2–11, 55 percent of the general public contends that "our laws should aim to . . . enforce the community's standards of right and wrong" rather than to "protect a citizen's right to live by any moral standards he chooses." If we turn to specific issues concerning sexual conduct and an individual's way of life, we find further evidence that many Americans are still intolerant of moral perspectives that differ from their own. On issues such as homosexual marriage, pornography, and the censorship of "obscene books," most members of the mass public continue to hold conventional beliefs about right and wrong, and in these matters, at least, want to limit the personal freedom of their fellow Americans (see Table 2–19). Although a plurality of the general public favors legalized prostitution and the right of women to choose abortion, sizable minorities continue to oppose these measures.

It would, in our view, be inappropriate to say that Americans who oppose the legalization of prostitution or pornography are failing to uphold the American value of individual liberty. As we have seen, libertarian values have not traditionally applied to most issues of sexual and moral freedom. It is nonetheless clear that the last two decades have witnessed a serious effort on the part of many political elites to extend the nation's libertarian creed so that it protects those who depart from society's moral conventions as well as those who depart from standard religious and political beliefs. It is precisely because the country's libertarian tradition is currently changing that the issues of sexual and moral freedom have particular interest for this study.

As our data suggest, some (though by no means all) of the opposition to the new forms of moral and sexual freedom appears to be rooted in the nation's religious heritage. Many spokesmen for these religious values claim that the traditional norms of moral conduct are expressions of God's will and, as such, are timeless and morally binding on everyone. They reject the idea that moral standards may be relative and subject to change; that unconventional sexual conduct may be freely advocated; or that forms of conduct that threaten family life, the moral order, religion, or "decency" may be practiced at the individual's discretion. Such ideas are, for them, expressions of skepticism that challenge the

Table 2-19   Attitudes of the general public and community leaders toward issues of moral freedom

	General public (N = 1,993)	Community influentials (N = 1,157)
1. Censoring obscene books:		
—is an old-fashioned idea that no longer makes sense	28	39
—is necessary to protect community standards	50	39
—Decline to choose	21	22
2. Selling pornographic films, books, and magazines:		
—is really a victimless crime and should therefore be left unregulated	23	31
—lowers the community's moral standards and therefore victimizes everyone	57	52
—Decline to choose	19	17
3. A homosexual couple who want to get legally married:		
—should have the same rights to marry as anyone else	22	25
—should be denied a marriage license because such a marriage would be unnatural	59	56
—Decline to choose	19	19
4. Abortion during the early weeks of pregnancy should be:		
—left entirely up to the woman	48	56
—prohibited except in extreme cases such as rape, the risk of a deformed child, or danger to the mother's life	40	28
—Decline to choose	13	16
5. In dealing with prostitution, the government should:		
—license and regulate it	47	49
—arrest or fine the people who have anything to do with it	30	24
—Decline to choose	23	27

Source: Civil Liberties survey, 1978–79.

foundations of religious faith and the truths upon which it is based. They often perceive people who depart from conventional forms of social behavior as misguided or wicked, lacking in self-discipline and moral rectitude. In their view, a society that countenances excessive moral freedom (or "license") risks its own demise.

But as important as the views of such religious spokesmen may be, Americans are less inclined to look to religious leaders for guidance than they once were. A host of lay opinion leaders— professional counselors, psychiatrists, writers of popular books and magazine articles, academics, television and film pro- ducers—now commonly espouse the view that social norms, in- cluding those pertaining to sex, are essentially matters of social convention. The norms, they argue, can and do change. Forms of conduct once considered sinful are now regarded as matters of personal preference; they represent the exercise of private choice and in themselves are neither good nor evil.

These observations lead us to expect that support for sexual and moral freedom should be weakest among those who are most committed to a traditionally religious view of the world, and strongest among those who have adopted a more secular outlook. Table 2–20 confirms this expectation. On a wide range of issues pertaining to sex and individual behavior, the conventionally re- ligious are much less likely to support the values of freedom than are those who take a more secular view of human conduct. Among the general public, for example, 49 percent of the more secular respondents regard the censorship of obscene books as old-fashioned and no longer sensible, while only 8 percent of the conventionally religious oppose such censorship.

Religiosity, of course, is not the only factor that influences a re- spondent's attitudes toward questions of moral freedom. Some people find sexual liberation morally offensive and oppose it on

Table 2–20 Effect of religiosity on support for moral freedom (percentage who are tolerant on each issue)

	General public		Community influentials	
	Highly secular (N = 274)	Highly religious (N = 143)	Highly secular (N = 193)	Highly religious (N − 94)
Censor obscene books[a]	49	8	58	15
Sell pornographic magazines	40	6	48	14
Legalize gay marriage	37	4	36	9
Allow abortion	69	19	76	23
Legalize prostitution	71	23	60	22

Source: Civil Liberties study, 1978–79.
a. The exact wording of the questions is given in Table 2–19.

grounds that have little to do with religion. Others, arguing from conservative premises, maintain that strong rules regulating sexual conduct are essential to maintain social order and keep human passions under control. Yet, even after we introduced statistical controls to take account of a respondent's age, education, and attitudes toward human nature, order, and stability, religiosity remained an important predictor of attitudes toward moral freedom.*

Even the most casual observation of recent trends in American society indicates that the traditional mores pertaining to sexual conduct and individual lifestyles have been greatly relaxed. The growing acceptance of homosexuality, the explicit portrayal of sexuality in films and magazines, the increase in abortion rates— all represent substantial changes in the traditional norms of conduct. Such changes might have occurred, of course, even if the United States had no libertarian tradition. But the country's libertarian heritage has undoubtedly helped to legitimate the trend. For one thing, it has provided the defenders of the new standards with a fund of ideas relating to individual rights and liberties that they can use to appeal to the public at large. For example, the notion that no one has a right to tell another how to lead his life has strong historical support in the American tradition; so does the notion that government has no business interfering in the private lives of its citizens. Although these ideas were not originally advanced with an eye to such matters as homosexuality and sexual freedom, no great leap of logic is required to extend their underlying principles to these issues as well.

The nation's libertarian tradition, as embodied in the Bill of Rights and the Constitution, has also enabled the higher courts to play a critical role in promoting freedom on moral issues. The Supreme Court, for example, has made it difficult (though not impossible) for would-be censors to proscribe books and films that are alleged to be obscene. It has defeated several attempts to restrict the availability of birth control information and devices. It has recognized the legality of abortion. It has even upheld the

---

* The zero-order correlation between the four-item religiosity index described earlier in this chapter and an eight-item morals tolerance scale was -0.57. The partial correlation, controlling for the variables described above, was -0.43. The items in the morals tolerance scale concerned pornography, abortion, obscenity, the rights of homosexuals, and the regulation of sexual practices among consenting adults.

right of citizens to possess the most unvarnished forms of pornography, provided they use it only within their homes. "Our whole constitutional heritage," the Court held, "rebels at the thought of giving government the power to control men's minds."[26]

Yet, despite the Court's wide-ranging efforts to enlarge the scope of individual freedom, it has also admitted that popular majorities may sometimes enact laws that regulate individual morality. Although communities may not prohibit the dissemination of an *idea*—for example, the advocacy of adultery in a film or publication—the Supreme Court has held that they may censor graphic sexual materials if such materials offend "community standards." On the whole, however, the Court has been instrumental in discouraging laws that aim to stifle individual liberty and has undoubtedly helped to promote greater popular support for freedom in the domain of moral conduct.

Evidence of the Court's powers of moral suasion is shown in Table 2–21. On issues on which the Court has taken a strong libertarian position, community influentials and the politically sophisticated members of the general public are more tolerant than the less sophisticated. On issues on which the Court has not taken a clear libertarian stand, however, elites and the more sophisticated are *not* consistently more tolerant than the unsophisticated. These results parallel our earlier finding on the Court's apparent influence on popular support for freedom of expression.

Obviously, the Supreme Court is not the only political agency that helps to shape popular beliefs on issues of individual freedom. Many other opinion elites play significant roles as well. Thus, when certain of these elites strongly contest the Court's decision on a particular issue—as some have done in attacking its rulings on abortion and school prayer—the Court's ability to influence public opinion on that issue will accordingly be diminished. In a later chapter we shall examine how politically sophisticated citizens respond to issues on which significant elites sharply disagree.

Summary and Conclusions

The growth of tolerance over the past two centuries has by no means eliminated the tensions between libertarian ideals and competing social and moral values. Instead it has simply shifted

Table 2-21   Effect of political sophistication on support for moral freedom

	General public			Community influentials (N = 1,157)	Legal elite (N = 487)
	Low soph. (N = 772)	Middle soph. (N = 755)	High soph. (N = 458)		
1. The movie industry:					
—should be free to make movies on any subject it chooses	34	49	58	69	81
—should not be permitted to make movies that offend certain minorities or religious groups	42	25	20	9	6
2. Censoring obscene books:					
—is an old-fashioned idea that no longer makes sense	20	31	38	39	54
—is necessary to protect community standards	57	50	43	40	26
3. Television programs that show people actually making love:					
—should be permitted as long as they are shown in the late evening, during adult viewing hours	29	31	29	31	42
—should not be allowed on television at all	56	56	59	54	45
4. In dealing with prostitution, the government should:					
—license and regulate it	40	51	53	49	61
—arrest or fine the people who have anything to do with it	36	27	24	25	16
5. A homosexual couple who want to get legally married:					
—should have the same rights to marry as anyone else	21	22	23	25	28
—should be denied a marriage license because such a marriage would be unnatural	59	59	61	56	53

Source: Civil Liberties study, 1978–79.

the focus of the debate, so that forms of freedom once controversial are now widely accepted and others once unthinkable have progressed to the point of being "merely" controversial. Thus Americans continue to argue about how much freedom they ought to allow, but the domain of protected liberties has grown significantly larger than it was in the past.

Major social and demographic changes, including the growth of a commercial, industrial society, a more heterogeneous population, mass education, and mass communication, account for much of the expansion of freedom. Urbanization, television, and the decline of rural life and the isolation that goes with it have also helped to fashion a society in which people are more exposed to unorthodox ideas and therefore less likely to be alarmed by new forms of nonconformity when they encounter them. The decline of a religious, God-centered view of the world and its replacement by a more secular view have also helped to render certain forms of unorthodoxy less offensive and hence more tolerable. Finally, the continual pull of libertarian ideals, especially as interpreted and reinterpreted by opinion elites, has induced many Americans to tolerate groups and ideas they actually dislike or fear.

We have suggested that neither the triumph of secular modes of discourse nor the prominence of libertarian ideals in the American ethos should be considered as given or inevitable features of American politics. Both, in the main, were spawned by "creative elites" and were subsequently learned by various segments of the mass public. Scientists, philosophers, and other intellectuals have labored for centuries to create the new ways of thinking about the world that we have described as secularism. As for the libertarian tradition, it originated in large measure among Europeans who were struggling to find ways to limit the power of their absolute monarchs. Transported to America, the doctrines of freedom were greatly elaborated, written into the federal and state constitutions, and reinterpreted and updated by succeeding generations of statesmen, judges, educators, and social commentators. Libertarian and secular values, as we have seen, have their greatest impact on the people most likely to have been exposed to them—opinion elites and the politically sophisticated. Few Americans, however, have entirely escaped the influence of these values.

3 Egalitarianism

Equality is, verbally at least, one of the two most honored values in the American democratic tradition—the other, of course, being liberty. The notion that all individuals are in some fundamental sense alike, that no person possesses greater intrinsic worth than another, and that all must be prized as members of a common humanity is a major presupposition of democracy. It underlies such democratic principles as popular sovereignty, the right of the governed to choose and hold accountable those who rule them, and the universal and inalienable nature of human rights, including minority rights. This belief in the equal worth and dignity of all human beings also underlies the modern welfare state, which aims to ensure that all citizens will possess the material necessities for a decent life.

During the eighteenth century, at a time when most Europeans, along with the rest of the world, still regarded equality as a radical and subversive idea, the American colonies proclaimed as a fundamental principle of just government that "all men are created equal." When Alexis de Tocqueville visited the United States half a century after the Declaration of Independence was adopted, he found American society dominated by a "passion for equality": "No novelty in the United States struck me more vividly during my stay there than the equality of condition. It was easy to see the immense influence of this basic fact on the course of society. It gives a particular turn to public opinion, and a particular twist to the laws, new maxims to those who govern and particular habits to the governed."[1]

Later students of American society have generally concurred with Tocqueville's judgment. James Bryce, for example, observed that "the United States are deemed all over the world to be pre-eminently the land of equality."[2] In the eyes of the millions who emigrated to the United States from all corners of the world, America represented not only the land of opportunity, but of *equal* opportunity. Anyone, however poor or humble his origins, could rise in station and achieve wealth and respectability. No one was to be excluded from the common legacy of American rights and opportunities.

But if equality is one of the most honored values in the American democratic tradition, it is also one of the most elusive and complex. No democratic society has ever achieved perfect equality, and most fall dramatically short of the ideal. Thus numerous Americans once condoned slavery, and even today many discriminate to varying degrees against blacks, women, and homosexuals. Economic inequality also exists and is widely accepted. Vast differences in wealth and access to "life chances" characterize American society no less than other societies that do not pretend to strive for equality. This condition results partly from the play of economic interests and the desire of those who have prospered to retain their advantages, and partly from the widespread acceptance of a powerful set of values associated with the private enterprise system that conflicts with egalitarianism.

One such cluster of values, for example, holds that those who exhibit greater initiative and talent, possess scarce skills, work more diligently, or take greater risks to advance themselves are entitled to retain the material wealth they gain by reason of these characteristics. Since individuals obviously differ in the traits likely to produce wealth, sharp economic inequalities are bound to result from the workings of a competitive economy. Once established, such inequalities tend to perpetuate themselves and to beget other forms of inequality. For example, people born into poverty are bound, regardless of their character and ability, to enjoy far less opportunity for economic gain than will the off-spring of wealthier families. Inequality of wealth, in other words, typically gives rise to inequality of opportunity.

This example only begins to illustrate the complexities and difficulties attending the notion of equality, a moral principle that is continually in conflict with the workings of the real world. People reconcile this conflict in different ways. Some argue that one must ignore individual differences in character, intelligence, sensibility, knowledge, and talent in order to serve the well-being of a common humanity. Others, claiming to be more realistic and practical, insist that individuals ought to be treated alike only insofar as they *are* alike; insofar as they differ in ability, achievement, or moral character, they should be treated differently. Still others hold that people should be treated as equal for certain purposes but not necessarily for others. Society should consider them equal before the law and recognize their right to enjoy, in exactly the same measure, the protections granted in the Constitution; but society is not obliged to guarantee them equal access to economic and social benefits if they have not earned them through appropriate demonstrations of character and ability.

Equality, then, is a broad, multifaceted, and often ambiguous concept that can take different forms and apply to different domains—legal, political, moral, and economic. Depending on the definition and context one chooses, it can refer to economic opportunities and life chances, to patterns of social stratification and deference, or to social justice, civil rights, the allocation of wealth, the right to participate in self-government, or the enjoyment of legal rights. The same person may hold strongly egalitarian attitudes toward some of these matters and inegalitarian attitudes toward others.

In order to show how Americans have responded to these competing notions, it is necessary to examine the tensions that exist between egalitarian values, on the one hand, and the competing values and hard social realities that impede the fulfillment of egalitarian ideals, on the other.

Equal Human Worth and Dignity

The principle of equality is rooted in the assumption that all human beings possess inherent worth and dignity. For many, this assertion of man's dignity arises from his association with the Almighty. Created by God in His own image, all people possess an eternal soul and enjoy His blessing. But the idea of the equal worth and dignity of all human beings is also embraced by secular thinkers who regard it as a moral presupposition for a just society. Conceding that men differ in station, capacity, skills, motivation, and conduct, they hold these differences to be less important than the common humanity shared by all. This assumption of the equality of human worth is so deeply ingrained in American political culture as to be axiomatic for most people. Commenting on the American view of equality, Perry has observed that: "Generic equality . . . is the idea that beneath the clothes they wear, and the status or occupation which organized society has bestowed upon them, all men are men, with the same faculties, the same needs and aspirations, the same destiny, and similar potentialities of development . . . no one will deny it, once the question is raised in this form."[3]

Contemporary public opinion surveys bear out Perry's contention. In the early days of opinion polling, Americans were occasionally asked directly whether they agreed with the idea that "all men are created equal." The results were so consistently lopsided—scarcely anyone could be found to deny so fundamental a tenet of the American creed—that pollsters rarely bothered to ask the question in subsequent surveys. One of the few times it was asked again was in 1958 when Americans were offered the options of endorsing or rejecting the claim that "all men are created equal." Table 3–1 shows that the vast majority of Americans fully endorsed the declaration of universal equality. Only white southerners, then embroiled in the initial phases of what was to become the civil rights revolution, differed from the national trend; yet even in the embattled South, only 6 out of 100 white respondents were willing to repudiate the egalitarian principle on which the nation was founded.

Table 3–1   Support for equality

	North		South	
	Whites	Blacks	Whites	Blacks
Do you think the Declaration of Independence was right, only half right, or not right at all when it stated that "all men are created equal"?				
—Right	82	75	67	83
—Only half right	10	12	17	8
—Not right at all	3	6	6	4
—No opinion	5	7	10	5

Source: Ben Gaffin and Associates, 1958.

The true meaning of such findings, nevertheless, remains somewhat unclear. The assertion of equality in the Declaration of Independence is so familiar to Americans that many may have
accepted it as "self-evident" without really considering its implications. It is uncertain, therefore, whether the popularity of the
famous phrase represents a genuine endorsement of egalitarian
principles, or merely a ritualistic nod to an American shibboleth.

Results from our recent surveys suggest that the earlier public
endorsement of the inherent equality of all people—as expressed
in abstract form, at least—was genuine. As the data in Table 3–2
demonstrate, egalitarianism continues to be strongly endorsed by

Table 3–2   Attitudes toward equality—equal worth and dignity

	General public	Opinion leaders
1. Teaching that some kinds of people are better than others:		
—goes against the American idea of equality	74	74
—only recognizes the facts	12	8
—Decline to choose	15	18
	(N = 938)	(N = 845)
2. Teaching children that all people are really equal:		
—recognizes that all people are equally worthy and deserve equal treatment	78	82
—teaches something that is obviously false	11	10
—Decline to choose	11	8
	(N = 1,026)	(N = 610)
3. Most of the people who are poor and needy:		
—could contribute something valuable to society if given the chance	78	80
—don't have much to offer society anyway	7	3
—Decline to choose	15	17
	(N = 938)	(N = 845)
4. A person who holds a position of great responsibility, such as a doctor, judge, or elected official:		
—should be treated the same as anyone else	64	63
—is entitled to be treated with special respect	29	25
—Decline to choose	8	12
	(N = 938)	(N = 845)

Sources: questions 1, 3, and 4, Opinions and Values of Americans survey, 1975–77;
question 2, Civil Liberties study, 1978–79.

both the American public and its opinion leaders: the ratio of egalitarian to inegalitarian responses often runs as high as five or ten to one.*

Results as one-sided as these cannot easily be dismissed. Although the items were worded to make an inegalitarian response as acceptable as possible, the vast majority of respondents nevertheless chose the egalitarian alternative. Evidently, a belief in the fundamental equality of all human beings can coexist with the widespread recognition that individuals differ in intelligence, character, and innate abilities. Beyond this, the data suggest agreement with what John Dewey and others have regarded as an article of democratic faith, namely, that despite differences in talent, every individual has the potential to contribute something of value to society.

But as impressive as these results are, they do not resolve the vexing issues associated with the ideal of equality. We observed earlier that one problem egalitarians face is that people do, indeed, vary greatly in their levels of achievement and in their possession of socially desirable traits. In light of such inequalities, what becomes of the proposition that all human beings are of equal worth?

From the perspective of the *ideal* of equal human value, the differences in individual characteristics present little difficulty. All people, regardless of endowment or social rank, are to be valued equally as human beings. Many features of American life are fully consistent with this ideal. When, for instance, James Bryce visited the United States in the late nineteenth century, he found great variations in wealth, status, and ability. He observed nonetheless that

> in America men hold others to be at bottom exactly the same as themselves. If a man is enormously rich . . . or if he is a great orator . . . or a great soldier . . . or a great writer . . . or a President, so much the better for him. He is an object of interest, perhaps of admiration, possibly even of reverence. But he is deemed to be still of the same flesh and blood as other men. The admiration felt for him may be a reason for going

* In calculating ratios, we discarded responses of "decline to choose" and considered only responses to the two substantive options.

to see him and longing to shake hands with him. But it is not a reason for bowing down to him, or addressing him in deferential terms, or treating him as if he were porcelain and yourself only earthenware.[4]

And yet social relations in America have not always been as entirely harmonious as Bryce indicates. Differences in achievement or status have often led to differences in the ascription of human worth. As in other societies, the wealthy, talented, and socially prominent are frequently treated as though they are indeed superior to others. Some of the less fortunate members of society, meanwhile, have been so poor and ill-educated that they have been unable to maintain a proper sense of their own worth and self-respect.

Prejudice and discrimination against racial, religious, and ethnic minorities have also been rampant in America. The nation's mistreatment of blacks and Indians has been so blatant and is so well known that it needs little recounting here. Although the instances are perhaps less well known, Germans, Irish, Asians, Italians, Poles, Jews, and Catholics have also been victims of discrimination at various times in the nation's history. For example, the Know-Nothings, a major third party movement of the 1850s, aimed at limiting the voting rights of Catholic immigrants. Ethnic prejudice was still widely defended as late as the 1920s, when groups such as the Eugenics Immigration League and the American Breeders' Association undertook a massive campaign to end the flow of foreign immigrants into the United States. In their rhetoric and expressed purpose, these and similar groups paid little heed to the ideal of equal human worth or to the sensitivities of the newcomers. The new immigrants—at this point largely southern and eastern Europeans—were, in the words of one writer in the popular press, "so much slag in the melting pot."[5] As one contributor to a popular weekly magazine wrote in 1923, the indiscriminate mixing of different nationalities would transform Americans into "a hybrid race of people as worthless and futile as the good-for-nothing mongrels of central America and Southeastern Europe."[6] Members of the scientific community enlisted in the anti-immigration campaign as well, attempting to prove from comparisons of skull sizes of people from different social groups and from the recently popularized IQ tests that the new immigrants were in fact inferior to older American stock.

One should not overstate the intensity of American ethnocentrism, however. Despite energetic efforts, "The movement toward racism," as the historian John Higham notes, "was an uphill fight in democratic America."[7] There was a good deal of loose talk in the late nineteenth and early twentieth centuries about the supremacy of Anglo-Saxon blood and culture, and widespread denigration of immigrant peoples and their cultures, but once the immigrants began to learn the language and customs of their adopted nation, they were usually able to win acceptance. Typical of the ambivalent attitudes that prevailed was this commentary in *The Press* of Philadelphia, a pro-restrictionist newspaper: "The strong stomach of America may, and doubtless will, digest and assimilate this unsavory and repellent throng . . . In time they catch the spirit of the country and form an element of decided worth."[8]

Many Americans, moreover, had always dissented from theories of racial inferiority, and the number became greater as time passed. "There is no better or nobler blood," wrote the sociologist Lester Ward, "there are no inferior people, only undeveloped or stunted ones."[9] Anthropologists like A. L. Kroeber and Franz Boas, with their emphasis on the vital importance of culture (which is learned) over race (which is inherited) in determining human behavior, argued effectively that all races were by nature equal and that no connection had been demonstrated between race and personality.[10] The views of thinkers like Ward, Kroeber, and Boas eventually triumphed over the old, ethnic ideas rampant in the nation's universities and in the popular media. Surveys of academics confirm that holders of race theories now represent a distinct minority in today's universities.

Still, academic opinion is not public opinion. Table 3–3 indicates that the ethnocentrism once common in the popular media still retained a hold on the public mind in the 1950s. Almost half the general public and the political influentials endorsed the proposition that "when it comes to the things that count most, all races are certainly not equal." A similar proportion agreed that "just as is true of fine race horses, some breeds of people are just naturally better than others." Whether such responses reflect

Table 3-3   Attitudes toward equality—human differences

	General public (N = 1,489)	Political influentials (N = 3,020)
1. When it comes to the things that count most, all races certainly are not equal.		
—Agree	49	46
—Disagree	51	54
2. Just as is true of fine race horses, some breeds of people are just naturally better than others.		
—Agree	47	46
—Disagree	53	54
3. We have to teach children that all men are created equal, but almost everyone knows that some are better than others.		
—Agree	59	55
—Disagree	41	45

Source: Political Affiliations and Beliefs study, 1958.

group prejudice or mainly recognition of differences in individual ability, their harshly inegalitarian tone is unmistakable.

In the two decades that have passed since these questions were asked, however, the nation has witnessed a flood of activity on behalf of equal rights for mistreated minorities. Great efforts have been made to prove the existence and adverse effects of social discrimination, and to prod government into actions that might help to correct the lingering effects of prejudice. According to the argument that has come to prevail in public discourse, minority groups would not lag behind the majority at all if it were not for discrimination, past and present. The campaigns for equal rights have stressed that all ethnic groups are similar in native talent and ability.

Although the arguments are not new, the overwhelming emphasis given to them in the equal rights campaigns of recent decades is almost certainly unprecedented. The extent to which political leaders now refrain from openly expressing anti-egalitarian or bigoted opinions should also be noted. Even George Wallace, when running for president in 1968, was careful to avoid any references that might suggest racial prejudice.[11] Popular levels of ethnocentrism, it seems plain, have also substantially declined. For example, a nationwide survey conducted in 1963 found that 31 percent of white respondents believed that "blacks are inferior to white people." In 1978 only 15 percent of whites still expressed this view. Likewise, 39 percent of the 1963 respondents, but only 25 percent of those surveyed in 1978, said they believed that "blacks have less native intelligence than whites."[12]

Two questions included in our 1978–1979 survey provide an interesting glimpse of contemporary American attitudes about individual differences. In Table 3–4, 70 percent of the general public attest that "no matter how we treat everyone, some people will turn out to be better than others." Seventy-seven percent of the community leaders likewise agreed that a certain amount of individual inequality appears to be inevitable. Yet, despite these attitudes, most Americans now refuse to endorse inegalitarian statements that flagrantly denigrate entire races, ethnic groups, or classes. For example, only 30 percent of the general public and 26 percent of the opinion leaders would say that "like fine race horses, some classes of people are just naturally better than others." Most Americans, it thus appears, acknowledge individual

Table 3–4   Two views of equality

	General public (N = 967)	Community influentials (N = 556)
1. Which of these opinions about equality comes closer to what you believe?		
—If we really gave every person an equal chance, almost all of them would turn out to be equally worthwhile.	21	16
—No matter how we treat everyone, some people will turn out to be better than others.	70	77
—Decline to choose	10	7
2. Which of these opinions do you think is more correct?		
—All people would be about the same if they were treated equally.	42	38
—Like fine race horses, some classes of people are just naturally better than others.	30	26
—Decline to choose	28	36

Source: Civil Liberties study, 1978–79.

differences in human capacities and talent but now reject the suggestion that entire categories of people are inherently inferior.

These findings lead us to conclude that although most Americans recognize individual differences in ability, they nevertheless believe that all people are, in some fundamental sense, equally worthy. Because of these conflicting perspectives, American attitudes toward equality are often ambivalent. Depending on how a question is phrased, what alternatives are offered, and especially whether the alternative to an egalitarian response has an invidious or categorical flavor, respondents may choose the egalitarian alternative on some questions and the inegalitarian alternative on others.

In what sense, then, do Americans believe that "all men are created equal"? Abraham Lincoln, when he was still an obscure Illinois politician, sought to resolve this question by arguing that when the Founding Fathers pronounced this "self-evident" truth, they were advancing not a literal description of reality but an *ideal*. They "meant to set up a standard maxim for a free society, which should be familiar to all, and revered by all; constantly looked to, constantly labored for, and even though never perfectly attained, constantly approximated, and thereby constantly spreading and deepening its influence and augmenting the happiness and value of life to all people of all colors everywhere."[13] The data we have presented in this chapter confirm Lincoln's observation about the "spreading and deepening" influence of the egalitarian ideal. An ideal that once applied mainly to native white Protestant males has been extended to include blacks, women, Catholics, Jews, immigrants, and other groups traditionally subject to discrimination. As a result, the American commitment to egalitarianism appears to be stronger and more inclusive today than at any previous time.

Belief in the equality of human worth implies belief in a number of principles, among them that every citizen should have an equal chance to participate in the political life of the nation, and that everyone must be accorded equal rights and opportunities under a system of impartial laws. While both principles have been part of the American ethos from its inception, both, as we shall see, have also been substantially modified and expanded as the nation has developed.

Egalitarianism and Popular Sovereignty

Although the United States was to become the world's first large-scale democracy, the men who drafted the Constitution were reluctant to provide for extensive popular participation in government. Some of the features they incorporated into the Constitution—the electoral college, separation of powers, a bicameral legislature that included an upper (or "aristocratic") house elected indirectly, an independent judiciary—were consciously designed to insulate the government from too much popular influence. Even the word *democracy* was, to some of the Founders and other notables of the late eighteenth century, a term of opprobrium, signifying "mob-ocracy" or "rule by the worst." As Hofstadter has observed, "Nowhere in America or Europe, not even among the great liberated thinkers of the Enlightenment . . . did democratic ideas appear respectable [in the eighteenth century] to the cultivated classes."[14]

Nevertheless, the American Revolution severely undermined the old aristocratic ideals and promoted the doctrines of political equality, liberty, and the right to self-government. The transformation, though not sudden, was far-reaching. When Tocqueville visited the United States in the 1830s, he found a society dominated by "a passion for equality" in all facets of life. Superior wealth, which had commanded political deference in colonial times, had become, by his day, "a real cause for disfavor and an obstacle to gaining [election to public office]."[15] Tocqueville traced the democratic revolution to feelings aroused by the War of Independence: "At that time society was shaken to the core. The people, in whose name the war had been fought, became a power and wanted to act on their own; democratic instincts awoke . . . a taste for every form of independence grew . . . customs and laws began to march in step to [that] goal."[16]

Institutional changes, as well as the decline of the patrician influence, tended to promote political equality. All adult white males were granted the vote, new forms of party organization arose to compete for popular favor, and informal barriers that discouraged the election of ordinary people to office were largely eliminated.

Today, of course, belief in popular sovereignty is firmly embedded in the American political culture (see Table 3–5). Roughly 95 percent of the respondents in Prothro and Grigg's study of American democratic values in the 1950s subscribed to the view that "every citizen should have an equal chance to influence government policy."[17] The public also overwhelmingly rejects any suggestion of one-man rule or a hereditary ruling class. Even during the Great Depression, 91 percent of the American public opposed dictatorship as a solution to the nation's problems, while only 3 percent endorsed the idea. Fully 98 percent of the respondents in a 1942 Gallup poll opposed the idea that certain men in the United States be invested "with titles like Lord, Duke, and Sir . . . the way they have in England." Political office, Americans believe, must be kept open to everyone. In Westie's Indianapolis

Table 3–5   Political equality

	General public
1. Every citizen should have an equal chance to influence government policy.	
—Agree	95
—Disagree; other	5
2. Would you like to see a dictatorship established in this country?	
—Yes	3
—No	91
—No opinion	6
3. Do you think it would be a good idea if we had titles like Lord, Duke, and Sir in this country the way they have in England?	
—Yes	0
—No	98
—Don't know	2
4. Everyone should have an equal right to hold public office.	
—Agree	91
—Disagree	8
—Undecided	1

Sources: question 1, James W. Prothro and Charles Grigg, "Fundamental Principles of Democracy: Bases of Agreement and Disagreement," *Journal of Politics,* 22 (May 1960), pp. 276–294; question 2, Gallup, 1937, cited in Hadley Cantril, ed., *Public Opinion, 1935–46* (Princeton, N.J.: Princeton University Press, 1951), p. 869; question 3, Gallup, 1942, cited in Cantril, *Public Opinion,* p. 868; question 4, Frank R. Westie, "The American Dilemma: An Empirical Test," *American Sociological Review,* 30 (1965), pp. 527–538.

study, 91 percent affirmed that "every citizen should have an equal right to hold public office."[18]

Although these data suggest that Americans strongly endorse popular sovereignty, they do not begin to illuminate the complications inherent in the notion. For example, how far are Americans prepared to go in extending equal voting rights to citizens who fail to comprehend the complexities of modern political life? The items in Table 3–6 pose this question in particularly acute form. Americans were asked whether they support voting rights for the illiterate, the poorly educated, and those who may know too little to vote intelligently. As the data show, most respondents favor equal voting rights even for poorly informed voters. They also oppose both minimal educational standards and literacy as

Table 3-6 Political equality—equal voting rights

	General public	Influentials
1. Who should be allowed to vote?		
—Only people who know something about the issues	10	7
—All adult citizens, regardless of how ignorant they may be	69	79
—Decline to choose	21	14
	(N = 1,993)	(N = 1,157)
2. People ought to be allowed to vote even if they can't do so intelligently		
—Agree	48	66
—Disagree	52	34
	(N = 1,484)	(N = 3,020)
3. Should people who cannot read or write have the right to vote?		
—Yes	56	—
—No	36	—
—No opinion	8	—
4. Some people say that only those people who have had at least five years of schooling should be allowed to vote. What is your opinion?		
—Agree	32	—
—Disagree	63	—
—No opinion	5	—

Sources: question 1, Civil Liberties study, 1978–79; question 2, Political Affiliations and Beliefs study, 1958; questions 3 and 4, Gallup release, March 19, 1965.

prerequisites for voting. When the public is asked to choose between extending the franchise to all adult citizens regardless of how "ignorant" they may be or restricting voting only to those "who know something about the issue," they opt, by a ratio of seven to one, for universal adult suffrage. Among the political influentials and the better educated, support for universal adult suffrage is even stronger. In this as in other matters, the politically sophisticated have internalized democratic and egalitarian norms more thoroughly than the general public.

The belief that "the people" are supreme and must rule themselves—either directly or through their chosen representatives—is the principal concept legitimizing democratic government. In their eagerness to defend this tenet, some champions of popular sovereignty have been inclined to invest "the people" with virtues well beyond anything they would be willing to attribute to the individuals who collectively make up this entity. They praise the people as possessing ultimate wisdom and a stainless character, viewing them as the infallible (or nearly infallible) beacon by which a wise nation will steer its course. Just as aristocrats of an earlier era were given to dismissing the people as a "stinking beast," so certain democrats have enshrined them as the most noble of "God's creatures," the repositories of the most exalted virtues—unspoiled by the urge for power and self-promotion that overtakes even the best-intentioned rulers.

The mystique of "the people" is for some democrats so strong that they tend to exclude from the ranks of the people those who are rich, influential, well-born, or highly successful, reserving the term instead for the so-called common or plain people, the "average man," or the "masses," and especially the most needy, disadvantaged, and powerless among them. It is the dispossessed members of the population whom they credit with the greatest wisdom and virtue. The dispossessed are presumed to be the least corrupted because they have largely been spared the temptations of greed and exploitation that so often entice the rich and powerful. Thus a portrait emerges of the common man as a near saint—a portrait not altogether unfamiliar, since many of its elements can be found in ancient Judaism and Christianity and have recurred in Rousseau's glorification of the "noble savage," in Tolstoy's reverence for the silent and dignified peasant, in Andrew Johnson's ennobled but unschooled farmer and artisan, and, of course, in Marx's idolization of the exploited proletarian. One scarcely needs to dwell on this portrait of "the people" to realize that it is just as arbitrary and unfounded as the portraits preferred by the overlords of earlier and more rigidly stratified societies. In the one case, the common people are scorned as "the great unwashed"—ignorant, swinish, and vile; in the other, they are exalted as the embodiment of all that is noble and generous in human nature.

As influential as these competing mystiques have been in the debates between the defenders and critics of egalitarianism and popular sovereignty, the American public, taken as a whole, does not fully accept either of them. As can be seen in Table 3–7, about half the public believe that most citizens are poorly informed or unsophisticated about politics, while the other half generally take a more favorable view of the electorate. For example, 48 percent say that "most people don't have enough sense to pick their own leaders wisely," while 52 percent disagree with this view. Similarly, about 46 percent say that the majority of voters "are too uninformed and emotional to make sensible choices," while 36 percent say that people "use their vote wisely most of the time."

The nation's opinion leaders are consistently—although not overwhelmingly—more optimistic than the general public about the wisdom of the electorate. Some 60 to 70 percent of the leaders appear to believe that the voters understand political issues, make sensible electoral choices, and really know their own best interests. On the other hand, 30 to 40 percent express doubts about the electorate's capacities. Clearly, despite the assertions of popular virtue and intelligence that have been commonplace in the American democratic context, there exists in American society a marked degree of uncertainty about the ability of the electorate to perform its civic duties effectively.

Owing, presumably, to their doubts about the wisdom of "the people," many Americans expect their elected representatives to exercise their own judgment on major issues rather than to adhere slavishly to what appears to be current public opinion. For example, when asked whether Congress or "the people" is "more often right in its views on broad national issues," 42 percent chose Congress and 40 percent chose the people (see Table 3–8). In addition,

Table 3-7 Political equality—wisdom of the people

	General public	Influentials
1. The majority of voters:		
—use their vote wisely most of the time	36	43
—are too uninformed and emotional to make sensible choices	46	34
—Decline to choose	18	23
	(N = 938)	(N = 845)
2. The main trouble with democracy is that most people don't really know what's best for them.		
—Agree	58	41
—Disagree	42	59
	(N = 1,484)	(N = 3,020)
3. Most people don't have enough sense to pick their own leaders wisely.		
—Agree	48	28
—Disagree	52	72
	(N = 1,484)	(N = 3,020)
4. "Issues" and "arguments" are beyond the understanding of most voters.		
—Agree	62	38
—Disagree	38	62
	(N = 1,484)	(N = 3,020)
5. Do you think that the majority of the people in this country are usually correct in their views on important issues?		
—Yes	38	—
—No	42	—
—Don't know	20	—

Sources: question 1, Opinions and Values of Americans survey, 1975–77; questions 2, 3, and 4, Political Affiliations and Beliefs study, 1958; question 5, Gallup, 1939, cited in Hadley Cantril, ed., *Public Opinion, 1935–1946* (Princeton, N.J.: Princeton University Press, 1951), p. 692.

53 percent said that "when making new laws, the government should pay most attention to . . . the opinions of people who really know something about the subject," while only a minority (22 percent) said that government should heed "the opinions of average citizens, regardless of how little they know."

Yet, from the standpoint of popular sovereignty, the most important finding in Table 3–8 is that, despite their reservations about the wisdom of the electorate, the vast majority of Ameri-

Table 3-8 How much influence on government decisions should the public have?

	General public	Community influentials
1. To be realistic about it, our elected officials:		
—know much more than the voters about issues, and should be allowed to make whatever decisions they think best	8	11
—would badly misuse their power if they weren't watched and guided by the voters	68	64
—Decline to choose	23	25
	(N = 1,026)	(N = 601)
2. When making new laws, the government should pay most attention to:		
—the opinion of the people who really know something about the subject	53	60
—the opinions of average citizens, regardless of how little they know	22	18
—Decline to choose	25	22
	(N = 1,026)	(N = 601)
3. Should people with more intelligence and character have greater influence over the country's decisions than other people?		
—Yes, because they have more to offer and can do more to benefit society.	39	45
—No, because every citizen must have an equal right to decide what's best for the country.	45	39
—Decline to choose	16	16
	(N = 1,026)	(N = 601)
4. Elections:		
—are mostly a waste of time and money, since the same people run things anyway	7	3
—are one of the best ways to keep elected officials on their toes	75	86
—Decline to choose	18	11
	(N = 967)	(N = 556)
5. Which group do you think is more often right in its views on broad national issues?		
—Congress	42	—
—The people	40	—
—Don't know	18	—

Sources: questions 1 through 4, Civil Liberties study, 1978–79; question 5, Gallup, 1939, cited in Hadley Cantril, ed., *Public Opinion, 1935–1946* (Princeton, N.J.: Princeton University Press, 1951), pp. 929–930.

cans believe that elections are essential "to keep elected officials on their toes," while only 7 percent dismiss elections as a "waste of time." Moreover, 68 percent of the public believe that elected officials "would badly misuse their power if they weren't watched and guided by the people." Although the public seems prepared to defer to the judgment of experts for certain purposes, it insists on its right to keep a close watch on elected officials and to retain the ultimate authority to hold its representatives accountable for their performance.

Equality of Rights, Opportunities, and Outcomes

The right of every citizen to participate equally in the choice of elected representatives now appears to be a settled principle of American democratic doctrine. Considerable controversy exists, however, over the question of whether individual equality also requires an equal (or more nearly equal) distribution of social and economic benefits. On one side of the argument are the advocates of free enterprise, who believe that while everyone must be free to compete economically, the social and economic inequalities that may arise from such competition are entirely legitimate. On the other side are those who believe that rewards ought to be somewhat more equalized and ought not to depend so heavily on differences in ability, opportunity, or social origins.

Few American opinion leaders have ever accepted the view— advocated, for example, by some socialists—that economic rewards ought to be distributed equally. In keeping with the nation's capitalist heritage, they have sought to guarantee that everyone enjoy the same right to acquire wealth under a system of fair rules uniformly applied. John Adams, a signer of the Declaration of Independence and the second president of the United States, articulated this position early in the nation's history: "That all men have one common nature, is a principle that will now universally prevail, and equal rights and equal duties will in a just sense, I hope, be inferred from it. But equal ranks and equal property can never be inferred from it, any more than [can] equal understanding, agility, vigor or beauty. Equal laws are all that can ever be derived from human equality."[19]

Adams, of course, was a leading spokesman for early American conservatism. Yet the sentiment he voiced has been reiterated and amplified by many important American thinkers of different ideological outlooks from the eighteenth century to the present. Even Herbert Croly, perhaps the most influential American liberal writer of the early twentieth century, observed that "American political thinkers have always repudiated the idea that by equality of rights they meant anything like equality of performance or power. The utmost varieties of power and ability are bound to exist and to bring about different levels of individual achievement. Democracy . . . requires an equal start in the race while expecting at the same time an unequal finish."[20]

A certain amount of social and economic inequality, therefore, has generally been considered compatible with the American conception of equality. Indeed, most Americans have tended to regard differences in wealth and status as evidence not of inequality per se, but of individual distinction, character, and achievement. As such, "earned" inequalities are, within limits, widely considered to be natural to democratic life. They are the just outcomes of fair competition among people of unequal talent, industry, and "character."

Nevertheless, the tendency to restrict equality to the idea of equal opportunity has not been without its critics. Some Americans are outraged by the inequalities of outcome that are permitted—or even encouraged—by the competitive ethic associated with private enterprise. Others resent what they consider society's arbitrary decisions about which talents to reward and which to ignore. Still others decry the greater advantages enjoyed by people who possess inherited wealth. An especially frequent criticism is that, given the obvious inequalities of wealth typical of modern capitalist societies, the granting of *formal* equality of opportunity is simply a sham.

It is natural to wonder whether a nation can genuinely uphold the ideals of political equality and equal opportunity on the one hand, and economic inequality on the other. A recent study by Verba and Orren indicates, nevertheless, that Americans at least try to maintain this uneasy combination of value preferences. These two authors collected quantitative indicators of political equality, equal opportunity, and economic inequality in the industrial democracies of the United States, Europe, and Japan.

After examining these indicators, which included class differences in rates of political participation, the availability of higher education to various segments of society, and the actual distributions of income, they concluded that "international comparisons of the extent of equality are difficult, for the measures are uncertain and the data are not always the best. No single measure will do, but comparisons across a range of indicators reveal that the United States ranks among the most open and participatory of modern democracies when it comes to politics and among the least egalitarian when it comes to economic matters. The nation embodies democratic polity and capitalist economy at their fullest!"[21]

Verba and Orren also investigated the efforts of governments in various industrial democracies to redress economic inequality. They found that, in most cases, the efforts in the United States lagged behind those of other countries. Yet they also discovered that "one area in which governmental spending in the United States has exceeded that in other nations is education. The United States ranks first in per capita spending on schooling and first in the percentage of the population that has received higher education. But educational expenditure differs from other outlays in that it promotes equal opportunity rather than equal results."[22]

Tables 3–9 and 3–10 present evidence about the views held by modern-day Americans on these matters. As the data show, most Americans strongly—even overwhelmingly—support the notion that everyone should have the same *chance* to "get ahead," but they are uniformly negative toward suggestions that everyone must end up with the same economic rewards. Indeed, the distinction between equal opportunity and equality of outcomes could scarcely be drawn more sharply than it is in these data.[23]

One should, however, interpret these results with caution. Many Americans endorse equal opportunity as an abstract value but fail to accept the specific measures that seem necessary to bring it about in practice. For example, Table 3–9 shows that in the early 1940s, 89 percent of the American public said that "Negroes in this town should have the same chance as white people to get a good education," while only 6 percent rejected the idea. Yet reflecting the conditions that prevailed at the time, a 1942 poll

Table 3-9   Equality of opportunity

	General public
1. Everyone in America should have equal opportunities to get ahead.	
—Agree	98
—Disagree	2
2. Children should have equal education opportunities.	
—Agree	98
—Disagree	1
—Uncertain	1
3. Do you think that Negroes in this town should have the same chance as white people to get a good education?	
—Yes	89
—No	6
—Qualified answers	3
—Don't know	2
4. Do you think Negroes should be given just as good a chance as white men to get ahead in the armed forces?	
—Yes	72
—No	22
—Don't know	6
5. Do you think a Negro doing the same work as a white man should get the same pay?	
—Yes	87
—No	10
—Don't know	3
6. As you know, there has been considerable discussion in the news lately regarding the rights of homosexual men and women. In general, do you think homosexuals should or should not have equal rights in terms of job opportunities?	
—Should	56
—Should not	33
—No opinion	11

Sources: questions 1 and 2, Frank R. Westie, "The American Dilemma: An Empirical Test," *American Sociological Review*, 30 (1965), pp. 527–538; questions 3–5, National Opinion Research Corporation, cited in Hadley Cantril, ed., *Public Opinion, 1935–1946* (Princeton, N.J.: Princeton University Press, 1951), pp. 509, 998; question 6, *The Gallup Poll, 1972–1977*, vol. 2 (Wilmington, Del.: Scholarly Resources, 1979), p. 1202.

Table 3–10 Equality of outcomes

	General public	Influentials
1. Under a fair economic system:		
—all people would earn about the same	7	5
—people with more ability would earn higher salaries	78	75
—Decline to choose	15	21
	(N = 938)	(N = 845)
2. Which would be fairer—to pay people wages according to:		
—their economic needs?	6	5
—how hard they work?	71	69
—Decline to choose	23	26
	(N = 967)	(N = 556)
3. Giving everybody about the same income regardless of the type of work they do:		
—would be a fairer way to distribute the country's wealth than the present system	5	5
—would destroy the desire to work hard and do a better job	85	84
—Decline to choose	10	11
	(N = 967)	(N = 556)
4. A person's wages should depend on:		
—how much he needs to live decently	20	11
—the importance of his job	45	43
—Decline to choose	35	45
	(N = 938)	(N = 845)

Sources: questions 1 and 4, Opinions and Values of Americans survey, 1975–77; questions 2 and 3, Civil Liberties study, 1978–79.

showed that 66 percent of the general public would have *denied* the right of black children to attend the same schools as whites.[24] Here we observe what is by now a familiar pattern: many respondents—in this case a vast majority—will solemnly endorse general ideals that they are reluctant to put into practice.

Instances of such discrepancies show up for other items in Table 3–9. During World War II, a large majority of Americans said that "Negroes should be given just as good a chance as white men to get ahead in the armed services." Yet only 41 percent of a national Gallup sample agreed that "Negroes and white soldiers [should] serve together in all branches of the armed services."[25] In the early 1940s, an overwhelming majority (87 percent) said that blacks and whites should receive the same pay for the same work—a principle inherent in the idea of equal opportunity. Other surveys of that period, however, reported that 39 percent did not want a black person hired to work alongside them; 31 percent said that their employer should not hire blacks as co-workers; and 25 percent said they would refuse to work alongside a black person.[26]

To be sure, considerable progress toward racial equality has been made in the United States since the 1940s. The discrepancies just reported between general ideals and more specific racial attitudes have now been somewhat reduced or resolved in ways that honor more fully the spirit of equal opportunity. Yet discrepancies between the abstract statements and particular applications of equality still appear. A 1977 Gallup Poll, for example, indicated that 56 percent of the American public endorse the general principle that homosexuals should have "equal rights in terms of job opportunities"; however, 65 percent of the same respondents would deny homosexuals the right to work as elementary school teachers.[27]

But if Americans were really opposed to equality of opportunity for blacks or homosexuals, what kept them from saying so? The reason, we believe, lies in the honorific status of equal opportunity as an American value and the sense of elementary fair play it embodies. Many are unwilling to admit even to themselves that they do not fully subscribe to this value. Often it is difficult for even the most prejudiced to deny that equal opportunity ought to be enjoyed by groups they dislike. One may consider such behavior inconsistent, but one must also recognize it as testimony to the power of the egalitarian norm in American life. Without it, public resistance to the civil rights movement might well have proved insuperable, and the civil rights advances of recent decades might never have occurred.

A 1960 study by the sociologist Frank Westie provides interesting corroborative evidence on this point.[28] Like other investigators, Westie found that respondents overwhelmingly endorsed general value statements such as "all people should be treated as equals in the eyes of the law" but frequently rejected parallel statements designed to measure support for these general values when applied to racial equality. For example, 60 percent said that people in a democracy "should be allowed to live where they please and can afford," but only 35 percent were willing to have a black family live next door. In a departure from previous research, Westie encouraged his respondents to compare the answers they gave to the two kinds of questions. On making these comparisons, many respondents became uncomfortable with the inconsistency in their attitudes and began to qualify or adjust one of their original statements. In 82 percent of the cases in which they recognized inconsistencies, the respondents modified their opinions on concrete issues to make them more consistent with their endorsement of general democratic values.

The Practical Meaning of Equality of Opportunity

Although the American commitment to the ideal of equal opportunity has endured for some 200 years, the precise meanings that have been attached to this ideal have changed as social and economic conditions have changed. To understand what Americans of the late eighteenth and early nineteenth centuries meant by equal opportunity, one must first appreciate their deep distrust of government. A powerful central government, they believed, would inevitably become the tool of the rich and the powerful, who would use their political influence to gain privileges for themselves and to mulct the less fortunate of their just earnings. As one nineteenth-century writer observed: "Experience will show that [the] power of government has always been exercised under the influence and for the exclusive benefit of wealth. It was never wielded in behalf of the community. Whenever an exception is made to the general law of the land . . . it will always be found to be in favor of wealth."[29]

The obvious solution to the problem of guaranteeing equal opportunity was to keep government small and the laws just. "The best government is that which governs least" became one of the most popular slogans of egalitarian reformers of this period. These reformers acknowledged that people varied in their innate capacities, but they insisted that if each person were left to fend for himself without any special aid from government, the distribution of wealth and property would be far more equal than it was. Direct government action, as one reform journal claimed, "has been the fruitful parent of nine-tenths of all the evil, moral and physical, by which mankind has been afflicted since the creation of the world, and by which human nature has been self-degraded, fettered and oppressed."[30]

The tendency to equate equal opportunity with minimal government was a response to the economic and political conditions during the nation's early history. But as the nation sharply accelerated its industrial development in the decades after the Civil War, attitudes toward equality of opportunity began to change as well. Reformers like Henry George, John R. Commons, and Lester Ward argued that the monopolistic practices of the new industrial conglomerates, combined with the inability of the urban working classes to obtain the education necessary for success, required a response from government that went far beyond the mere equal protection of the laws. George, for example, said that adhering to the old conception of equal opportunity under the new conditions of the late nineteenth century was like insisting that "each should sink or swim for himself in crossing a river, ignoring the fact that some had been artificially supplied with corks and others artificially loaded with lead."[31]

The reforms enacted during the late nineteenth and early twentieth centuries may seem rather minor in retrospect, consisting as they did mainly of laws intended to break up a handful of monopolies and to end other blatantly anticompetitive business practices. Nevertheless, these reforms represented a profound departure from past belief and practice. For the first time, leading members of both political parties—the Republican Theodore Roosevelt as well as the Democrat Woodrow Wilson—acknowledged that positive government action was sometimes essential for realizing the ideal of equal opportunity. This was a critical turn in the evolution of the American political tradition.

The idea that government had a vital role to play in promoting equality of rights and opportunities developed much further during the New Deal, and still further in the 1960s during the public debates over poverty and racial and sexual discrimination. Perhaps the most far-reaching of these public discussions were the debates over racial inequality and segregation. With the passage of landmark civil rights bills in 1964, 1965, and 1968, the federal government undertook aggressive efforts to end racial discrimination in public education, employment, housing, interstate transportation, travel accommodations, and voting rights—to end, in short, the most egregious forms of *de jure* and *de facto* discrimination.

The civil rights revolution of the 1960s, to be sure, did not end racial discrimination in the United States. It made significant inroads on the problem, however, and it put an end to virtually all *de jure* discrimination by public agencies. The adoption of the new civil rights regulations, moreover, helped to discredit open Southern resistance to integration and, in doing so, effectively deprived racial prejudice of its last public defenders. Today few if any public figures of significant stature openly maintain that blacks and whites ought to live in different neighborhoods or attend different schools, that local communities have a right to discriminate if they wish to do so, or that blacks ought to be denied equal access to certain jobs or professions. Many issues involving racial equality obviously remain unsettled, but debates now center on how best to overcome *de facto* or covert discrimination, and how best to remedy the effects of past discrimination.

The 1960s also witnessed a major, and in certain respects parallel, assault on sexual discrimination. Partly as a result of the 1964 Civil Rights Act, which prohibited sex discrimination by government or by institutions receiving public funds, many barriers to equal opportunity for women have fallen or been weakened. Private opposition to women's rights survives, of course, but today one rarely encounters any public defense of such prejudice. The struggle to strengthen the rights of women will doubtless continue, fortified increasingly by the nation's egalitarian tradition.

The principle of equal opportunity took on still another aspect in the public debate over President Lyndon Johnson's so-called War on Poverty. Johnson and his liberal allies argued that millions of Americans were so deeply mired in poverty that they were effectively denied an adequate chance to help themselves or to advance economically. Rather than attacking the big trusts and monopolies, as the Progressives had done, Johnson sought to open opportunities to the disadvantaged through business loan programs, vocational training programs, and remedial and supplementary education to help them acquire the knowledge needed for success in a modern industrial society. The names of these antipoverty programs—Head Start, A Better Chance (ABC), Educational Opportunities Program, Operation Bootstrap—expressed the self-help philosophy they embodied.

In linking such themes as competition, self-help, and individual achievement to the principle of equal opportunity, liberal reformers sought to tie the War on Poverty to traditional American values. Nevertheless, what they were proposing represented, in at least one respect, a departure from those values. Whereas leading Americans in the eighteenth and nineteenth centuries had argued that everyone would have a chance to prosper if government did not interfere, Johnson and other liberals were now saying that genuine equality of opportunity could be achieved under the conditions of modern industrial society only if government helped to raise the poor to a level of independence. As Johnson explained the War on Poverty:

> The young man or woman who grows up without a decent education, in a broken home, in a hostile or squalid environment, in ill health or in the face of racial injustice—that young man or woman is often trapped in a life of poverty.
>
> He does not have the skills demanded by a complex society. He does not know how to acquire those skills. He faces a mounting sense of despair . . .
>
> The War on Poverty is not a struggle simply to support [such] people, to make them dependent on the generosity of others . . . It is a struggle to give [them] a chance.[32]

The effort to extend equality of opportunity also led to the introduction of "affirmative action," government-enforced policies to compensate women, blacks, and other minorities for the disadvantages they had suffered and continued to suffer because of discrimination. In discussing this notion, Whitney Young explained that "a conscious, planned effort must be made to bring qualified Negroes into entrance jobs in *all* types of employment . . . This approach suggests that if a business never hired Negroes in its offices or plants and two equally qualified people apply, it should hire the Negro to redress the injustice previously visited upon him."[33] Note that Young asked only that *qualified* blacks be given preferential hiring treatment, and that they be appointed to *entry-*

level jobs, after which blacks would presumably be expected to compete for promotion on the same terms as anyone else. Thus he was proposing a form of equal opportunity rather than equality of outcomes between blacks and whites.

These attempts to redefine the meaning of equality of opportunity during the 1960s have provoked strong opposition from several directions. Many critics of the War on Poverty were less opposed to equal opportunity as such than to the rising costs of government and the intrusion of federal agencies into new social domains. The growth of government activity was attacked not only as undesirable in itself, but as an attempt to undermine the freedom, independence, and self-reliance of the people. The policy of affirmative action has been even more controversial than the War on Poverty. Many people find it incompatible with the principle of equal opportunity to give preference to a given race or sex, even when the the avowed purpose is to compensate the disadvantaged. Affirmative action, the critics claim, favors the minority by handicapping the majority.

As these observations suggest, the meaning of "equal opportunity" has undergone several changes over the years. But which, if any, of these definitions and redefinitions of the term do the American people presently support? Our data provide some answers to this question. Table 3–11 shows that a majority of Americans and their opinion leaders agree that "efforts to make everyone as equal as possible . . . should be increased"; only a small fraction—10 percent—want them decreased. A sizable plurality of Americans, furthermore, believe that "if some people are born poor, the community . . . should help them to become equal with others." By a margin of over three to one in the general public and more than ten to one among opinion leaders, Americans also feel that "spending tax money to provide a college education for those who can't afford it is . . . a good idea," while only small fractions of either group oppose it.

Popular attitudes toward government assistance to the disadvantaged are nevertheless marked by ambivalence. Almost 60 percent of the mass public say that "laws guaranteeing equal opportunities for blacks and other minorities sometimes go too far." Although most Americans think that government should intervene positively to promote social and economic equality, they also

Table 3-11 Attitudes toward increasing equality

	General public (N = 938)	Opinion leaders (N = 845)
1. Efforts to make everyone as equal as possible should be:		
—increased	57	60
—decreased	10	8
—Decline to choose	33	32
2. If some people are born poor, the community:		
—should help them to become equal with others	44	57
—should simply accept the fact that not everyone can make it	23	13
—Decline to choose	33	30
3. Spending tax money to provide a college education for those who can't afford it is:		
—a good idea	53	68
—a bad idea	16	6
—Decline to choose	31	26
4. The laws guaranteeing equal job opportunities for blacks and other minorities:		
—should be made even stronger	19	37
—sometimes go too far	59	36
—Neither/undecided	22	27

Source: Opinions and Values of Americans survey, 1975–77.

believe that the primary responsibility for personal advancement ought to remain with the individual. Americans, in other words, have not abandoned their traditional commitment to economic individualism, nor are they ready to endorse all government programs that advertise themselves as equal opportunity programs. Table 3–12 indicates that most Americans believe that poor people, blacks, and women should rely more on their own resources and initiative than on government to help them overcome the effects of discrimination and economic disadvantage. By a two to one margin, the general public says that the poor "should help themselves" rather than "receive special government help"; by more than three to one, they say that blacks and women should fight discrimination by developing their own talents and abilities rather than by relying on group pressure.

Table 3–12   Individual responsibility

	General public	Opinion leaders
1. In order to improve their conditions, the poor:		
—should receive special government help	22	43
—should help themselves	53	19
—Decline to choose	25	38
	(N = 938)	(N = 845)
2. Which of these statements do you agree with?		
—The best way for blacks to overcome discrimination is through pressure and social action.	18	—
—The best way to overcome discrimination is for each individual black to be even better trained and more qualified than the most qualified white person.	72	—
—Decline to choose	10	—
	(N = 2,248)	
3. Which of these statements do you agree with?		
—The best way to handle problems of discrimination is for each woman to make sure she gets the best training possible for what she wants to do.	74	—
—Only if women organize and work together can anything really be done about discrimination.	21	—
—Decline to choose	5	—
	(N = 2,248)	

Sources: question 1, Opinions and Values of Americans survey, 1975–77; questions 2 and 3, University of Michigan, National Election Study, 1976.

Most Americans also reject the principle of affirmative action (see Table 3–13). Some 53 percent of the public contend that "laws requiring employers to give special preference to minorities when filling jobs are . . . a bad idea," while only 15 percent consider such laws desirable. In another recent national survey Americans say by equally large margins that affirmative action on behalf of blacks and women would be "unfair" to qualified whites and to men. And as numerous surveys over the past decade attest, Americans overwhelmingly oppose the busing of school children away from neighborhood schools as a means of promoting equal educational opportunities.

Table 3–13 shows, in addition, that opinion leaders tend to op-

Table 3-13   Affirmative action

	General public	Influentials
1. Laws requiring employers to give special preference to minorities when filling jobs are:		
—a good idea	15	33
—a bad idea	53	31
—Decline to choose	32	37
	(N = 938)	(N = 845)
2. Laws requiring employers to give special preference to minorities when filling jobs are:		
—necessary to make up for a long history of discrimination	10	26
—unfair to qualified people who are not members of a minority	76	62
—Decline to choose	15	12
	(N = 1,026)	(N = 601)
3. Laws requiring employers to give special preference to women when filling jobs are:		
—only fair, considering how often they have been discriminated against in the past	9	12
—unfair to men who may be more qualified	76	76
—Decline to choose	15	12
	(N = 1,993)	(N = 1,157)
4. In the matter of racial integration, which policy would you favor?		
—Busing children to schools outside their own neighborhoods to achieve racial balance	6	25
—Keeping children in neighborhood schools	83	50
—Decline to choose	11	25
	(N = 938)	(N = 845)
5. More minority students should be admitted to our college:		
—even if it means lowering standards of admission	5	8
—only if normal standards of admission are met	85	81
—Decline to choose	10	12
	(N = 1,026)	(N = 601)

Sources: questions 1 and 4, Opinions and Values of Americans survey, 1975–77; questions 2 and 3, Civil Liberties study, 1978–79; question 5, Civil Liberties study, 1978.

pose affirmative action almost as strongly as do most members of the general public. Verba and Orren have turned up similar findings in their study of economic and political equality. Support for racial quotas among businessmen, leading media figures, Republican elites, farm leaders, and "intellectuals" was generally weak. Support for affirmative action was strong only within certain elite groups: "Three out of four of the black leaders favor [quotas] . . . and they are supported by a slight majority of feminist leaders. Among groups generally allied with blacks and feminists, though, there is little support for racial quotas. Only three out of ten Democratic leaders and college youths support such quotas, as do only one in four labor leaders."[34]

Taken together, these data suggest that although Americans favor equality of opportunity, including government programs to promote it, they do not favor equality at the expense of discouraging individual achievement, or penalizing nonminorities. A 1977 poll conducted for the *New York Times* and CBS News further confirms these findings. Ninety-four percent of the respondents in a national survey said that racial discrimination is "wrong," and 73 percent supported laws that would "see to it that blacks have equal job rights." But on the issue of affirmative action, the public took a decidedly negative stance. Only 22 percent of those surveyed said that blacks should be given "extra consideration" in job hiring in order to "make up for past discrimination."[35]

Similar attitudes are apparent in Table 3–14. A majority of Americans favor remedial education programs to help women and minorities score higher on college entrance and job placement tests. They insist, however, that "ability" rather than special preference be the final criterion for admitting them to college and placing them in jobs—a criterion that stresses formal equality of opportunity for people of equal talents.

Summary and Conclusions

American opinion has, from the early days of the Republic, regarded equality of opportunity as a fundamental principle of the civic culture. Like their forebears, contemporary Americans believe that a person's success in life should depend on his own ef-

Table 3-14 Equal opportunity for jobs and college

1. Some people say that to make up for past discrimination, women and members of minority groups should be given preferential treatment in getting jobs and places in college. Others say that ability, as determined by test scores, should be the main consideration. Which comes closest to your point of view?

	Men	Women	Whites	Nonwhites
—Special preference	13	17	10	38
—Ability	80	78	85	49
—No opinion	7	5	5	13

2. Would you favor or oppose the federal government's offering special educational or vocational courses, free of charge, to enable members of minority groups to do better in tests?

	General public
—Favor	60
—Oppose	29
— No opinion	11

Sources: Gallup, 1979; *San Francisco Chronicle,* April 5, 1979.

forts and abilities rather than on his social standing at birth. As we have shown, however, attitudes have changed about how best to attain equal opportunity. When, as in the nineteenth century, the impediments to equality appeared to result from government-sanctioned privilege, Americans believed that a policy of minimal government was the best way to promote equal opportunity. In the twentieth century, when the impediments to equal opportunity seemed to arise from the stratifications of industrial capitalism, most Americans came to favor government intervention to help the disadvantaged overcome these impediments.

The concept of equality itself, moreover, has been greatly broadened, so that the number of people thought to be entitled to equal opportunity has dramatically increased. Numerous public opinion surveys indicate that contemporary Americans are far less prejudiced toward minorities and women than they were forty or fifty years ago. Moreover, majorities now *favor* government action to combat many forms of discrimination once widely accepted as normal.

Part of the reason for this change obviously lies in the efforts of blacks, women, and other deprived groups to improve their own conditions. In addition, the rise in overall levels of national wealth and productivity has perhaps made it easier to distribute economic rewards and life chances to broader segments of the population, including those who had suffered discrimination in the past. But as important as these factors may have been in promoting equality, we believe that democratic ideals themselves have also played a vital role. Consider, for example, President Johnson's plea on behalf of the civil rights legislation of 1964:

> We believe that all men are created equal. Yet many are denied equal treatment . . .
> We believe that all men are entitled to the blessings of liberty. Yet millions are being deprived of those blessings—not because of their own failures, but because of the color of their skin . . .
> [This] cannot continue. Our Constitution, the foundation of our Republic, forbids it. The principles of our freedom forbid it. Morality forbids it.[36]

One encounters this kind of appeal to traditional democratic ideals throughout the history of race relations in the United States. For example, in the nineteenth-century debate over the proposed Fifteenth Amendment to the Constitution forbidding discrimination against blacks in voting, a Kentucky senator had enumerated a list of reasons why blacks were allegedly inferior to whites. Daniel Clark of New Hampshire rose to reply:

> Here is the difficulty: the negro is a man! and however degraded, inferior, abject, or humble, it is our duty to elevate and improve him, and to give him the means of elevation or improvement; and the Senator from Kentucky may assert and prove that there are thirty-six, or fifty-six, or a hundred and six points of difference between him and the white man, but until he shows that he is not a man, the negro will be entitled to be treated by us as a man, and to demand and enjoy the same political privileges as other men.[37]

Speeches of this kind, rooted in the assumption of the essential worth of all people, have not always carried the day, but in appealing to values that no American could easily ignore, they have been able to command a hearing and even, at times, to persuade audiences to take a more tolerant stance than they otherwise might have.

The Westie study, referred to earlier, provides useful empirical evidence of the power of egalitarian values to shape public opinion. Westie found that when survey respondents were forced to confront inconsistencies between the values of the American ethos and their own prejudices, most modified their attitudes to make them more consistent with egalitarianism.

In explaining changing American attitudes toward racial and sexual equality, one must also take into account the vital role played by political elites in promoting egalitarian values. Although many local opinion leaders, particularly in the South, made political careers for themselves by echoing the race prejudices of their constituents, other more nationally oriented leaders often resisted or openly fought such prejudices. Particularly in the past forty years, national opinion leaders—in the civil rights movement, the press, the universities, and the federal government—have been at the forefront of the struggle to achieve racial equality. Beginning in the 1930s, when the federal government began pressing southern social workers to distribute relief benefits fairly, the national government (prodded, to be sure, by the civil rights organizations) has chipped away at the southern caste system and at the patterns of discrimination that remained in other parts of the nation. The civil rights acts of the 1960s were in many respects the culmination of this effort.

Decisions by the courts also played a critical role in promoting school desegregation and other forms of racial equality. The courts, of course, are not only the institution most insulated from popular pressures but also are the most attentive to the constitutional principles that embody the nation's egalitarian tradition.

Because so much of the impetus toward racial equality has emanated from the elite centers of the nation's political culture, one should expect that the people who pay most attention to the activities of those centers—namely, the politically sophisticated and involved—will exhibit the greatest support for equal rights. This expectation is borne out by Table 3–15, which shows that the politically sophisticated are more likely than the unsophisticated to oppose segregation and to favor government programs promoting equal rights for blacks and women.

Yet, as we have observed, the nation's political elites have not reached agreement on all issues relating to equality; they are

Table 3-15   Effect of political sophistication on support for clear egalitarian norms[a]

	Political sophistication				
	Low	Medium-low	Middle	Medium-high	High
1. If an employer is forced to lay off some employees, he should:					
—treat men and women employees exactly the same	48	53	61	62	69
—let the women go first, especially if they are married	43	30	31	28	17
—Decline to choose	9	17	8	10	14
	(N=183)	(N=186)	(N=186)	(N=186)	(N=185)
2. If minorities aren't receiving equal treatment in jobs or housing:					
—the government should step in to see that they are treated the same as everyone else	41	53	48	55	65
—they should try to act better so that they will be accepted	30	30	31	20	14
—Decline to choose	29	17	21	25	21
	(N=154)	(N=177)	(N=178)	(N=178)	(N=182)
3. Should the government support the right of black people to go to any hotel or restaurant they can afford, or should it stay out of this matter?					
—Go anywhere	44	54	57	63	75
—Stay out of this matter	31	29	31	26	20
—Don't know/no interest	26	17	12	11	6
	(N=436)	(N=405)	(N=488)	(N=428)	(N=637)
4. Which of these statements would you agree with?					
—White people have a right to keep black people out of their neighborhoods if they want to.	31	22	18	12	9
—Black people have a right to live wherever they can afford to, just like anyone else.	55	68	74	81	86
—Don't know/no interest	14	10	8	8	5
	(N=436)	(N=405)	(N=488)	(N=428)	(N=637)
5. What about you? Are you in favor of desegregation, strict segregation, or something in between?					
—Desegregation	20	26	33	42	58
—In between	50	54	49	47	37

Table 3–15 (continued)

	Political sophistication				
	Low	Medium-low	Middle	Medium-high	High
—Segregation	24	17	17	10	5
—Don't know/no interest	6	3	1	1	1
	(N = 436)	(N = 405)	(N = 488)	(N = 428)	(N = 637)

Source: questions 1 and 2, Opinions and Values of Americans survey, 1975–77; questions 3–5, University of Michigan, National Election Study, 1972.

a. Blacks have been excluded from the tabulations on items concerning racial equality. No appreciable differences exist between men and women on the issue of sexual equality; hence, all respondents are included in the results.

sharply divided on matters such as busing to achieve school integration and affirmative action. Although the Supreme Court has sanctioned certain forms of affirmative action and has generally upheld busing, many congressmen and several presidents have resisted such policies. The effects of these divisions within the elite are apparent in Table 3–16. In the absence of an elite consensus favoring particular egalitarian norms, the politically sophisticated members of the general public are *not* more likely to support those norms than the unsophisticated. (For a further discussion of the role of opinion elites in promoting the values of the ethos, see Chapter 8.)

If, as we maintain, the egalitarian values of the ethos have played a significant role in helping disadvantaged groups to achieve a measure of equality, certain other values in the ethos have served to obstruct policies aimed at equalizing opportunities. In particular, demands for affirmative action have run afoul of traditional capitalist values that stress individual merit, private enterprise, and personal responsibility. Moreover, some egalitarians believe that the pursuit of equality by means of racial and sexual quotas is actually inconsistent with the American ideal of equal opportunity. Having noted these exceptions, we must nevertheless stress that the values of the ethos have on the whole greatly helped rather than hindered the efforts of blacks and other disadvantaged groups to achieve equality: the civil rights revolution of the past few decades could scarcely have occurred without the powerful influence of the egalitarian tradition.

Table 3-16   Effect of political sophistication on support for egalitarian policies when elites are divided[a]

	Political sophistication				
	Low	Medium-low	Middle	Medium-high	High
1. Laws requiring employers to give special preference to minorities when filling jobs are:					
—necessary to make up for a long history of discrimination	7	8	4	6	11
—unfair to qualified people who are not members of a minority	69	79	88	87	81
—Decline to choose	24	14	8	7	8
	(N = 192)	(N = 160)	(N = 180)	(N = 192)	(N = 215)
2. Laws requiring employers to give special preference to women when filling jobs are:					
—only fair, considering how often they have been discriminated against in the past	15	9	7	7	8
—unfair to men who may be more qualified	64	76	82	85	81
—Decline to choose	21	16	11	8	11
	(N = 429)	(N = 338)	(N = 372)	(N = 383)	(N = 485)
3. In the matter of racial integration, which policy would you favor?					
—Busing children to schools outside their own neighborhoods to achieve racial balance	3	2	3	6	8
—Keeping children in neighborhood schools	89	93	88	86	76
—Decline to choose	8	5	9	8	18
	(N = 154)	(N = 177)	(N = 178)	(N = 178)	(N = 182)

Sources: questions 1 and 2, Civil Liberties study, 1979; question 3, Opinions and Values of Americans survey, 1975–77.

a. Blacks have been excluded from the tabulations on items concerning racial equality. No appreciable differences exist between men and women on the issue of sexual equality; hence, all respondents are included in the results on this question.

4 The Cultural Foundations of Capitalism

Just as the United States is widely regarded as the first political democracy in the modern world, so it is also viewed—along with Great Britain—as a model of the capitalist economic system. Capitalist values have been so pervasive in American life and so deeply etched into the national consciousness that they must be considered the second of the two major strands of thought that compose the American ethos.

Capitalism in American Life

A passion for business is as old as the nation itself. "There is probably no people on earth," wrote Francis J. Grund, a nineteenth-century Austrian immigrant to the United States, "with whom business constitutes pleasure, and industry amusement, in an equal degree with the inhabitants of the United States of America." He continued, "Business is the very soul of an American; he pursues it, not as a means of procuring for himself and his family the necessary comforts of life, but as the fountain of all human felicity; and shows as much enthusiastic ardour in his application to it as any crusader."[1]

Few observers of life in the United States are likely to challenge this claim. Since colonial days Americans have cheerfully conceded their drive toward economic gain, and they have been irrepressible in their pursuit of it through business. President Coolidge once summarized the prevailing attitude: "The business of America is business."

Although America's devotion to business has resulted in impressive economic achievements, American business does not enjoy an altogether favorable public image. For the past century, its nature and role in American life have often been topics of public controversy. Questions rarely arise about the social desirability of the small, individually owned or family owned business, such as a neighborhood store or small manufacturing plant; but as business grows and takes on the characteristics of "big business" and large-scale capitalism, it awakens anxieties among many Americans. They worry about monopolies, excessive power and profits, misleading advertising, ruthless competitive practices, depression, and unemployment. Thus, for example, when Americans are asked whether business has "too much power" in American life, only about 35 percent say yes. But when they are asked about "big business," the figure rises to 82 percent.[2]

The term *capitalism* itself seems even less well regarded. One rarely encounters the word at all in popular print except when it is used to attack the capitalist system. Many businessmen consciously avoid the term. For example, a former president of the United States Chamber of Commerce, speaking for his colleagues, conceded that "We fear that the word capitalism is unpopular. So we take refuge in a nebulous phrase and talk about the 'Free Enterprise System.' "[3]

In this volume we employ the word *capitalism* as a neutral term that best evokes the system of values, principles, and practices characteristic of the private enterprise economy in its "pure" or ideal-typical form. We attach neither honorific nor pejorative significance to the word but merely consider it an informative, useful, and appropriate descriptive term. Our definition of capitalism refers to a form of economic organization in which entrepreneurs—owners, managers, and, in general, those who stand to reap economic rewards from the success of a business venture—seek profit through the private ownership and management of the instruments of production and distribution, such as factories, farms, banks, and transport. The free competitive market, operating according to economic laws of supply and demand, determines which goods and services are produced or made available, the price at which they sell, the profits earned on their sale, and the wages paid to workers.

The proponents of capitalism contend that the market allocates resources and distributes goods and services in the fairest and most efficient manner possible. Capitalism in the ideal form is also a "rational" economic system in the sense that owners and managers continually strive to increase efficiency, to achieve the highest level of productivity at the lowest unit cost, to set prices at a level that will improve their competitive position in the market, and ultimately, of course, to maximize profits. Investment decisions are made without reference to tradition, sentiment, ideology, aesthetics, or personal likes and dislikes: what counts most is their potential economic return. In short, all economic decisions are rationally calculated to yield the largest possible return for the smallest possible cost. A share of the profits that are the fruit of successful competition is then reinvested in new enterprises or new machinery in a ceaseless effort to improve efficiency, expand production, and increase profits further. Thus the inherent dynamic of capitalism is that of perpetual economic growth.

This brief description of capitalism is, of course, an abstract, ideal-typical account. In practice, many capitalist entrepreneurs depart in some way from the principles stated. Describing the system in its idealized form, nevertheless, provides a useful baseline from which to explore the attitudes of Americans toward their country's economic system in practice and toward the cultural values that underlie it.

The Protestant Ethic

As the history of underdeveloped nations in the twentieth century has repeatedly shown, the fashioning of democratic societies among people unfamiliar with democracy can rarely be accomplished quickly or easily. In order for such free societies to work, elites and a fair proportion of ordinary citizens must learn complex and difficult norms. Much the same can be said about capitalism and its institutions. As Max Weber has argued in his classic study, *The Protestant Ethic and the Spirit of Capitalism,* capitalism requires both an instinct toward self-aggrandizement and a willingness to channel that instinct into such constructive values as investment, sober economic calculation, efficiency, frugality, self-denial in the private use of capital, scrupulous adherence to contracts, and—perhaps above all—diligent toil at one's calling. According to Weber, Protestantism was crucial to the development of a climate in which these and other values intrinsic to capitalism could flourish.

Weber's thesis is especially appropriate for an understanding of American capitalism. America was, from the beginning, a predominantly Protestant nation, and many of its business leaders have attributed their own economic success to the cluster of beliefs that Weber called the "Protestant ethic." Perhaps the most influential settlements in the New World were those of the New England Calvinists, more commonly known as Puritans. In few parts of the world were the values of Protestantism and early capitalism so mutually reinforcing as in the Puritan colonies.

Protestantism, especially in its Calvinist manifestation, was haunted by a fear of man's sinfulness and the need to enforce strict moral codes that would tame man's boundless appetites and passions. Order, strict adherence to principle, and the importance of willpower and self-restraint were endlessly lauded; unchecked emotion, spontaneity, and even play met with suspicion and hostility. Puritanism enforced its demanding ascetic and spiritual values as strongly perhaps as it was possible to do in a rudimentary society set into a wilderness. In countless sermons, the Puritan settlers were exhorted to shun worldly pleasure, mortify their appetites, and conform to "Godly ways."

In its original stark form, Puritanism survived barely a century in the North American wilderness. Nevertheless, its staunch moralistic orientation, its fear of the Dionysian spirit, and its efforts to subject human feelings and passions to rational control appear to have left a lasting imprint on American culture (see Table 4–1). For example, more than 80 percent of those responding to one of our national surveys thought that "a person's emotions should always be held in check by the moral code." Over 60 percent agreed to the even stronger assertion that there is "no such thing as being 'too strict' where conscience and morals are concerned." More than 85 percent of the general public and 89 percent of a sample of American political leaders held that "in dealing with other people, it is better to be guided by principle than by affection for them."

For all its severity, however, Puritan moralism differed in de-

Table 4–1   Attitudes toward elements of the Protestant ethic

	General public (N = 1,484)	Political influentials (N = 3,020)
1. A person's emotions should always be held in check by the moral code.		
—Agree	84	84
—Disagree	17	16
2. There is no such thing as being "too strict" where conscience and morals are concerned.		
—Agree	62	54
—Disagree	38	46
3. In dealing with other people, it is better to be guided by principle than by affection for them.		
—Agree	85	89
—Disagree	15	11
4. I believe we are made better by the trials and hardships of life.		
—Agree	91	92
—Disagree	9	8

Source: Political Affiliations and Beliefs study, 1958.

gree rather than in kind from that of other religions. What most set the Protestant sects apart from the rest of the Judeo-Christian tradition was their manner of coping with the human frailty and sin that so obsessed them. Rather than counseling the faithful to escape the weaknesses of the flesh by retreating to convents and monasteries, as the Catholic church did, or concentrating on prayerful meditation and preparation for the next life, the Puritans, along with other Protestants, resolved to "mortifie these our affections" by plunging into a life of unremitting worldly toil.[4] They determined that men and women must discharge their earthly duties with such dedication, discipline, and steadiness as to leave no opening for sin to enter their lives. Hence the struggle to earn a livelihood was no longer viewed as either a burden or a distraction from spiritual life. It was transformed, instead, into a "calling" by God, who regarded work as a vital form of moral activity. The virtuous life was exemplified by the hardworking, sober, and thrifty artisan, merchant, or entrepreneur who had amassed large stores of material goods from the "zeal and diligence" of his daily industry. One's economic achievements thus became, in effect, a measure of one's moral standing.

This radical new religious perspective had important secular implications. Most important, perhaps, was that the deliberate pursuit of wealth and material goods—disdained by the hereditary aristocracy and viewed with suspicion by the Catholic church—had attained powerful religious sanction.

An obvious affinity existed between the Puritan emphasis on moral restraint and the values emphasized by the emerging bourgeois class: temperance, sobriety, thrift, purification through honest labor, fulfillment of one's contractual duties and obligations, and prudence in personal conduct and business affairs. Also important was the emphasis on channeling one's energies into a form of disciplined economic endeavor that was more congenial to a rational, impersonal, and efficiency-oriented economy like capitalism than to the more leisurely and custom-bound production routines of traditional societies.

The thesis connecting the rise of capitalism to the Protestant Reformation, most fully developed by Weber, was questioned in certain respects by R. H. Tawney, who argued that it was not so much the effects of a new religious vision that produced capitalism but the development of a new social and economic vision among the growing merchant classes.[5] Tawney maintained that these merchants, by reason of their greater wealth, exerted strong influence on the congregations and ministers of the new Protestant churches, pressing them to adopt views in which wealth came to be regarded as a divine reward for Calvinist virtues, while poverty was a sign of moral delinquency. Whether one prefers Weber's interpretation or Tawney's, however, the central point remains that the Protestant denominations, and particularly their Calvinist strains such as American Puritanism, gave enthusiastic sanction to forms of entrepreneurial endeavor that were formerly suspect.

It is ironic that Protestant theologians valued wealth not for the comforts or pleasures it might afford but for the arduous *process* by which it was acquired. This process, as Protestant ministers repeatedly stressed, tamed the passions, kept one occupied, instilled good habits, and enabled one to avoid the temptations of sin. John Cotton remarked on this irony in a sermon to his Puritan congregation: "There is [a] combination of virtues strangely mixed in every lively holy Christian. And that is, Diligence in worldly businesses, and yet deadnesse to the world; such a mystery as none can read, but they that know it. For a man to [take] all opportunities to be doing something early and late . . . go any way and bestir himselfe for profit, this will he doe most diligently in his calling . . . And yet bee a man deadhearted to the world."[6]

The admonition to achieve worldly success but not to enjoy it—to remain "dead hearted to the world"—was characterized by Weber as a doctrine of "worldly" or "active asceticism." At the heart of the doctrine—and of the Protestant ethic as a whole—are two normative injunctions: one should work zealously, dutifully, and methodically in order to avoid sin and demonstrate one's worth; and one should acquire good habits such as frugality, sobriety, humility, and simplicity in conduct in order to demonstrate one's capacity for self-restraint, self-denial, and devotion to one's calling and one's God. As Weber observed, the Protestant ethic provided, in effect, the rationale by which acquisitiveness could be reconciled with restraint.

This tendency to view toil as a calling, as a blessing rather than a curse, was thought by Weber to be the "most characteristic" feature of "the social ethic of capitalistic culture."[7] Though stripped of its theological moorings, this view of work has been widely incorporated into the American value system. Long after the strictly theological tenets of Puritanism had lost their status as behavioral imperatives, many Americans continued to view work and wealth through the moral prism of the Calvinist creed. Thus, one group of American social scientists writing about American values in the 1950s observed that in the American heritage, "Continuous, narrow application to work . . . is not just a concession to the unpleasant demands of practical life; it is a positive value in itself . . . This confidence that work in an occupation may in itself be a legitimate and rewarding focus of a man's best energies and not merely a means of 'higher' things is deepset in American values."[8]

That most Americans, workers as well as those we call influentials, still believe in the intrinsic value of exertion and hard work is evident from the data in Table 4-2. Approximately seven out of ten Americans, for example, feel that "laziness is almost like a

Table 4-2   Attitudes toward work

	General public	Political influentials
1. There is something wrong with a person who is not willing to work hard.		
—Agree	75	71
—Disagree	25	29
	(N = 1,484)	(N = 3,020)
2. A man who does not show the highest sense of duty toward his chosen work hardly deserves to be respected.		
—Agree	78	83
—Disagree	22	17
	(N = 1,484)	(N = 3,020)
3. I sometimes feel that laziness is almost like a sin.		
—Agree	77	67
—Disagree	23	33
	(N = 1,484)	(N = 3,020)
4. People should place more emphasis on working hard and doing a good job than on what gives them personal satisfaction and pleasure.		
—Agree	63	—
—Disagree	23	—
—Mixed, unsure	15	—
5. If you were to get enough money to live as comfortably as you like for the rest of your life, would you continue to work or would you stop working? (Asked of employed persons only.)		
—Yes, would continue working	66	—
—No	30	—
—Unsure	4	—

Sources: questions 1, 2, and 3, Political Affiliations and Beliefs study, 1958; question 4, Roper Survey, 1981, cited in "Opinion Roundup," *Public Opinion* (August 1981), p. 25; question 5, National Opinion Research Corporation survey, 1973, cited in Connie De Boer, "The Polls: Attitudes towards Work," *Public Opinion Quarterly*, 42 (Fall 1978), p. 419.

sin." Majorities of close to 75 percent say that "there is something wrong with a person who is not willing to work hard." An even larger number (78 percent) express the opinion—familiar to Calvinism but otherwise extraordinary—that one cannot respect a man "who does not show the highest sense of duty toward his chosen work." Recent surveys conducted by national polling organizations reveal that almost two-thirds of the American people subscribe to the view that "people should place more emphasis on working hard and doing a good job than on what gives them personal satisfaction and pleasure." Equally striking is the response of two-thirds of employed Americans who claim they would want to continue working even if they had enough money to live comfortably for the rest of their lives.

These results are noteworthy because they are by no means the universal response of mankind to the necessity for toil. Not all societies have venerated work or considered idleness a sign of inferiority; among many primitive societies, the contrary attitude has prevailed. Similarly, among the societies of antiquity, especially those that were sharply stratified and dominated by a noble or warrior class, leisure was regarded as a mark of high status while labor was relegated to menials and inferiors. Even in medieval Europe, work was rarely considered a virtue: among those who led a spiritual life, the preferred values were prayer and contemplation; among those in the secular realm, the goals were luxury, leisure, and (if possible) idleness. Noblemen and ecclesiastical lords who possessed the resources to lead such lives did so without shame. Such attitudes, however, have never been dominant in America. Even the wealthy rarely aspired to idleness or a life of leisure. Rather, as Tocqueville observed in the early nineteenth century, "In the United States, a wealthy man thinks that he owes it to public opinion to devote his leisure to some kind of industrial or commercial pursuit or to public business. He would think himself in bad repute, if he employed his life solely in living."[9]

Recent research indicates that this attitude still prevails. Even among the elites we have tested, as well as the general public, the value of work, of mental or physical exertion, is repeatedly endorsed. To be unemployed, to live on welfare, or even to enjoy the life of a wealthy sybarite is to invite disdain. Whereas work is perceived as honorable and purifying, idleness (especially at public expense) is regarded as dishonorable, a mark of character weakness. A 1979 survey of college-bound high school seniors suggested that the commitment to work is as strong among young people as it is among the population as a whole. Three-fourths of this sample affirmed that "I expect work to be a very central part of my life," while only 15 percent acknowledged that "to me, work is nothing more than making a living." More than four out of five also said they would want to work even if they had all the money they needed to live comfortably.[10] The status of the work ethic does not appear, from these figures, to have declined very much (if at all), despite the presumed "alienation" or "disillusionment" of the sixties, and despite current stereotypes concerning the alleged rejection of the parent culture by young people.

We are not saying, of course, that Americans now embrace capitalist values in the same spirit of "worldly asceticism" that characterized Puritanism. Any suggestion that most contemporary Americans, with their obvious desire for comfort, consumer goods, and pleasure, are religious ascetics would be absurd. Nevertheless, the values associated with the Protestant ethic continue to make their presence felt in the attitudes Americans express toward the economy. For example, Table 4-3 shows that although support for capitalist values is strong in all segments of the public, respondents who score high on a summary measure (or "scale") of Calvinism are more likely to support the principles of free-enterprise capitalism than are those who score low on the Calvinism scale. Competition, private property, unregulated business enterprise, resistance to government ownership of industry—all are endorsed

Table 4-3 Calvinism and support for business values

Business attitudes	Calvinism scale[a]					
	General public			Political influentials		
	Low (N = 347)	Middle (N = 699)	High (N = 438)	Low (N = 893)	Middle (N = 1,330)	High (N = 797)
1. Our freedom depends on the free enterprise system.						
—Agree	77	82	87	75	92	93
—Disagree	23	18	13	25	8	7
2. It is having to compete with others that keeps a person on his toes.						
—Agree	79	90	93	75	95	97
—Disagree	21	10	7	25	5	3
3. Private property is necessary for economic progress.						
—Agree	78	83	91	76	93	95
—Disagree	22	17	9	24	7	5
4. Men would not do their best if government owned all industry.						
—Agree	76	84	88	72	89	90
—Disagree	24	16	12	8	11	10

Source: Political Affiliations and Beliefs study, 1958.
a. Examples of the items in this scale may be found in Table 4-2.

most frequently by respondents who are most deeply attached to Calvinist values.[11] Data from other parts of our study also show that, particularly among elites, Calvinist attitudes are positively associated with support for probusiness political candidates and for the Republican party, the party most identified with business. Among the political influentials, the correlation between the Calvinist scale and an index of beliefs distinguishing Republicans from Democrats is strong, 0.50; among the general public (which is less attuned to ideological and value distinctions), the correlation is weaker, but nevertheless significant, 0.38. On the available evidence, in short, Calvinism—as defined by the values Weber labeled the "Protestant ethic"—continues to be associated with support for the values of business and capitalism.

The values of the Protestant ethic, of course, are not the only cultural forces that help to sustain capitalist institutions in the United States. The country's secular tradition of economic individualism also plays an important role in sustaining capitalism.

The Heritage of Individualism

When Toqueville set out to characterize the novel social orientation he found in the United States in the 1830s, he described it as "individualism." Although the word seems never before to have appeared in the English language, it so aptly characterized American culture that within a few years it was widely accepted as one of the nation's most distinctive traits.[12] As Toqueville originally defined it: "Individualism . . . disposes each citizen to isolate himself from the mass of his fellows and withdraw into the circles of family and friends; with this little society formed to his taste, he gladly leaves the greater society to look after itself . . . Such folk owe no man anything and hardly expect anything from anybody. They . . . imagine that their whole destiny is in their own hands."[13] Toqueville was no admirer of this form of individualism. In his view it atomized society, led to personal isolation, and undermined public virtue. Many other educated Europeans shared his evaluation, regarding American individualists as incessant self-seekers and worshipers of the "almighty dollar." Individualism, for them, was a term of opprobrium.

Americans, however, saw the concept more favorably, hailing it as the social principle that would simultaneously liberate men from the tyrannies of the Old World and lead them to great and unique accomplishments of their own. Whereas many Europeans regarded the term as synonymous with selfishness, it signified for Americans "self-determination, moral freedom, the rule of liberty, and the dignity of man."[14]

Why should individualism have been so much more attractive to Americans than to Europeans? One answer is that European societies in the eighteenth century, dominated by hereditary aristocracies and authoritarian regimes, were largely inhospitable to freedom. Most people in Europe were locked into rigid social structures that prevented them from changing vocations or rising to higher stations. In the eyes of Europe's governing classes, most men were too unruly, ignorant, and brutish to handle freedom responsibly or to manage their own lives, much less to participate in governing the society. The "common good," therefore, required that ordinary people be held under firm control rather than left to their own initiatives.

As Americans compared their own society to that of Europe— an exercise in which they engaged frequently and with obvious condescension and pleasure—they could not help noticing that their own country was more prosperous than any nation in Europe. Historians have attributed American prosperity variously to the natural wealth of the continent, to the great frontier and the availability of rich land, to the sturdy character of the early American settlers, and to the influence of Calvinist religious beliefs. All these factors doubtless played a role, but to many eighteenth- and nineteenth-century Americans who confronted the question, the answer lay mainly in the nation's free democratic institutions and in the spirit of self-reliance and individualism that made those institutions possible. Americans believed, in other words, that the prosperity of their nation was the result of a system in which each man moved ahead on his own, free of the myriad legal and social restrictions that were still widely defended in Europe as essential to the maintenance of social order and cohesion. Beyond this, Americans believed that everyone *ought* to be able to get ahead on his own. Contrasting individualism in the United States with the prevailing conditions elsewhere, one nineteenth-century American declared: "Ours is a country, where men . . . can attain to the most elevated position, or acquire a large amount of wealth, according to the pursuits they elect for themselves. No exclusive privileges of earth, no entailment of estates, no civil or political disqualifications, stand in their path; but one has as good a chance as another, according to his talents, prudence, and personal exertions. This is a country of self-made men, than which nothing better could be said of any state of society."[15]

By the end of the nineteenth century the notion of individualism had achieved such popularity and esteem that many regarded it as virtually a one-word summary of the American creed. The term captured the idea that society exists to serve the individual, who must be free to speak his own mind, to manage his own affairs, and—within the limits of laws that apply equally to everyone—to pursue his own idea of the good life. The emphasis on private achievement and maximum individual freedom embodied in this view of individualism was obviously in harmony with capitalist notions of individual initiative, economic competition, personal profit, and narrowly limited government. From this perspective, individualism incorporated capitalist values and restated them as moral imperatives.

Individualism, however, was not invented solely by the emerging business classes, nor was it exclusively identified with economic enterprise. It was an idea that was also thought to promote political freedom, equality, religious toleration, due process of law, and the rights of privacy. In the eighteenth and nineteenth centuries it was embraced both by the country's foremost democrats and by its entrepreneurs as a progressive and liberating idea, and as an essential element of economic freedom and independence. Individualism thus provided the rationale for personal independence in both the political and economic spheres, serving the values of capitalism on the one side and democracy on the other.

Throughout the history of the Republic, appeals to individualism have furnished the basis for countless political and social movements. Individualism was invoked by Abolitionists to reject the dominion of master over slave, and by slave owners to justify their right as individuals to own and use "property" as they pleased, free of external interference. Industrialists, of course, have drawn on the doctrine of individualism to justify their vast economic power, while Social Darwinists have argued that, in the struggle for existence, a society should mainly seek to advance the well-being of individuals who have demonstrated their fitness to survive. Liberal reformers, meanwhile, have insisted on the supreme worth of every individual human being, and on the right of each to share equitably in society's benefits.

The democratic perspective on individualism is exemplified by writers such as Emerson. Claiming that the gift of genius has to some degree been bestowed on everyone, Emerson urged that all men devote themselves unsparingly to the development of their own individuality. He was an outspoken enemy of all collective systems, beginning with society itself. In a spirit suggestive of certain movements of the 1960s, he wrote: "I appeal from your [society's] customs. I must be myself. I cannot break myself any longer for you . . . I will not hide my tastes or aversions . . . I do this not selfishly but humbly and truly. It is alike your interest, and mine, and all men's, however long we have dwelt in lies, to live in truth."[16]

The economic perspective on individualism is exemplified in the following tribute delivered in 1911 by Senator Chauncey Depew to the millionaire railroad magnate, Cornelius Vanderbilt: "The American Commonwealth is built upon the individual. It recognizes neither classes nor masses . . . We have thus become a nation of self-made men . . . Commodore Vanderbilt is a conspicuous example of the product and possibilities of our free and elastic conditions . . . He neither asked nor gave quarter. The same . . . open avenues, the same opportunities which he had before him are equally before every other man."[17]

America, it seems, has been awash with every variety of philosophical belief about individualism. Such beliefs have served to justify every form of social organization, from the anarchy of radical individualists to the economic oligarchy of rugged individualists. But individualism, as a broad concept relevant to economic life, encompasses a number of other more specific notions associated with the capitalist tradition, such as ambition, achievement, the pursuit of profit, and the salutary effects of competition.

Ambition and Achievement

In the older, traditional societies of Europe, most people plied the same trades as their fathers and forefathers. The children of serfs were forced to cultivate the same land as their ancestors. The sons of craftsmen usually had little choice but to become apprentices in their fathers' trade. To aspire to higher social status was contrary to tradition—and often impeded by existing laws.

Although some of these attitudes were initially carried over to the New World, they proved impossible to maintain under American social and economic conditions. Ambition and the desire for social advancement were no longer denigrated but became instead the new ideal. "The idea instilled into the minds of most boys, from an early age, is that of 'getting on,' " wrote an observer of American life around 1850.[18] Countless sermons, homilies, and popular tracts conveyed the gospel of worldly success. Like the heroes of Horatio Alger novels, nineteenth-century Americans were continually entreated to strive for personal achievement and preferment.

The possibility that ambition might degenerate into unscrupulous greed was recognized, of course, but many Americans seemed to have a greater fear that ambition might be petty than that it might be overweening. As Lyman Abbot, a popular minister of the nineteenth century, wrote:

> The ambition to succeed may be and always ought to be a laudable one. It is the ambition of every parent for his child. It is emphatically an American ambition; at once the national vice and the national virtue. It is that mainspring of activity; the driving wheel of industry; the spur to intellectual and moral progress. It gives the individual energy; the nation push. It makes the difference between a people that are a stream and a people that are a pool; between America and China. It makes us at once active and restless; industrious and overworked; generous and greedy. When it is great, it is a virtue; when it is petty, it is a vice.[19]

Modern social scientists have often claimed that an emphasis on achievement is an integral feature of American culture. S. M. Lipset, for example, has presented cross-cultural data from which he has inferred that Americans are more achievement-oriented than the people of other nations, such as England, Canada, or Australia[20]—a claim also advanced by David McClellan in his work on the achievement motive.[21] Robin Williams, Jr., in his comprehensive study of American values, concludes that American culture is "marked by a central stress upon personal achievement."[22]

Data from our own research provide some perspective on such claims. The traditional idea that son should follow father in the same occupation and social station finds scant support in twentieth-century America. Three-fourths of the general public and four-fifths of the influentials assert, on the contrary, that everyone "should try to amount to more than his parents did." Nearly identical proportions also affirm that they regard themselves as "rather ambitious . . . at heart." And almost half the respondents confessed disdain for a man "who is satisfied to stay where he is all his life."

Yet two of the items in Table 4–4 show that support for the value of achievement is neither unequivocal nor uniformly distributed throughout the population. Seventy percent of the general public say that security is more important to them than

Table 4–4   Personal achievement and ambition

	General public (N = 1,484)	Political influentials (N = 3,020)
1. Everyone should try to amount to more than his parents did.		
—Agree	74	80
—Disagree	26	20
2. I guess you could say I am a rather ambitious person at heart.		
—Agree	74	82
—Disagree	27	18
3. I have no use for a man who is satisfied to stay where he is all his life.		
—Agree	47	46
—Disagree	53	54
4. Security is more important to me than advancement.		
—Agree	70	33
—Disagree	30	67
5. It is better just to be "one of the group" than to be singled out for special attention.		
—Agree	61	37
—Disagree	38	63

Source: Political Affiliations and Beliefs study, 1958.

advancement—scarcely an overwhelming endorsement of the importance of achievement—while more than two-thirds of the influentials (who on the average enjoy higher incomes) opt for advancement over security. Similar differences turn up regarding individual recognition. Respect for ambition and achievement, then, is stronger among the leaders of public affairs than among the general public.

A central methodological concern in systematic studies of political culture involves the question of how much popular support must be registered before one can certify that a particular value has, so to speak, "broad popular acceptance." Our results ought to be viewed in light of this problem: even in a society that has long and justly been known for its comparatively important emphasis on achievement, general support for this value is not uniformly strong. Although this finding may not surprise some observers, it is useful to keep it in mind when evaluating popular attitudes toward other values in the ethos. Cultural values may exist and exert an important influence on a society even though popular support for them is somewhat uneven and less than unanimous.

The Pursuit of Profit and Self-Interest

Committed as they were to ambition, achievement, and the right of each individual to manage his own affairs, most nineteenth-century Americans appear to have had little difficulty accepting the related proposition that each man ought to be free to make as much money as possible. "The only principle of life propagated among young people is to get money," wrote an observer of American life in 1784, "and men are esteemed according to what they are worth—that is, the money they are possessed of."[23] Some fifty years later Tocqueville claimed to find a similar acquisitive tendency among Americans. "No stigma attaches to love of money in America," he wrote. "The American will describe as noble and estimable ambition that which our medieval ancestors would have called base cupidity."[24] At the end of the nineteenth century, an English visitor to America observed that the American ideal of success was still, more than anything, the possession of great wealth.[25] A society in which this view predominated was bound to attract large numbers of restless people eager to make their fortunes.

This preoccupation with wealth, of course, is fully in keeping with the spirit of capitalism, which depends on the desire for economic gain as the driving force of the economy. Yet American attitudes toward the pursuit of economic self-interest are more complicated than these brief remarks suggest. Since the rise of big business, for example, Americans have frequently complained about excessive profits that have been unfairly wrung from the consuming public. American society, moreover, has always harbored values that tended to keep the quest for profit within certain limits—although these countervailing influences, ironically enough, have existed within the same traditions that have also encouraged acquisitiveness and profit making. Russell Conwell, an influential religious moralist of the early twentieth century, made a considerable effort to instruct the readers of his best-selling book, *Acres of Diamonds,* how to become rich, while simultaneously admonishing them that "the man that worships the dollar instead of thinking of the purposes for which it ought to be used, the man who idolizes simply money, the miser that hoards his money in the cellar, or hides it in his stocking, or refuses to invest it where it will do the world good, that man who hugs the dollar until the eagle squeals . . . has in him the root of all evil."[26] Warnings like this recur throughout American history, perhaps because Americans in practice have paid them so little heed. The drive to amass wealth, both for the pleasure it affords and the success it evidences, has coexisted with misgivings about the corrupting effects of pursuing wealth as an end in itself.

Modern survey research bears out the ambivalence with which the craving for wealth is regarded. For many years, and especially since the emergence of a counterculture in the late 1960s, it has been fashionable among the young to decry the materialistic bent of American society. Between 1968 and 1973, for example, the percentage of college students who said they would "welcome less emphasis on money" rose from an already high 65 percent to 80 percent. But when college students were asked in a survey covering part of the same period (1970 to 1973) what they would most look for in a job after graduation, the number of students who listed "the money you can earn" as among their most important objectives rose from 36 percent to 61 percent. The desire to make money, it seems, was growing at least as rapidly as the concern to deemphasize it.[27]

Findings of this kind leave the impression that despite the turbulence of the past fifteen years, Americans remain strongly committed to the private pursuit of wealth. As always, however, one must be careful not to overstate the point. It can be seen from Table 4–5, for example, that popular support for the principle of unrestricted economic gain is strong, but not uniformly so. Some 95 percent of Americans surveyed in the late 1950s agreed that "there's nothing wrong with a man making as much money as he honestly can." In 1976 a similar view was expressed by 91 percent of the American work force.[28] And in another recent survey, 70 percent of the sample expressed the belief that "profits are necessary for economic growth."[29] In our 1978–79 survey, only 11 percent of the public wanted to set limits on the amount of profit a business can earn, while 73 percent said that profits should be as large as business can fairly earn. Despite these attitudes, however, many Americans express skepticism about the value of unlimited profits. Only a plurality was willing to assert that "everyone profits in the long run" when business makes as much money as it can, and 24 percent thought that unlimited profits would mean that "workers and the poor are bound to get less." Similarly, while only a minority embraces the strongly critical view that profit seeking "brings out the worst in human nature," many respondents are reluctant to express enthusiastic approval for the profit system in general or for unlimited business profits in particular. These results recall our earlier discussion of the public's ambivalence toward certain features of capitalism. In this case, although some Americans are wary of the profit system, very few favor fundamental alterations of the system, much less its abolition.

Competition

The profit system, of course, begets a number of economic and social inequalities—in wealth, to begin with, but also in social status, material comforts, personal power, and opportunities for the creative use of freedom. How does one justify such inequalities within an ethos that announces as one of its central propositions that "all men are created equal"?

Table 4–5   Attitudes toward the acquisition of income and profits[a]

	General public	Influentials
1. There is nothing wrong with a man trying to make as much money as he honestly can.		
—Agree	95	96
—Disagree	5	4
	(N = 1,484)	(N = 3,020)
2. The government should limit the amount of money any individual is allowed to earn in a year.		
—Agree	9	
—Disagree	91	
	(N = 1,370)	
3. The profits a company or business can earn should be:		
—strictly limited by law to a certain level	11	8
—as large as they can fairly earn	73	79
—Decline to choose	16	13
	(N = 1,026)	(N = 601)
4. When businesses are allowed to make as much money as they can:		
—workers and the poor are bound to get less	24	18
—everyone profits in the long run	42	50
—Decline to choose	34	32
	(N = 1,995)	(N = 1,166)
5. The profit system:		
—brings out the worst in human nature	16	11
—teaches people the value of hard work and success	54	48
—Decline to choose	29	41
	(N = 938)	(N = 845)

Sources: question 1, Political Affiliations and Beliefs study, 1958; question 2, Kay Schlozman and Sidney Verba, *Injury to Insult* (Cambridge, Mass.: Harvard University Press, 1979); questions 3 and 4, Civil Liberties study, 1978–79; question 5, Opinions and Values of Americans survey, 1975–77.

a. In this and subsequent tables, the numbers of respondents for the Civil Liberties samples will vary somewhat, since some questions were asked of all respondents, some of half the respondents, and some of the other half.

The doctrines derived from the Protestant ethic provide one kind of answer. They hold that great wealth and the several forms of inequality to which it gives rise reflect differences in personal virtue. The virtuous thrive not only because of their dutiful habits, but because of divine recognition of their moral worth.

The creed of individualism provides another answer. If everyone has the same chance to compete for society's rewards, the resulting distribution of those rewards, however equal or unequal, may be considered just. The challenges and rewards of competition apply equally to individual businessmen who rival one another directly, and to hundreds of thousands of workers who compete against each other through the impersonal mechanisms of the free labor market.

Despite its central place within the capitalist creed, competition was not an idea that figured prominently in the writings of the Founding Fathers. But with the burgeoning of laissez-faire theory in the early nineteenth century and the vogue of Social Darwinism later in the century, competition assumed a position of commanding doctrinal importance. At a time when rapid industrialization was creating scores of new industrial barons and millions of impoverished factory families, William Graham Sumner, the most influential Social Darwinist in America, put the case for unchecked economic competition in characteristically blunt language:

> Many . . . are frightened at . . . competition, which they elevate into a bugbear. They think it bears harshly on the weak. They do not perceive that here "the strong" and "the weak" are terms which admit of no definition unless they are made equivalent to the industrious and the idle, the frugal and the extravagant. They do not perceive, furthermore, that if we do not like the survival of the fittest, we have only one possible alternative, and that is the survival of the unfittest. The former is the law of civilization; the latter is the law of anti-civilization. We have our choice between the two.[30]

Millionaires, according to Sumner, are the products of natural selection, and their ascendancy to positions of economic dominance benefits the entire society. Their great fortunes are earned rewards for the extraordinary services they render society. Today few Americans still contend—though many may inwardly believe—that competition alone can legitimate all material inequality, however extreme.[31] The competitive system, however, continues to be widely admired by the proponents of capitalism for its manifold benefits. Competition, they claim, forces companies to strive for ever-greater efficiency and for better, more attractive products. It compels all firms, large and small, to remain alert to the desires of the customer and to satisfy them as far as humanly possible. Even monopolies must constantly upgrade their products lest an innovative competitor break into their market. Competition also offers tangible incentives for creative thought and hard work, while penalizing idleness and sloth. A competitive system, therefore, stimulates each individual to work up to his or her abilities.

Arguments of this kind have become so commonplace in American society that many may be unaware that they are, after all, only arguments—and that their empirical status and normative warranty are by no means beyond dispute. Nevertheless, the public opinion data presented in Table 4–6 strongly suggest that Americans generally accept them. Almost 90 percent of respondents in our PAB survey stated that competition "keeps a person on his toes." Only a handful of respondents in our 1975–1977 surveys found competition "wasteful and destructive," while the vast majority said that competition is a stimulus to "better performance and a desire for excellence." Thus it is easier to understand why Americans, accepting competition as they do, also accept the inequalities of reward that are the inevitable outcome of economic competition.

Table 4–6   Perceptions of competition

	General public	Influentials
1. It is having to compete with others that keeps a person on his toes.		
—Agree	88	89
—Disagree	12	11
	(N = 1,484)	(N = 3,020)
2. Competition, whether in school, work, or business:		
—is often wasteful and destructive	8	14
—leads to better performance and a desire for excellence	81	68
—Decline to choose	11	19
	(N = 938)	(N = 845)

Sources: question 1, Political Affiliations and Beliefs study, 1958; question 2, Opinions and Values of Americans survey, 1975–77.

Decline of Capitalist Values?

Despite their support for capitalism, various observers throughout American history have expressed concern that its emphasis on material accumulation would have a corrosive effect on certain values of the Protestant ethic. For example, John Wesley, founder of the largest Protestant denomination in America, had occasion to lament that as the Methodists grow diligent, "they increase in goods . . . in the desires of the flesh, the desire of the eyes, and the pride of life."[32] John Adams, an arch Puritan throughout his lifetime, voiced a similar concern in a letter to Jefferson: "Will you tell me how to prevent riches from producing luxury . . . how to prevent luxury from producing effeminacy intoxication extravagance Vice and folly?"[33]

Similar concerns are voiced today. The sociologist Daniel Bell, a leading student of American values, has written that capitalism "has destroyed the Protestant ethic by zealously promoting a hedonistic way of life."[34] He believes that early in the twentieth century, "the Protestant ethical was undermined not by modernism, but by capitalism itself. The greatest single engine in the destruction of the Protestant ethic was the invention of the installment plan, or instant credit. Previously one had to save in order to buy. But with credit cards, one could indulge instant gratification."[35] From a somewhat different perspective, the historian Christopher Lasch reaches a similar conclusion: "The Protestant virtues no longer excite enthusiasm. Inflation undermines the horror of indebtedness, exhorting the consumer to buy now and pay later. As the future becomes more menacing and uncertain, only fools put off until tomorrow the fun they can have today."[36]

To many writers, these trends toward a "hedonistic way of life" signify not only a decline in the "worldly asceticism" once identified with the Protestant ethic, but a weakening of the cultural underpinnings of capitalism. Why this concern?

The Protestant ethic, as we have seen, viewed wealth as the direct result of ascetic self-restraint. Inequalities of material wealth were thus tied, at least in theory, to differences in moral worth. With the decline of this ascetic spirit, however, commentators like Bell and Irving Kristol worry that wealth is now associated by many Americans with greed rather than with moral entitlement, and that capitalism, because of this association, is losing its popular legitimacy. Thus Kristol contends that Americans "will not live for long in a society in which power, privilege and prosperity are not distributed according to some morally meaningful criteria."[37] In a similar vein, Bell argues that "American capitalism . . . has lost its traditional legitimacy, which was based on a moral system of reward rooted in the Protestant sanctification of work."[38]

One can scarcely quarrel with the claim that capitalism and worldly success no longer enjoy the explicitly *religious* sanction they once had. In the nineteenth century it was not uncommon to encounter rhetoric asserting that wealth comes "only to the man of morality";[39] that the rich are rich because they are honest and most deserving; that "pauperism and vagrancy are crimes";[40] and that "poverty comes from vice, rather than vice from poverty."[41] According to Henry Ward Beecher: "There may be reasons of poverty which do not involve wrong; but looking comprehensively through city and town and village and country, the general truth will stand, that no man in this land suffers from poverty unless it be more than his fault—unless it be his *sin.*"[42] Today, however, as Table 4–7 shows, the unequivocal identification of personal virtue with worldly success or failure—an identification at the heart of the Protestant ethic, as well as of Social Darwinism—is embraced by only a minority of the American public. When respondents were asked, for example, whether the most successful businessmen of the early twentieth century should be held up as models of character, only 37 percent of the general public thought they should. Among the influentials, who are better informed than the general public about the careers of men like Rockefeller, Ford, and Morgan, the proportion expressing admiration for these financial and industrial magnates was even smaller (21 percent).

If Americans are disinclined to admire some of the nation's most conspicuously successful capitalists, Table 4–7 indicates that they are even less willing to assign unequivocal blame to the economically unsuccessful. Only about 30 percent of the general public are inclined to castigate the poor as "lazy" and lacking in self-discipline, or as unwilling to "try hard enough to get ahead." Among elites, the proportion embracing a moralistic interpretation of economic failure is even lower.

Table 4-7 Economic status and moral worth

	General public (N = 938)	Influentials (N = 845)
1. Men like Henry Ford, Andrew Carnegie, J. P. Morgan, and John D. Rockefeller should be held up to young people as:		
—selfish and ambitious men who would do anything to get ahead	11	10
—models to be admired and imitated	37	21
—Decline to choose	52	70
2. The poor are poor because:		
—the wealthy and powerful keep them poor	21	13
—they don't try hard enough to get ahead	24	9
—Decline to choose	55	78
3. When people fail at one thing after another, it usually means they:		
—weren't given a good enough chance to begin with	15	11
—are lazy and lack self-discipline	34	19
—Decline to choose	52	70

Source: Opinions and Values of Americans survey, 1975–77.

The language employed in these questions is, by the standards of the nineteenth century, fairly mild. The reluctance of most Americans to identify worldly success (or failure) with superior (or inferior) moral character thus lends support to the contention that the Protestant ethic no longer functions as strongly as it once did to legitimate the great material inequalities associated with capitalism. Perhaps a more important issue, however, is whether this development signifies, as some believe, that capitalist society has "lost its transcendental ethic"—and hence, presumably, its legitimacy.[43]

Taken as a whole, the data available to us do not seem to warrant this conclusion. Note, for example, that although few Americans are willing to blame the poor for their plight, even fewer blame the economic system for making them poor. Between half and three-fourths of our respondents in Table 4–7 decline to take either of the substantive options offered them. One could, perhaps, construe such indecision as signifying confusion about values or, alternatively, as a crisis of confidence in the capitalist system. But it is at least equally tenable to conclude that the pattern of responses shown in Table 4–7 reflects a realistic appreciation that poverty in America is a complex phenomenon not adequately accounted for by either the moralistic explanations of nineteenth-century Protestantism or the critical appraisals of capitalism by the radical left.

One must also be careful not to overstate the magnitude of the changes that are presumed to have occurred. A recent replication of a survey originally conducted more than fifty years ago should give pause to anyone viewing the country's attachment to capitalist values as in precipitous decline. In the early 1920s Helen and Robert Lynd administered a small battery of questions to the students of the local high school in their famous study of "Middletown." In 1977 two sociologists returned to the same school and, finding its social and ethnic composition relatively unchanged, readministered parts of the same questionnaire.[44] Table 4–8 shows that remarkably little change had occurred in the responses students gave to the two questions about individual responsibility for success and failure. Then as now, about half the students attributed responsibility for personal success or failure to the individual himself; then as now, only a minority cared to challenge the legitimacy of the distribution of wealth in the United States.

These observations still leave open the question of the present status of capitalist values. One might point out, for example, that even if the Puritan influence were to disappear entirely (which it has not done), capitalism as an economic form can draw on other values with which it has been associated. Popular support continues to be strong for such values as personal independence, indi-

Table 4–8 Responsibility for success or failure, percentage answering "true," 1924 and 1977

	1924	1977
1. It is entirely the fault of the man himself if he cannot succeed.	47	47
2. The fact that some men [in 1977: people] have so much more money than others shows there is an unjust condition in this country that ought to be changed.	30	34

Source: From Theodore Caplow and Howard M. Bahr, "Half a Century of Change in Adolescent Attitudes: Replication of a Middletown Survey by the Lynds," *Public Opinion Quarterly,* 43 (Spring 1979), pp. 1–17, table 1.

vidual ambition, achievement, competition, hard work, and initiative in the quest for private profit. We have also seen that Americans overwhelmingly endorse the key capitalist notion that remuneration ought to be geared to the quality and scarcity of economic skills. They also believe that no limits ought to be placed on the acquisition of wealth. Indeed, available data suggest that opposition to this principle may be decreasing: in a 1939 survey, 24 percent of the general public favored laws "limiting the amount of money any individual could earn in a year," whereas in 1976 the number favoring such a limitation had dropped to 9 percent.[45]

Summary and Conclusions

The Protestant ethic was a distinctive contribution to American culture by the early Puritan settlers of New England. But in the eighteenth and nineteenth centuries, other more secular values such as individualism and competition also became prominent. By the second half of the nineteenth century—perhaps the apogee of laissez-faire capitalism in the United States—the economic system rested on a secure foundation of both religious and secular values.

Today, however, capitalism appears to derive its legitimacy less from the ascetic features of the Protestant ethic than from secular values such as individualism and economic efficiency. This development should occasion little surprise in light of the tendency over the past few centuries for religious modes of thought to play an ever-smaller role in explaining or evaluating social, economic, and scientific affairs. The declining tendency to identify worldly success with religious salvation may simply mark another stage of this general retreat. Strong secular values now remain to perform the role formerly filled by religious beliefs. The Protestant ethic in its fully realized sixteenth-century form may have helped to establish capitalism in an age that was dominated by theological metaphors. But, as Weber himself acknowledged, the Protestant ethic need not be retained in its original form in order to ensure the survival of capitalism under the conditions of modern secular society.

It appears, then, that the cultural values on which capitalism relies are solidly in place. Americans may not approach economic enterprise in exactly the same spirit as their forebears, but our data show that they remain strongly committed to values associated with capitalist enterprise. As we shall argue more fully in later chapters, the survival of capitalism in the United States will depend far more on its effectiveness as an economic system—on its ability to produce goods and services efficiently and to distribute them equitably—than on the status of the religious values that once served to legitimate it.

5 Capitalism as an Economic System

"Can capitalism survive?" Joseph Schumpeter opened his analysis of the future of capitalism in his classic 1942 study, *Capitalism, Socialism, and Democracy,* with this question. His reluctant answer was "No, I do not think it can."[1] An astute observer of capitalism, Schumpeter had become convinced, to his dismay, that socialism was "the likely heir apparent." Though he offered no precise date for the demise of capitalism, he left the impression that it was likely to occur within a few decades.

Insofar as it applied to the United States, Schumpeter's somber prognosis has not, of course, been borne out. At least until now, capitalism has obviously survived, both in America and elsewhere. Moreover, the advanced capitalist nations have, on the whole, achieved economic growth, productivity, innovation, efficiency, and standards of living well beyond those of the socialist or communist nations of the world. Yet Schumpeter's analysis has in other ways proved sufficiently discerning to lead one to wonder whether his forecast about the extinction of capitalism is as far from the mark as it seems. Forty years after its original publication, *Capitalism, Socialism, and Democracy* continues to be widely read and discussed,[2] and one may well ask why.

Schumpeter's thesis has particular interest for students of politics and public opinion. Unlike most Marxists, who believed that capitalism would fail largely for economic reasons—a view bolstered by the depth and tenacity of the Great Depression—Schumpeter thought the sources of its failure would be primarily political. He believed that capitalism, if left to function freely without government interference, could generate enough economic growth to raise all social classes to a decent, continually improving, standard of living. But Schumpeter doubted that capitalism would be left to function freely. He expected public opinion to demand ever-higher levels of government interference with the economy in order to "improve" the performance of capitalism; the resulting policies would fail "to take account of the requirements of the capitalist engine and become a serious impediment to its functioning."[3] Schumpeter further predicted that the public, led by alienated and irresponsible intellectuals, would become increasingly angry over the economic problems brought about by its own demands for government control of the economy, and increasingly impatient with the chronic dislocations of the business cycle and the insecurities to which it gave rise. The status of capitalism, therefore, was precarious. Any momentary faltering could generate public demands for measures that would cripple the system, or result in its outright abolition.

Much of Schumpeter's analysis still commands respect. Government has dramatically increased its regulation of business, and has done so in ways that, in the opinion of many businessmen, hamstring and seriously deter business enterprise. Popular attitudes toward capitalism seem also to have developed along lines foreseen by Schumpeter. Many Americans have grown increasingly critical of business and businessmen, pressing for a variety of new government economic regulations.[4] Observing these developments, the proponents of capitalism have often turned deeply pessimistic, if not apocalyptic, in their outlook. Irving Kristol, a prominent publicist for business causes, concluded in the mid-1970s, for example, that the modern corporation is headed toward imminent destruction. As he wrote in the *Wall Street Journal:* "In every way, the large corporations look more and more like a species of dinosaur on its lumbering way to extinction. The cultural and political environment becomes ever more hostile; natural adaptation becomes ever more difficult; possible modes of survival seem to be beyond its imaginative capacity."[5] Similarly, Leonard Silk and David Vogel reported in a recent study of leading American business executives that the typical attitude among them is one of despondency and fear. "Every day in a piecemeal way," according to one executive, "the public unwittingly destroys the free market." Another observed that "the American capitalist system is facing its darkest hour." Summarizing the dominant sentiment expressed by businessmen toward the public, Silk and Vogel wrote that "many leading business executives, feeling the intense public pressures upon them, have begun to wonder whether democracy and capitalism are compatible."[6]

How valid are these concerns? Are business enterprises as beleaguered by adverse public opinion as many businessmen believe? Has the American public begun to reject capitalism and its values? Is the public demanding new types of government interference with the economy that will destroy capitalism?

Given the present state of knowledge, we cannot offer conclusive answers to such questions. We do not know, for example, how successfully the economy will respond to the problems that now challenge it. Nor can we say which of the demands the public makes on capitalism seriously impede its performance and which are reasonable and workable. We *are* in a position, however, to estimate the depth of popular support for capitalism and the kinds of economic changes the public favors.

In making these estimates, one must keep in mind that criticism of business has been a recurrent theme in American history. For example, Andrew Jackson, the dominant political figure in the United States in the 1820s and 1830s, kept up a steady verbal and legislative assault on the interests of the business classes during the eight years he served as president. He opposed tariffs that were designed to protect American industries from destructive foreign competition; he vetoed a bill, strongly desired by business, for a centralized national banking system; and he curtailed federal support for the road and canal system favored by businessmen eager to develop an integrated national economy. Jackson's political speeches, moreover, were peppered with fulminations against the abuses of "the monied interests," the "paper aristocracy" (that is, bankers), those who "desire to amass wealth without labor," and the "rich and powerful who too often bend the acts of government to their selfish purposes."[7]

The antibusiness tone of the Progressive era was, if anything, even more pronounced. Muckraking journalists treated the new industrial system with a degree of critical venom that had rarely been seen in American journalism. Every real or imagined failing or abuse of American business was zealously paraded before the reading public—the sharp competitive practices of large corporations, the unsafe and unsanitary conditions in many factories, the shoddy products manufactured in those factories, and the illicit ties between self-serving businessmen and shady politicians. By 1914 Walter Lippmann was able to write that "the only real question among intelligent people is how business methods are to be altered, not whether they are to be altered. For no one, unafflicted with invincible ignorance, desires to preserve our economic system in its existing form."[8]

Despite the strong antibusiness attitudes expressed in both the Jacksonian and Progressive eras, closer examination of the reform movements in those periods discloses little opposition to the essential principles of capitalism as such. A commitment to laissez-faire, for example, and a desire to divorce government from economic affairs lay at the heart of Jackson's political program. This meant, at the time, that government should refuse to enact measures such as centralized banking that would benefit large, nationally oriented business organizations at the expense of smaller, local enterprises. Jackson, in short, was not hostile to business or capitalism per se; his sympathies lay with the small local entrepreneurs, growers, and merchants who were his staunchest supporters, and it was to assure their prosperity that he championed the principles of unfettered enterprise.

Similar observations hold for the Progressive reformers of the early twentieth century. Though shocked by the unfair and corrupt business practices exposed by the muckrakers, they remained unequivocally attached to the institutions and values of capitalism. The paramount goal of the Progressive reformers, as Richard Hofstadter has shown in his penetrating study, *The Age of Reform,* was to reinstate, insofar as possible, the business climate of pre-industrial America—a time when (as the Progressives saw it) success depended solely on individual talent and integrity, and a small-scale entrepreneur could prosper without fear of "cutthroat competition" from giant corporations. It was to achieve these results that the Progressives advocated such measures as the Clayton Anti-Trust Act, which aimed not to break up or abolish large corporations but to compel them to adhere to fair competitive practices and the principles of the free market.

Table 5-1 The free enterprise system

	General public	Influentials
1. In your opinion, is the free enterprise system necessary for free government to survive?		
—Probably not	6	12
—For the most part, yes	80	83
—Decline to choose	14	5
	(N = 1,026)	(N = 601)
2. The private enterprise system:		
—mostly leads to depression and widespread poverty	7	6
—is generally a fair and efficient system	63	66
—Decline to choose	30	28
	(N = 938)	(N = 845)
3. The free enterprise system:		
—survives by keeping the poor down	5	6
—gives everyone a fair chance	65	60
—Decline to choose	30	34
	(N = 967)	(N = 556)
4. Our freedom depends on the free enterprise system.		
—Agree	82	87
—Disagree	18	13
	(N = 1,484)	(N = 3,020)
5. On the whole, our economic system is just and wise.		
—Agree	77	89
—Disagree	23	11
	(N = 1,484)	(N = 3,020)
6. If the system of private industry were abolished:		
—most people would work hard anyway	21	23
—very few people would do their best	48	39
—Decline to choose	31	39
	(N = 938)	(N = 845)

Sources: questions 1 and 3, Civil Liberties study, 1978–79; questions 2 and 6, Opinions and Values of Americans survey, 1975–77; questions 4 and 5, Political Affiliations and Beliefs study, 1958.

In light of this historical record, it is not surprising that modern public opinion surveys have turned up ambivalent attitudes toward business. Suspicion of business, in particular, is still widespread. As we reported earlier, a 1976 poll found that 82 percent of Americans expressing an opinion on the subject complained that big business had "too much power" in society—a result that made big business the least trusted of the twenty-four groups about which the public was questioned.[9]

Levels of public confidence in business were higher in the more prosperous decade of the 1960s: as late as 1968, for example, 70 percent of the public expressed confidence that "business tries to strike a fair balance between profits and the interests of the public," compared with only 15 percent in 1977.[10] Yet more recent criticism ought not to be viewed as signifying the outright rejection of capitalism or opposition to its essential values. Surveys taken at different times over the past two decades confirm that the vast majority of Americans (80 percent) regard private enterprise as necessary for the survival of free government. Some 90 percent of the respondents in a recent national survey assert that they are prepared to make sacrifices if necessary to preserve the free enterprise system. As shown in Table 5–1, about two-thirds believe that the private enterprise system is "generally fair and efficient," while fewer than 10 percent say that it "mostly leads to widespread poverty and depression." An even smaller number endorse the familiar Marxist charge that capitalism causes war, and that wars would disappear if capitalism were abolished. A plurality of the American public thinks that the abolition of private industry would undermine the willingness of people to work hard. Nearly two-thirds of the general population say that capitalism "gives everyone a fair chance"—a surprisingly strong endorsement in light of the persistence of poverty and racial discrimination in the United States—while only 5 percent accept the radical belief that the system "survives by keeping the poor down." Taken together, these results give little evidence that Americans living in the fourth quarter of the twentieth century are on the verge of abandoning the private enterprise system.

This conclusion is strongly bolstered by the response of the American public and its leaders to such frequently recommended alternatives as socialism and communism. Both are overwhelmingly and repeatedly repudiated by the American people. As Table 5–2 illustrates, only a scattering of respondents believe that if communism were adopted in the United States, the average person would benefit. In fact, more than 80 percent say that communism would make life worse for most people. Similarly, all but

Table 5-2 Communism and socialism

	General public	Influentials
1. If adopted here, the main features of communism would:		
—greatly benefit the average person	3	4
—make things worse for most Americans	82	82
—Decline to choose	15	14
	(N = 967)	(N = 560)
2. Some form of socialism would certainly be better than the system we have now.		
—Agree	11	4
—Disagree	89	96
	(N = 1,484)	(N = 3,020)
3. Communism or socialism may not be perfect, but they certainly would be improvements over the dog-eat-dog systems people have lived under until now.		
—Agree	11	2
—Disagree	89	98
	(N = 1,484)	(N = 3,020)
4. The communist countries will go down in history as:		
—countries that reached a new and higher stage of progress	5	5
—dictatorships that crushed human freedom	68	54
—Decline to choose	27	42
	(N = 938)	(N = 845)
5. The sacrifices made by the people in the communist countries are:		
—necessary and will benefit the people in the long run	8	10
—not really in the people's interests	62	41
—Decline to choose	30	50
	(N = 938)	(N = 845)
6. There are a great many things in the Soviet Union that could be copied by this country with much benefit to the common people.		
—Agree	16	—
—Disagree	84	—
	(N = 1,064)	

Sources: question 1, Civil Liberties study, 1978–79; questions 2 and 3, Political Affiliations and Beliefs study, 1958; questions 4 and 5, Opinions and Values of Americans survey, 1975–77; question 6, Marginal Believer survey, 1955 (for sample characteristics on the MB survey, see Herbert McClosky, "Personality and Conservatism," *American Political Science Review*, 52 (1958), pp. 27–45.

11 percent of the general public and only a handful of the political influentials reject any suggestion that socialism or communism would be preferable to the present economic system. Only 5 percent of Americans think of the communist countries as having reached a new and higher stage of progress—one of the major claims communists make for the superiority of their system. An overwhelming majority of 84 percent doubt that there is anything in the Soviet Union worth copying that would benefit the average American. At no point in the survey data of the past forty years does one encounter significant support among Americans for socialist or communist "solutions." On the contrary, these alternatives are largely reviled, in sharp contrast to the response Americans make to capitalist values and institutions.

These data serve to underscore a fact long evident to even the casual observer of American life: the United States has never produced a large-scale radical movement or a significant measure of popular support for socialism, communism, or any other system proposed by the radical left (or, for that matter, the radical right). Nevertheless, the data also indicate that despite their continuing commitment to private enterprise, Americans tend to be highly critical of big business and various business practices.

Some observers may consider the two sets of findings inconsistent or surprising. But, as we have noted, a certain ambivalence toward business—a mixture of admiration and distrust—has been common in American history. Nor is business the only institution about which Americans have mixed feelings. Like the people of many other nations, Americans habitually voice disdain toward politics and politicians, which frequently does little to prevent them from returning incumbents to office. Indeed, as recent survey data make plain, Americans express qualms about many important social and political groups—including doctors, lawyers, bankers, and clerics—but when the occasion requires, they entrust their lives or personal well-being to them. To what extent these expressions of skepticism reflect a deep-seated distrust of authority and to what extent they represent a form of ritualistic cynicism, a *pro forma* "style of response" typical of the culture—or the *Zeitgeist*—is difficult to say.[11] In any event, suspicion of business institutions has not led to efforts to alter them radically, much less to eliminate them.

In evaluating public attitudes toward existing economic values and practices, one should keep in mind that notions like capitalism and socialism represent extremely complex bodies of ideas—so complex that it would be unrealistic to expect most Americans to understand, much less to favor, all the ideas embodied in such terms. For example, only 28 percent of the general public in our OVS survey could correctly select from the two choices offered a correct description of so familiar an economic notion as inflation. Similar signs of ignorance or misinformation about vital concepts and public issues recur throughout our surveys. Professions of support for capitalist values by many members of the public, therefore, may indicate not so much a carefully considered evaluation of the merits and demerits of capitalism as an economic system, but a form of traditional attachment to a familiar set of practices to which one responds without much reflection. Doubtless, too, many endorse the symbols and values of the economic system simply because they have personally prospered under it.[12] The survival of capitalism, in other words, does not depend on widespread public appreciation of the fine points of economic policy or on a subtle understanding of the pros and cons of economic competition and the complex workings of the free market. However, even unexamined attachments to prevailing values can have a significant bearing on the course of public policy, as can be seen by examining the popular response to the key capitalist institution of private property.

Property

From the earliest years of the American republic, the notion of private property has enjoyed extraordinary popular favor. Like other features of early American life, freehold ownership of the land represented, in effect, a rejection of certain Old World institutions. Among other things, it signified the repudiation of a system in which almost all productive land was owned by a small aristocratic minority or by the Church, but was cultivated by the labor of peasants and landless tenants. The European system, as Benjamin Franklin once characterized it, was one in which wealth was "pinched off the backs and out of the bellies of the miserable inhabitants" by a class of avaricious overlords.[13]

Except in the slave-holding states, those who tilled the soil in America were usually freeholders—owners of private property, rather than tenants or serfs. Ownership of the land not only freed a great many Americans from material privation but enabled them to attain a level of dignity and independence that was impossible for the vassal or tenant of an aristocratic overlord. To Americans of Franklin's day, property thus seemed to be an essential institution of democratic society. As Crevecoeur exulted in his *Letters from an American Farmer:*

> The instant I enter on my own land, the bright idea of property, of exclusive right, of independence, exalt my mind. Precious soil, I say to myself, by what singular custom of law is it that thou wast made to constitute the riches of the freeholder? What should we American farmers be without the distinct possession of that soil? ... No wonder Europeans who have never been able to say that such portion of land was theirs cross the Atlantic to realize that happiness: This formerly rude soil has established all our rights; on it is founded our rank, our freedom, our power as citizens, our importance as inhabitants of such a district. This image, I must confess, I always behold with pleasure and extend them as far as my imagination can reach: for this is what may be called the true and only philosophy of an American farmer.[14]

This American reverence for private property led Tocqueville to observe that in "no other country in the world is the love of property keener or more alert than in the United States, and nowhere else does the majority display less inclination toward doctrines which in any way threaten the way property is owned."[15]

In Tocqueville's day, commercial property was mainly landed property, and—outside the southern plantation regions—was typically owned by independent freeholders in relatively small parcels. Thus property represented both home and livelihood for many Americans. Even commercial property consisted for the most part of owner-operated shops and small, individually owned plants. The growth of modern industrial capitalism changed this pattern drastically: thereafter the most visible and important forms of commercial property were large corporate concentrations of mineral and manufacturing wealth that bore little resemblance to the family farms and shops of the early nineteenth century.

Aside from the sheer increase in the size of corporate property holdings, two other important changes in the nature and significance of property stand out.[16] One is that the new forms of property less often served to encourage independence and self-reliance among the populace, or to protect ordinary citizens from being exploited by the wealthy and powerful. On the contrary, when concentrated in the hands of large, impersonal corporations, private property tended to undermine the very values it had promoted in the formative years of the Republic.

A second, related difference is that modern corporate property is normally owned by thousands or even millions of stockholders who, though "owning" it in the technical sense, have little effective voice in its management. The two major attributes of property ownership in the past—legal title to property and actual control over its use—are thus often divorced. As Walter Lippmann observed, the modern shareholder who "may never [even] see his property . . . is a very feeble representative of the institution of private property."[17]

Questions about the property rights of stockholders were pointedly raised by A. A. Berle, Jr., and Gardner Means in their 1932 classic, *The Modern Corporation and Private Property*. Must we not recognize, they asked, "that we are no longer dealing with property in the old sense?"[18] By surrendering direct control over their "property," Berle and Means maintained, the owners (that is, the shareholders) of modern corporate property "have released the community from the obligation to protect them to the full extent implied in the doctrine of strict property rights."[19] Hence the community may legitimately abridge the traditional rights of property when it is in the public interest to do so.

Berle and Means are not the only—or the first—American thinkers to make suggestions of this kind. A number of social philosophers and reformers, including Henry George, Edward Bellamy, and John Dewey, had urged that traditional notions of property be reformulated to take account of the new forms of corporate ownership and control that emerged in the late nineteenth and early twentieth centuries. The lack of impact of these appeals on the abstract notions of private property held by the American people is, however, striking. Even under the changed conditions of the industrial age, most Americans continue to adhere to the traditional conception of property as the bulwark of individual

Table 5-3 General value of private property

	General public	Influentials
1. Private ownership of property is necessary for economic progress.		
—Agree	84	88
—Disagree	16	12
	(N = 1,484)	(N = 3,020)
2. Private ownership of property:		
—is as important to a good society as freedom	78	63
—has often done mankind more harm than good	7	14
—Decline to choose	15	24
	(N = 938)	(N = 845)
3. Private ownership of property:		
—is as important to a good society as freedom	87	74
—has often done mankind more harm than good	4	10
—Decline to choose	9	16
	(N = 967)	(N = 556)
4. As long as we have a system of private ownership, we will be in serious danger of losing our freedom.		
—Agree	11	3
—Disagree	89	97
	(N = 1,484)	(N = 3,020)

Sources: questions 1 and 4, Political Affiliations and Beliefs study, 1958; question 2, Opinions and Values of Americans survey, 1975–77; question 3, Civil Liberties study, 1978–79.

freedom and the source of economic well-being. As Table 5–3 demonstrates, more than four out of five respondents in our 1958 survey agreed that "private ownership of property is necessary for economic progress." Likewise, the vast majority of respondents in the national surveys we conducted in the late 1970s thought that private property "is as important to a good society as freedom," while only a scattering of respondents felt that it "has often done mankind more harm than good." Consistent with these views, almost 90 percent (and an even higher number among the influentials) reject the familiar radical charge that the system of private ownership represents a danger to freedom.

Impressive though these results are, they do not tell us whether Americans are simply endorsing the right of ordinary people to own their own homes, land, tools, and personal belongings, or whether they also support the property rights of large industrial corporations and agribusinesses. Table 5–4 helps to answer this question. By an overwhelming margin, Americans of the late 1950s rejected the suggestion that the country's farmland be redivided "so that no one could own land except the people who actually do the farming." By smaller though still substantial margins, respondents in our two surveys in the late 1970s likewise preferred that the nation's land be left in the hands of private owners rather than "turned over to the people." Sentiment for public ownership of large-scale industry is also weak: in one national survey, only a fifth of the population said it would be "a good idea," and about half flatly opposed it; in another survey, 74 percent rejected the view that "the country would be better off if big business were taken over by the government as in certain European countries."[20]

Table 5–4   Redistribution of property

	General public	Influentials
1. The farmland of this country should be redivided so that no one could own land except the people who actually do the farming.		
—Agree	17	5
—Disagree	83	95
	(N = 1,484)	(N = 3,020)
2. The land of this country should be:		
—left in the hands of private owners	54	67
—turned over to the people	12	5
—Decline to choose	33	28
	(N = 967)	(N = 556)
3. Public ownership of large industry would be a:		
—good idea	22	17
—bad idea	45	51
—Decline to choose	33	31
	(N = 938)	(N = 845)

Sources: question 1, Political Affiliations and Beliefs study, 1958; question 2, Civil Liberties study, 1978–79; question 3, Opinions and Values of Americans survey, 1975–77.

Our data thus suggest that the owners of private property—even those who own or manage vast concentrations of property—have little reason to fear that an angry public is waiting sullenly in the wings for an excuse to confiscate their holdings. On the contrary, popular support for private ownership of property remains strong.

Obviously this does not mean that private property is safe from *all* public interference. Since at least the mid-nineteenth century, American government at all levels has become increasingly active in setting restrictions on the uses of property. This is especially true of landed property, which is now subject to zoning laws and environmental safeguards that are often detailed and stringent. Even the various forms of corporate property—factories, warehouses, and transportation systems—are now viewed by government as "affected with a public interest" and therefore properly subject to public regulation. As Paul Samuelson comments: "It is obvious that in the years ahead, the so-called private corporation will find itself increasingly subjected to external constraints never dreamed of at the Harvard Business School. Not only will the corporation president find he cannot follow policies that will pollute the atmosphere; he will also discover that hundreds of traditional ways of making business decisions will simply no longer be available to him. Society will expand business's responsibilities and take increasing part in deciding how they are to be met."[21]

American public opinion generally supports regulation of the use of property, but in a curious and revealing way. Although the majority continue to agree that an individual has the right to use his property as he pleases, they also endorse many of the specific measures that property owners perceive as violating traditional property rights. The two items in Table 5–5 serve to illustrate this. By a ratio greater than two to one, a majority of the general public assert that "the way property is used should mainly be decided . . . by the individuals who own it" rather than by "the community." One might assume, on evidence of this kind, that most Americans are firmly wedded to the traditional interpretation of property rights. But the second item in Table 5–5 points in a contrary direction: only a fifth of the general public agree that "a lumber company has the right to cut down enough trees to protect its investment," while three-fifths assert that the number of

Table 5-5   Control of private property

	General public (N = 938)	Influentials (N = 845)
1. The way property is used should mainly be decided by the:		
—individuals who own it	58	36
—community, since the earth belongs to everyone	22	30
—Decline to choose	20	34
2. A lumber company that spends millions for a piece of forest land:		
—should, nevertheless, be limited by law in the number of trees it can cut	63	71
—has the right to cut down enough trees to protect its investment	21	11
—Decline to choose	16	18

Source: Opinions and Values of Americans survey, 1975–77.

trees a company can cut should "be limited by law." These data show that, although Americans remain attached to the old and familiar notion of private property, many are willing to compromise that value when pressed by a strong competing value, such as environmental protection.

The persistence of traditional attitudes toward property has doubtless made the recommendations of economic reformers like Berle and Means extremely difficult to enact. In America, in contrast to some other parts of the world, the conception of property ownership does not usually conjure up images of avaricious landlords, exploitation of the common people, or opposition to the principles of equality and democratic government. Nor, despite the animadversions of generations of social critics, is property widely viewed in the United States as a symbol of entrenched privilege and the private expropriation of public goods. American traditions, as well as the widespread ownership of land, housing, and small businesses, have led most Americans to perceive private ownership of property as beneficent and even ennobling. The images that spring to mind when the word *property* is mentioned are mainly the positive images that were formed in the late eighteenth and early nineteenth centuries, when property was viewed as a bulwark of democratic freedom and independence. The effect of these honorific associations is to make Americans wary of expropriating farmland, nationalizing banks or industry, or interfering in other ways with the key capitalist institution of private property.

Laissez-Faire and the Role of Government in the Economy

The free market lies at the heart of capitalist economy. In theory, it determines not only wages and prices but the type, quality, and amount of goods and services to be produced. Since each individual is free to make his own economic decisions—to choose a vocation, to save or invest capital, to manufacture, buy, or sell products, to offer his labor at whatever price he can command—the market also determines in great measure who succeeds in business and who does not.

A free market may seem too amorphous an institution to bear such complicated and difficult responsibilities. Yet, following Adam Smith's arguments in *The Wealth of Nations,* and those of other classical economists, American influentials have believed for more than two centuries that a system that leaves each buyer and seller free to arrive at the transaction most favorable to his own interests will lead, as though guided by an "invisible hand," to the optimal use and distribution of economic resources. In short, ideas that originated in the realm of economics have been integrated into the American political culture as well.

Still somewhat controversial in the early years of the Republic, the creed of laissez-faire found distinguished champions in statesmen like Jefferson and philosophers like Emerson. It reigned almost unchallenged throughout most of the nineteenth century in America, where the science of economics was so firmly wedded to laissez-faire doctrines that they virtually became the test of whether one was, indeed, an economist at all.[22]

Laissez-faire also appealed to commentators, statesmen, clergymen, and other leaders of nineteenth-century opinion, but largely for its vaunted political and moral significance. The belief, for example, that the state should play a minimal role in the economy was entirely compatible with the deep-seated American suspicion of government as an inherently despotic institution. Laissez-faire was also consistent with the values of Protestantism and the burgeoning philosophy of individualism, both of which placed the individual entrepreneur at center stage. The doctrine of laissez-faire strongly supported the belief that individuals should bear sole responsibility for their own economic affairs and should neither seek nor receive help from government or any other external agency. Laissez-faire was thus perceived not only as scientifically valid but as wholly in keeping with fundamental national values. As the historian Yehosha Arieli has observed: "Almost all significant American political thought in the nineteenth century centered on the radical concept of *laissez faire* as the natural order of society which harmoniously fused social justice and liberty. It animated the reform movements of the Jacksonian era—the Free Soilers, the Loco-Foco, and the 'Barnburners'—no less than those of the Greenbackers, the Single-Taxers, the Populists, and Bryan's and Wilson's Democracy . . . The vision of a new society fashioned on the natural order of freedom was the center of the national idea."[23]

One might suppose that a principle appealing to so many intellectual and cultural strains—the Protestant ethic, economic science, individualism, competition, and fear of government— would prove to be one of the most enduring principles in the American political tradition. Surprisingly, however, this has not been the case. By the late nineteenth century, industrial growth and other drastic economic changes had so profoundly altered the character of American society that Smith's "invisible hand" no longer seemed capable of performing the regulative functions its proponents claimed for it. Disagreements over the proper role of government intruded increasingly into the public debate. Taking one side of the issue were the progressive reformers, liberal intellectuals, and spokesmen for the working class, all of whom urged that government intervene to smooth out swings in the business cycle and remedy the social ills, such as poverty, that seemed beyond the effective reach of market forces. Taking the other side in the debate was a coalition of conservative and business interests, who fervently argued that economic regulation by government must be held to a minimum.

The result of this conflict has been a continuing series of setbacks to laissez-faire. Merely to name some of the problem areas for which government now takes significant responsibility would be to list the defeats that the proponents of laissez-faire have had to endure: unemployment insurance, regulation of the hours of labor, mandatory collective bargaining, consumer protection laws, environmental safeguards, prohibition of racial and sexual discrimination in employment, job safety legislation, restrictions against unfair economic competition and monopoly, and many more. Government now concerns itself even with such vital business issues as interest rates, corporate mergers, and the regulation of prices and wages.

Nor are most of these forms of interference with laissez-faire unpopular. Although current levels of government regulation of business are, by historical standards, high, most Americans support them. As Table 5–6 shows, large majorities approve the present levels of government regulation of key industries, and many favor even greater regulation. These findings and other data throughout our own surveys leave little doubt that the public's belief in laissez-faire has substantially declined.

Popular support for laissez-faire capitalism appears surprisingly weak even at a relatively abstract level, as Table 5–7 testifies. In our survey from the late 1950s, 74 percent of the general

Table 5–6 Federal regulation of specific industries

Industry	Percentage in favor of federal regulation	Percentage in favor of increased regulation
Drug	80	48
Oil	73	49
Food	73	49
Utilities	71	42
Chemicals	68	34
Airlines	67	31
Steel	66	31
Banking	66	30
Automobiles	64	35
Tire and rubber	64	27
Cigarettes and tobacco	63	33
Electrical appliances	62	25
Computers	54	21
Average	67	35

Source: Louis Harris and Associates, 1976, cited in S. M. Lipset and William Schneider, "The Public View of Regulation," *Public Opinion* (January 1979), p. 8.

Table 5-7 General attitudes toward government regulation of business

	General public	Influentials
1. Most things would run pretty well by themselves if the government just didn't interfere.		
—Agree	25	30
—Disagree	75	70
	(N = 1,484)	(N = 3,020)
2. We need a strong central government to handle modern economic problems efficiently.		
—Agree	74	54
—Disagree	26	46
	(N = 1,484)	(N = 3,020)
3. Every time another government regulation over industry is adopted, we take one more step toward collectivism.		
—Agree	43	39
—Disagree	57	61
	(N = 1,484)	(N = 3,020)
4. Government regulation of business:		
—is necessary to keep industry from becoming too powerful	45	42
—usually does more harm than good	28	35
—Decline to choose	27	23
	(N = 1,993)	(N = 1,157)
5. The way business is behaving, we need the government to keep an eye on them.		
—Agree	62	—
—Disagree	28	—
6. Government has to play an increasingly active role in regulating business and industry because of the increasing size of corporations and the complexity of the U.S. economic system.		
—Agree	59	—
—Disagree	33	—
—Other	8	—

Sources: questions 1, 2, and 3, Political Affiliations and Beliefs study, 1958; question 4, Civil Liberties study, 1978–79; question 5, *U.S. News and World Report*, 1977, cited in S. M. Lipset and William Schneider, "The Public View of Regulation," *Public Opinion* (January 1979), p. 10; question 6, Opinion Research Corporation, 1978, cited in Lipset and Schneider, "Public View of Regulation," p. 8.

public and more than half the political influentials affirmed that "we need a strong central government to handle modern economic problems efficiently." Large majorities also rejected the opinion that "most things would run pretty well by themselves if the government just didn't interfere."

Comparable results turn up in the 1970s. By a margin of two to one, Americans reject the contention that government regulation of business "usually does more harm than good." Such regulation, they say, is "necessary to keep industry from becoming too powerful." By similar margins, Americans say that in view of the way business enterprises behave, we need the government "to keep an eye on them." A 1978 survey by the Opinion Research Corporation reports that three-fifths of the American public believe that government should take an increasingly active role in regulating business "because of the increasing size of corporations and the complexity of the U.S. economic system." Depending on how the question is phrased, national surveys also indicate that some 40 to 60 percent of the American public support the idea of government wage and price controls.[24]

The overall pattern, then, seems fairly clear: only a small number of Americans are so deeply opposed to business that they favor replacing private enterprise with public ownership of large businesses and industry. At the other end of the opinion spectrum, another small group—perhaps 10 to 20 percent—wants a return to laissez-faire and a sharp reduction in government regulation of the economy. The balance—a substantial majority of Americans—seems reasonably satisfied with the present intermingling of business independence and government intervention.

These attitudes, of course, represent a substantial departure from the opinions about laissez-faire that dominated public discourse in the nineteenth century. What accounts for this change? As a first step in answering this question, recall that in the early eighteenth and nineteenth centuries, laissez-faire was popularly associated with the ideals of individual rights, equality, and democracy. With the rise of industrial capitalism in the late nineteenth century, however, this association began to weaken as laissez-faire came to be identified with economic uncertainty and hardship for the average American while the wealthy few enjoyed unlimited opportunities. This ideological shift, as we shall argue more fully in the next chapter, profoundly undermined public confidence in laissez-faire.

Intellectuals, ministers, and members of the fledgling professions of economics and sociology were among the first to challenge the ideal of laissez-faire. Beginning in the 1870s they began turning out books and pamphlets arguing that a strong and active central government was necessary to cope with the conditions of a large-scale industrial economy. The new spirit that infused economic thought in this period was described by Richard T. Ely, a leader of the movement, in this fashion: "This younger political economy no longer permits the science [of economics] to be used as a tool in the hands of the greedy and the avaricious for keeping down and oppressing the laboring classes. It does not acknowledge *laissez faire* as an excuse for doing nothing while people starve, nor allow the all-sufficiency of competition as a plea for grinding the poor."[25] Spotlighting, among other problems, unsanitary conditions in the food industry, safety problems in new industrial plants, and the corruption of local and state governments by business, a generation of muckraking journalists called for a government strong enough to force business to honor accepted standards of moral conduct. As proposals for reform gathered force and popularity, the great Boston patrician William James accurately observed that "stroke upon stroke, from pens of genius, the competitive regime so idolized 75 years ago seems to be getting wounded to death."[26]

Even a number of businessmen, though reluctant to admit it, began to lose some of their enthusiasm for unqualified laissez-faire. Unregulated competition, they found, gave rise to a degree of uncertainty that made it difficult to plan their industrial activities efficiently. As a result, some of them—particularly those engaged in moderate or small-sized enterprises—demanded that government establish laws and regulatory agencies to prevent monopolies, enforce competitive standards, and help stabilize their markets.[27]

But even though the ideal of laissez-faire came under sustained attack, it was not easily defeated. In the period between the 1870s, when pressure for greater government regulation of the economy began to build up, and the late 1930s, when the Supreme Court shifted its predominant orientation to permit such regulation, laissez-faire was the focal point of intense social and political strife. There is little point in reviewing in detail here the events that marked this struggle—the agrarian revolts, strikes and urban riots, and bitter legislative and judicial conflicts. It suffices to say that the traditional norms associated with laissez-faire were a major obstacle to the adoption of measures that many economists and social reformers considered necessary to ameliorate the problems of an industrial society.

A comparison with European conditions might serve to emphasize the point. With their long-established traditions of strong government, European countries moved relatively quickly to involve government in the conduct of economic life under the new industrial conditions. In a few cases—Bismarck in Germany and Disraeli in Great Britain readily come to mind—even conservatives participated in these efforts to some extent. In the United States, on the other hand, where laissez-faire, personal freedom, and individualism were deeply etched into the national creed, even liberal-minded reformers were for many years reluctant to urge government intervention in the economy. Having been reared on the hallowed doctrines of small, limited government preached by democrats like Thomas Jefferson and Andrew Jackson, they hesitated to involve the state in activities that (as they saw it) might only serve to strengthen the entrenched interests against the common people. Measures to regulate (or assist) the economy were thus resisted in the United States, while countries with traditions of more powerful government moved more rapidly to enact them.

Whether events in this case were shaped by existing values or whether values were altered by events (an old issue in the social sciences) cannot be known with certainty. It seems plain, however, that each seems to have influenced the other. By what seems a fair reading of the historical evidence of the late nineteenth and early twentieth centuries, the popularity of laissez-faire doctrine functioned to delay and, in some instances, to block most efforts to make government responsive to the new industrial conditions. Here traditional values appear predominantly to have influenced events, rather than the reverse. Yet, when adherence to laissez-faire failed to resolve the recurrent problems of industrial society, faith in it grew weaker, new approaches involving government intervention were tried, and new attitudes were gradually formed. In this case, events seem predominantly to have influenced political values.

Modern poll data add important details to this general outline. Numerous surveys, as we have just seen, confirm that the public now demands many forms of government activity that violate traditional laissez-faire doctrine. Public opinion, for example, strongly favors regulations to protect the environment, guarantee job safety, and assure the quality of food and drugs. However, surveys also show that the public maintains a lingering attachment to the idea of laissez-faire. Lipset and Schneider, for example, report that American opinion, though favoring government intervention in numerous economic spheres, has typically failed to press for abandonment of laissez-faire principles as such. Incongruous as it may seem, forty years of public opinion research turns up few if any instances in which a majority of Americans advocate increased government regulation of the economy as a desirable goal *in its own right.*

Other data further emphasize the ambivalent nature of the popular response to the growth of government regulation. Although present levels of regulation are widely accepted, solid popular majorities still complain that "the more government regulation there is, the less efficiently companies can operate." A plurality of the general public (though not of the influentials) likewise say that "one reason modern governments have grown so big and complicated is that they do things people should do for themselves" (see Table 5–8).

Survey data thus highlight several aspects of public opinion about government regulation that might easily be overlooked if one were making judgments only on the basis of the historical decline of laissez-faire practice. Americans, though skeptical of unrestrained capitalism, still seem to maintain a distinct preference for private management of the economy—unless, in their opinion, private mechanisms fall short and public remedies appear to be the only effective alternatives. As Lipset and Schneider argue:

> The fact that regulation is widely supported does not mean that most Americans have confidence in government planning and management. Americans still endorse free market

Table 5–8   Attitude toward government

	General public	Influentials
1. The more government regulation there is, the less efficiently companies can operate.		
—Agree	65	—
—Disagree	22	—
—Other	13	—
2. One reason modern governments have grown so big and complicated is that they do:		
—so many things people need and want	24	49
—things that people should do for themselves	46	26
—Decline to choose	31	25
	(N = 938)	(N = 845)

Sources: question 1, *U.S. News and World Report,* cited in S. M. Lipset and William Schneider, "The Public View of Regulation," *Public Opinion* (January 1979), p. 10; question 2, Opinions and Values of Americans survey, 1975–77.

economic values, particularly free enterprise and individual competition. They favor regulation not because they want the government to run the economy, but because they have become increasingly concerned with what they view as the "bad citizenship" of business—or, perhaps, because they have become increasingly sensitive to the social costs of traditional business practices. Regulation is aimed at ending these abuses, not at telling people how to run their affairs.[28]

Public opinion surveys also help to shed light on the dynamics of mass opinion change toward issues relating to laissez-faire. For example, when President Nixon suddenly announced support for wage and price controls in 1971, the polls showed a shift of approximately 20 percentage points toward greater public support for such controls. An even larger shift, from 37 percent to 82 percent, occurred among a sample of Republican business and political leaders, who, of course, tend to pay far more attention to presidential pronouncements than do most members of the general public.[29] These results are consistent with one of the hypotheses of this study, namely, that opinion elites (in this case the president and his administration) play a vital role in influencing public attitudes toward traditional political values.[30]

Some may wonder, in view of the responsiveness of public

opinion to elite influence, whether there is reason to attach much significance to public attitudes toward capitalism. We believe there is. The capacity of leaders to influence public opinion is obviously limited—though it is difficult to say to what degree and under what circumstances. Leaders are aware of this limitation and are usually reluctant to push policies that depart too far from the attitudes of the electorate. More important, the continuing public preference for limited government helps to sustain a political culture in which private business still exercises great influence.

Self-Interest and Support for Capitalism

From Adam Smith to the present, the defenders of capitalism have argued that the private enterprise system is the most efficient system ever devised. They usually claim, in addition, that the system pays large and equitable dividends to all segments of the population—so that even the working classes are better off under capitalism than they would be under socialism or communism. Since, however, capitalism does not reward everyone equally, the question arises whether support for the system is as strong among those who earn relatively little as it is among those who enjoy high financial rewards. Is there, as one would expect, a strong relationship between income and support for capitalism?

Our data offer only modest support for the existence of such a relationship. As can be seen in Figure 5–1, support for capitalism as measured by our 29-item capitalism scale tends to rise as an individual's income rises.[31] The increase, however, is both uneven and fairly small. One can get a sense of the magnitude of the differences shown in Figure 5–1 by bearing in mind that the lowest possible score on our capitalism scale is zero and the highest possible score is +58 (a score of +58 would mean that the respondent took all possible procapitalist responses). The mean score on the capitalism scale for people with incomes under $6,000 was 29.7, while the mean score for people with incomes over $30,000 was 36.7—a difference of only seven points, or slightly more than half a standard deviation.

If we examine specific issues involving capitalist values (as we

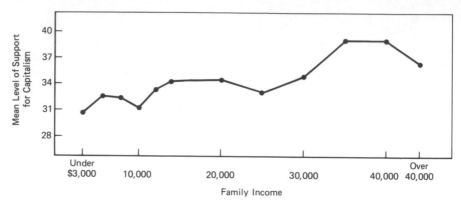

Figure 5–1 Effect of income on support for capitalism among the mass
public (standard deviation on support for capitalism scale is
9.5). *Source:* Opinions and Values of Americans survey, 1975–77.

have in Table 5–9), income appears to have a relatively large impact on attitudes toward some issues and no effect at all on others.
Its impact seems to be largest for those issues that most directly
reflect economic self-interest. For example, 69 percent of the
high-income respondents but only 34 percent of the low-income
respondents believe that the low pay given to manual workers is
"about right, considering the amount of skill involved." The two
groups differ by similar margins on the amount of influence workers ought to have over management decisions. Yet Table 5–9 also
shows that, verbally at least, Americans of lower income support
the essential principles of capitalism—the rights of property
owners, the value of competition, the importance of hard work in
achieving success—almost as strongly as do more affluent Americans. Thus, even among the lower-paid groups, 76 percent of the
respondents say that "people with more ability [should] earn
higher salaries"; among the affluent, 84 percent choose this response.[32] In short, while the American working classes tend to
want higher wages and a greater voice in the management of industry, they nonetheless exhibit almost as much support for the
fundamental values and institutions of capitalism as do members
of the wealthier classes.

One note of caution is in order: these results do not mean that
all Americans agree about the desirability and effectiveness of

Table 5–9 Effect of income on attitudes toward capitalism among the general public

	Family income	
	Under $6,000 (N = 128)	Over $35,000 (N = 51)
1. Unskilled workers (such as janitors, dishwashers, and so on) usually receive wages that are:		
—much too low for the dirty work they do	49	14
—about right, considering the amount of skill required	34	69
—Decline to choose	17	17
2. The private enterprise system:		
—mostly leads to depression and widespread poverty	10	6
—is generally a fair and efficient system	51	84
—Decline to choose	39	10
3. When it comes to making decisions in industry:		
—workers should have more to say than they do now	36	28
—the important decisions should be left to management	33	59
—Decline to choose	31	13
4. Public ownership of large industry would be a:		
—good idea	21	16
—bad idea	37	64
—Decline to choose	42	20
5. The way property is used should mainly be decided by the:		
—community, since the earth belongs to everyone	18	20
—individuals who own it	68	60
—Decline to choose	14	20
6. A lumber company that spends millions for a piece of forest land:		
—should, nevertheless, be limited by law in the number of trees it can cut	59	68
—has the right to cut down enough trees to protect its investment	25	14
—Decline to choose	16	18
7. Competition, whether in school, work, or business:		
—is often wasteful and destructive	9	12
—leads to better performance and a desire for excellence	77	73
—Decline to choose	17	15

Table 5-9   (continued)

	Family income	
	Under $6,000 (N = 128)	Over $35,000 (N = 51)
8. Under a fair economic system:		
—all people would earn about the same	9	2
—people with more ability would earn higher salaries	76	84
—Decline to choose	17	14
9. Getting ahead in the world is mostly a matter of:		
—getting the breaks	19	8
—ability and hard work	63	64
—Decline to choose	18	28

Source: Opinions and Values of Americans survey, 1975–77.

capitalism. Certain differences exist among them, but as we shall see in later chapters, they are better explained by factors related to social learning and ideology than by theories of class interest or conflict.[33]

Concluding Remarks

Can capitalism survive? Or more to the point, to what extent does American public opinion represent a threat to the private enterprise system?

No one, of course, can offer a conclusive answer to this question, but one can perhaps rule out certain contingencies. One of the important lessons of the 1930s, for example, is that even under prolonged conditions of severe depression the American public and its political leaders have been able to resist pressure to transform the economy in some wholesale fashion, preferring instead to experiment with limited reforms, gradual measures, and, in retrospect, modest adjustments in existing economic institutions. Survey data give further evidence of this cautious attitude. A vast majority of Americans (70 percent of the general public and 91 percent of the influentials) affirmed, even during the economic recession of 1958, that America could restore prosperity "without changing the private enterprise system very much." Nearly the same proportions rejected the contention that "without sweeping changes in our economic system, little progress can be made in the solution of social problems" (see Table 5–10).

This predominantly cautious orientation toward fundamental economic change should allay some of the fears businessmen harbor about public attitudes toward the economy. Some businessmen and economic commentators, however, believe that the most serious danger to private enterprise is not that Americans will embrace radical solutions, but that they will demand so many government services and economic regulations that private enterprise will be stifled. They fear, in other words, that capitalism might be destroyed by piecemeal "reforms" that, although individually moderate, would amount in the end to a radical change. Those who follow Schumpeter in holding this view may not find much comfort in the data just presented. A majority of Americans support, or at least are willing to accept, economic policies calling for wide-ranging government intervention in the economy. Even probusiness Republicans often accede to measures that laissez-faire economists regard as pernicious. What, then, should one conclude about Schumpeter's pessimistic prognosis?

So far, at least, Schumpeter seems to have been correct on one major point of his analysis and wrong on two others. He was clearly correct in believing that the American people would demand government intervention and regulation of the economy

Table 5–10 Attitudes toward economic change

	General public (N = 1,484)	Influentials (N = 3,020)
1. We can do everything needed to get prosperity without changing the private enterprise system very much.		
—Agree	70	91
—Disagree	30	9
2. Without sweeping changes in our economic system, little progress can be made in the solution of social problems.		
—Agree	39	15
—Disagree	61	85

Source: Political Affiliations and Beliefs study, 1958.

whenever the free market seemed incapable of functioning effectively on its own. As our data clearly attest, most Americans are simply unwilling to wait patiently until business works out its own solutions to such problems as unemployment, poverty, inflation, pollution, unsafe products, or dangerous working conditions.

Schumpeter appears to have been wrong, however, in his evaluation of how the government regulations demanded by the public would affect economic performance. Although confronted with increasingly stringent regulations, the American economy—measured by improvements in the overall standard of living of the average American—has performed well in the era since World War II. Despite inflation, unemployment, and other economic difficulties in the late 1970s and early 1980s, few reputable economists believe that the American economy is in danger of imminent collapse as a result of overregulation. Many economists maintain, on the contrary, that the success of the private enterprise system over the past four decades is partly due to just those forms of government intervention that Schumpeter feared.

Schumpeter also appears to have overemphasized the significance of the public's chronic hostility toward business and its consequent willingness to impose government limitations on private enterprise. In analyzing the available data, we sought to correct this emphasis by describing the more complex pattern of beliefs and values that shape American attitudes toward business. We observed, for example, that outbreaks of popular hostility toward business have recurred throughout American history, and that they have not signified a desire on the part of the public to overturn capitalism. We also pointed out that popular distrust of the motives of business has usually been matched—both historically and in modern survey data—by high levels of distrust toward government. In assessing the likelihood that antibusiness feeling will lead to pressure for a government takeover of the private economy, one would do well to recall Ralph Nader's remark that Americans think "the only thing worse than having a car built by General Motors is to have one built by the government."[34]

Nor is the traditional American fear of government the only value that tends to counteract chronic suspicion of the motives of business—particularly big business. Americans, as we saw, profess a continuing commitment to such values and institutions as individualism, competition, achievement, private property, the profit system, differential incomes, and the unlimited acquisition of wealth. Hence, despite their disillusionment with the performance of certain aspects of private enterprise, Americans are still attached to the values constituting the moral and economic underpinnings of capitalism. It would appear, therefore, that Schumpeter overstates the magnitude of the threat to capitalism posed by public opinion.

This does not mean, of course, that the commitment of most Americans to traditional capitalist values is irrevocable. Popular support for capitalist ideas, institutions, and practices, like support for the more demanding aspects of the democratic tradition, is to some degree fragile and subject to shifts under stress. We have already reported data that demonstrate the instability lurking beneath the surface of American public opinion with respect to business: a 45 percentage point increase over a period of a few weeks in the support expressed for a policy of wage and price controls among Republican influentials; a 55 percentage point drop (from 70 percent to 15 percent) over the period of a decade in the confidence Americans express in the willingness of business to strike a fair balance between profits and public interest; and a virtual turnabout in American attitudes toward laissez-faire over a period of fifty to seventy-five years. From the standpoint of the supporters of pure capitalism, such changes will doubtless appear to represent a serious decline in popular support for business. Can we be certain that in some future economic crisis, popular support for, say, private profits or private property will not also decline dramatically?

The answer, obviously, is that we cannot be certain. But having said this, we should keep the nature of our uncertainty in perspective. The data available up to now furnish little reason to believe that public support for fundamental capitalist values and institutions is likely to erode—assuming, of course, the absence of a prolonged economic crisis. Even now, despite numerous strains in the system and complaints about its deficiencies, no socialist or other radical party has managed to attract significant support. As Lipset and Schneider observe:

The United States is the only economically developed society without an effective socialist, communist, or labor party, and unions are weaker here than in most other industrialized countries. Both the socialist and trade union appeal have declined in the United States as compared to the past. High taxation, which so disturbs business here, still leaves the United States behind every other industrialized nation except Japan in the proportion of the Gross Domestic Product absorbed in taxes. Although it is difficult to get precise estimates of total public spending on social welfare, the available evidence also indicates that few other countries devote as low a proportion of their national income to this purpose as the United States.[35]

None of this is to deny, however, that capitalism may be undergoing an important long-term transformation. Certainly the expanded role of government in economic affairs, among many other developments, makes American capitalism in the third quarter of the twentieth century a different system from that of a hundred years ago, and one would be foolish to deny the possibility of large changes in the future. What sorts of changes are they likely to be? What forces lie behind them, and how will Americans respond to them? The opinions and values held by contemporary Americans, as we shall see in the chapters that follow, may provide some insights into these questions.

6 Capitalism and Democracy in Conflict

Having outlined American attitudes toward the essential principles of capitalism on the one hand and democracy on the other, we propose in this and subsequent chapters to explore more fully the status of the two traditions in American life—their relative standing in popular esteem, their future prospects, and the complex relationship between them. We shall also examine the process by which Americans acquire their views about capitalism and democracy and why, in some cases, they support one of the traditions more strongly than the other. Clarification of these questions, we believe, can shed considerable light on the dynamics of American public policy, past and present.

In their formative years, capitalism and democracy were for the most part allied in the struggle to throw off the countless restrictions on human conduct that had grown up over centuries of feudalism and aristocratic rule. Yet the two traditions have not always coexisted harmoniously. Especially since the mid-nineteenth century, events in both Europe and the United States have frequently pitted them against each other. Modern industrial capitalism, for example, has spawned great concentrations of wealth, which threaten such democratic values as social and political equality. Popular majorities, on the other hand, have demanded that government enact various regulations that greatly impinge on the workings of the free market.

Although we have touched upon these conflicts in earlier chapters, they are sufficiently far-reaching to warrant closer examination. In what ways, for example, are the values of capitalism and democracy congenial, and in what ways do they clash? Are the conflicts so severe as to threaten the foundations of popular support for either capitalism or democracy? To what extent is it possible to be an enthusiastic supporter of both traditions—a firm believer, for example, in both social equality and unlimited private profits, in popular sovereignty and the concentration of economic power in the hands of a few?

To simplify the presentation of evidence dealing with these questions, we will employ the two scales of capitalist and democratic values described in Chapter 1 and in Appendixes I and II. Each respondent, it will be recalled, was given a score that reflects the number of instances in which he chose a procapitalist (or prodemocratic) answer to a large set of policy questions that concern capitalist (or democratic) values. Individuals scoring among the highest third of all respondents in the general public were classified as "high" in their support for capitalist (or democratic) values; those falling in the bottom third of the distribution of scores were classified as having scored "low" on these measures; while those scoring in the mid-ranges of the distribution have been labeled "middle" scorers.[1] These scales, it should be noted, contain few items that express principled opposition to capitalism or democracy per se. Thus a respondent could score low on the capitalism measure not because he wished to overthrow capitalism, but because he favored a form of welfare capitalism that limited certain privileges of business, such as freedom from government regulation. Similarly, a person might score low on the democracy scale because he preferred to limit or qualify the enforcement of certain democratic values rather than to abolish them.

With the help of these indexes we can now address the central issue of harmony or disharmony between the two traditions, beginning with the question of how support for democratic values relates to support for the values of capitalism. The evidence on this point is unequivocal: people who are most firmly attached to democratic values tend to exhibit the least support for capitalism. Those, on the other hand, who most ardently support the values of capitalism display the least overall support for democratic values. Although we shall explore the dimensions of this negative

Table 6-1 Capitalism and democracy in conflict

Index of support for the values of capitalism	Index of support for democratic values[a]					
	General public			Opinion leaders		
	Low (N = 323)	Middle (N = 295)	High (N = 320)	Low (N = 51)	Middle (N = 153)	High (N = 641)
Low	20	32	53	8	20	53
Middle	33	32	26	8	24	25
High	47	36	21	84	57	22

Source: Opinions and Values of Americans survey, 1975–77.
a. For details of index construction, see Chapter 1 and Appendixes I and II.

relationship more fully, the data presented in Table 6–1 furnish a rough and preliminary idea of its magnitude.

Among members of the general public scoring high on the index of democratic values, only 21 percent score high on the index of capitalist values; among those scoring low on democratic values, 47 percent score high on capitalist values—a difference of 26 percentage points. Among the opinion leaders, who more often organize their political beliefs in keeping with some general principle, the negative relationship between the two indices is even stronger: among those scoring high on the index of democratic values, 22 percent are high on the capitalist index; but among those scoring low on the democratic index, 84 percent score high on capitalist values—a difference of 62 percentage points.

While these findings may disappoint those who deny the existence of tension between capitalism and democracy, their full meaning is by no means self-evident. Why do these differences in opinion exist, and what is their significance for the operation of the American political system? To answer these questions, we must first consider the theoretical and historical relationship between the two traditions.

Capitalism and Democracy in Harmony

Capitalism and democracy, as we have noted, share similar historical origins. Each, in its own way, represented an effort to break out of the confines of the mercantilist order and to throw off the anachronistic restraints by which individuals were circumscribed and closely controlled. Within its respective sphere, each system sought to free individuals from the crushing weight of ancient institutional impediments. Each aimed to secure for every individual the right to manage his own affairs and to participate in the larger economic and political decisions that shaped his own life and that of the nation.

As one might expect of traditions with such parallel histories, capitalism and democracy came to share many values. Both, for example, emphasized the principles of competition and freedom of exchange—in the one case, a free (or competitive) market for the manufacture and sale of goods; in the other, a free market for the exchange of ideas. Both denied that any central authority ought to possess the power to dictate what people should produce and purchase, or what they should think, read, and advocate. Accordingly, both traditions assigned a high place to such values as individualism, personal freedom and independence, and individual advancement on the basis of merit rather than status, prescription, or group membership.

Both capitalism and democracy also aspire to be "rational" systems, fashioned on the principle of rational decision making. Neither system attributes sacred or mystical powers to leaders or any other individuals or classes. Each chooses, from the several alternatives available to it, the solution it considers best calculated to resolve a given problem. Each attempts to calculate costs and benefits in selecting one alternative policy over another. Both systems depend on rational exchange and rational choice.

Though it is often overlooked, capitalism also shares with democracy a commitment to certain forms of equality. Both systems grew out of a broad social movement that aimed to put an end to special privileges related to birth, caste, entitlement, or social status. Both aimed to achieve rational social arrangements that included the recognition of equal rights and opportunities. Capitalism, in fact, has in some ways helped to promote social and political equality. As Milton Friedman has observed:

> It is a striking historical fact that the development of capitalism has been accompanied by a major reduction in the extent to which particular religious, racial, or social groups have operated under special handicaps in respect of their economic activities . . . The substitution of contract arrangement for status arrangement was the first step toward the

freeing of the serfs in the Middle Ages. The preservation of Jews through the Middle Ages was possible because of the existence of a market sector in which they could operate and maintain themselves despite official persecution. Puritans and Quakers were able to migrate to the New World because they could accumulate the funds to do so in the market despite disabilities imposed on them in other aspects of their life.[2]

Thus, when one is mainly concerned with maximizing profits, questions of status, birth, race, or religion usually become secondary or irrelevant—possibly even a nuisance.

The work ethic underlying capitalism is also essentially egalitarian. Prior to the rise of capitalism, the ideal of worldly success was the life of a *grand seigneur*—a life of leisure, luxury, and pleasure seeking, largely if not entirely free of toil. Among the nobility, labor was considered demeaning and distasteful, the curse of the low-born. But the adherents of capitalism, as we have seen, deplored the idleness of the gentry, upholding instead the diligent bourgeois and the industrious artisan and yeoman. Implicit in the selection of these models, and in the Protestant ethic that idealized them, was a tendency toward leveling. Nothing in the capitalist creed suggested that everyone should stand on the same moral or material plane, but all were to be equal in their opportunity for gain and in their obligation to labor for their own good and the good of society.

Today capitalism connotes to some a society so marked by economic inequalities and the domination of the weak by the strong that democratic life is all but impossible. But few Americans living in the late eighteenth and early nineteenth centuries appear to have shared this view. To them, the values associated with free enterprise provided the foundations for a democratic and largely egalitarian social order. Economic competition, for example, implied almost literally the elimination of special privileges. Everyone, regardless of birth, wealth, or political influence, presumably stood on an equal plane before the neutral forces of the free market.

Another key capitalist institution, private property, was also seen by early nineteenth century Americans as an essential feature of democracy. In the Jeffersonian tradition of agrarian democ-

racy, private property provided citizens with a source of livelihood and personal autonomy, thereby helping to ensure that government could not become oppressive or tyrannical. Moreover, as
Robert Dahl notes, "Democracy is and has always been closely
associated in practice with private ownership of the means of production. It is an arresting fact that even today in *every* country governed by polyarchy [that is, democratic institutions] the means
of production are for the most part owned 'privately.' "[3]

Eventually, of course, the operation of the free-market economy
was to produce new class divisions and new forms of privilege. But
in the years when the American political tradition took form, capitalism was still predominantly an economy of independent
small-scale entrepreneurs, craftsmen, artisans, and farmers who
operated out of their own shops or worked their own land. Even
when spectacular business successes occasionally led to the accumulation of large personal fortunes, they were usually too short-
lived to pose a serious challenge to egalitarian values. Wealth, as
Tocqueville observed, circulated in America "with incredible ra-
pidity."[4] In the fluid conditions of an expanding and still predominantly rural society, the personal resources necessary to compete
successfully in economic life were available to many, if not to everyone.[5] A man could go far with a bit of imagination, hard work,
and a strong right arm. Wages remained high, land was readily
available and cheap, and credit was relatively easy to obtain. Reflecting the prevailing faith in the harmony between private enterprise and egalitarianism, one mid-nineteenth-century
politician boasted that "our country is a country of busy men.
Whatever gives facility and expansion to labor, benefits every
class of the community. Unlike the European states, we have no
piles of hoarded wealth destined to be transmitted en masse to
posterity. Opulence, among us, is a gilded pyramid that stands
upon a pedestal of ice, and its foundations are perpetually melting in the sun; the stream that flows from them may fertilize the
land."[6]

The early nineteenth century was, of course, a time of bitter political and economic divisions, many of which were closely related
to the values of capitalism and democracy. As the Jacksonian
movement illustrates, however, the people who took strong stands
in favor of free competition and unfettered enterprise were, by

and large, the same people who championed popular sovereignty, equality of rights, and individual freedom.[7]

Capitalism and Democracy in Tension

If American life in the early nineteenth century exemplified the generally harmonious union of capitalism and democracy, events by the end of the century had brought to the surface many of the tensions that were latent in their association. Whereas the free-enterprise economy in pre-industrial America had promised equal opportunity and (by European standards) a broad distribution of wealth and property, it led in the industrial age to gross disparities in economic status and power. Widespread poverty, unemployment, and economic depression, formerly rare, were now chronic problems. By 1906 the inequality of wealth had become so acute that the German sociologist Werner Sombart observed: "It may be said indisputably that the absolute contrasts between poor and rich are nowhere in the world anything like as great as they are in the United States."[8]

In addition, values common to the traditions of capitalism and democracy began to take on new meanings and to be applied in novel ways. Individualism, for example, once synonymous with freedom and independence for the common man, was reformulated by the defenders of capitalism as "rugged individualism," in which form it served to justify the vast economic power of entrepreneurs. The traditional faith in minimal government, originally associated with the desire to prevent the powerful from subjugating the weak, was now invoked to strengthen the economic power of the wealthy few. Thus capitalism and democracy, once allies against the inequities of the old European order, increasingly diverged.

The immediate sources of this divergence were plainly the vast changes in social and economic conditions that developed in the late decades of the nineteenth century—the transition from a predominantly rural and agricultural economy to a predominantly urban and industrial one. In its early stages, capitalism had (in effect) promised to free the individual from the suffocating restrictions imposed by the old order. In this, it unquestionably succeeded. But in the course of destroying traditional limitations on freedom, capitalism created new limitations that in some ways resembled the old. The increasing division of labor and its concentration in larger production units, for example, often diminished the personal independence so ardently championed by the early proponents of both democracy and capitalism. Work in the factories became for many a new form of dependence. Social and economic mobility also declined as workers were locked into unskilled and poorly paid jobs.

The great inequalities of wealth and opportunity that resulted from these changes had a deleterious effect on the conduct of democratic life. They tended, for example, to divide more sharply the wealthy from the poor, and to create barriers between social classes that led to resentment, hostility, and fear. The great personal fortunes of the new "captains of industry" set them apart socially from other Americans and fostered even sharper inequalities in political power and influence. It was in this period, for example, that the United States Senate came to be described as a "millionaire's club."

Although the political system remained in principle accessible to the poor as well as to the wealthy, the former obviously functioned at a severe disadvantage. Not only did they lack the financial resources to participate effectively in the election of candidates or the enactment of legislation, but they also lacked *social* resources, such as education, that are vital to political effectiveness. They retained the right to vote, of course, but many were, by virtue of their low social status, effectively disfranchised and without significant influence on the political system.

Another, more subtle conflict between the values of capitalism and democracy also emerged in this period. Democratic doctrine presumes that citizens have the right to control their own lives and, indirectly at least, the institutions (including economic institutions) that shape their lives. Only then can they hope to ensure social justice and promote the common good. Capitalist doctrine, on the other hand, holds that in the sphere of economics, the owners and managers of private enterprise must be free to set wages and prices, accumulate capital through savings, decide on how to invest their wealth, and organize the workplace. Hence government must refrain from interfering in the operation of the free market, since in the capitalist view such interference not only violates the principles of laissez-faire but weakens the ability of private enterprise to function effectively. Thus, while democracy asserts the right of the people to rule, capitalism in effect limits this right by removing economic affairs from popular control.

To speak of conflict between the values of capitalism and democracy is, to be sure, to elevate the issues of the new industrial age to a relatively high level of ideological abstraction. Many Americans, probably the majority, were unconscious of such a conflict. For them the issues that mattered were the concrete problems of everyday life—finding a decent job, obtaining food and housing, educating their children, or, from the perspective of business, keeping taxes low, labor unions weak, and government regulation of the economy minimal. Yet, when spokesmen for these conflicting interests aired their cases in public, they often invoked the values of either capitalism or democracy. Businessmen insisted on their "right" to be free of government regulation, and to use their property in any way they chose. Spokesmen for farmers and the working classes, on the other hand, protested that the barons of industry were trampling on the rights of the people and undermining their chances for social and political equality. Thus, to a far greater degree than before, the values of capitalism and democracy appealed to opposing political interests and stood for sharply different programs of action.

Woodrow Wilson typified the progressive politicians of the early twentieth century who focused public attention on the conflict between the two traditions. In running for the presidency, he promised to wage "a crusade against the powers [that is, the trusts] that have governed us—that have limited our development—that have determined our lives—that have set us in a straightjacket to do as they please." The crusade, he promised, would be nothing less than "a second struggle for emancipation."[9]

Similar contentions were repeated some twenty-five years later by President Franklin D. Roosevelt: "In 1776, we sought freedom from the tyranny of a political autocracy—from the eighteenth century royalists who held special privileges from the crown." Now, however, freedom was threatened by "economic royalists" who had impressed the whole structure of modern society into their "royal service." Then, playing directly on the theme of tension between capitalism and democracy, he charged that "the hours men and women worked, the wages they received, the conditions of their labor—these had passed beyond the control of the people, and were imposed by this new industrial dictatorship. . . The royalists of the economic order have conceded that political freedom was the business of the Government, but they have maintained that economic slavery was nobody's business." Government intervention, in his view, was necessary to ensure citizens their basic economic rights. What was at stake, he claimed, was nothing less than "the survival of democracy."[10]

While political leaders such as Wilson and Roosevelt advocated limits on private enterprise in order to preserve democratic values, few prominent public figures were willing to argue the reverse case, namely, that in order to protect capitalism, free speech should be proscribed, political equality forgotten, or free elections suspended. If there were leaders who favored such measures, they rarely expressed their feelings in public and never sought to have them incorporated into the program of a major political party. The reluctance of conservatives, Republicans, and other champions of capitalism to attack the democratic tradition in the same way that liberal democrats criticized laissez-faire suggests that, in the competition between democratic and capitalist values, the former enjoyed greater favor than the latter.

One possible reason for this asymmetry is that, in a political system based on competitive elections and universal suffrage, it is easier to attack values identified with the interests of a wealthy minority than to attack those associated with the interests of the people as a whole. Then, too, democratic ideals were the primary inspiration for the founding of the American republic and were embodied in the nation's most cherished documents, such as the Declaration of Independence and the Bill of Rights. Capitalism, though valued, played a lesser role in establishing the new nation and inspired no comparable manifestos.

In the decades since the New Deal, the conflict between the two traditions has received somewhat less attention from politicians and opinion leaders than it did in the earlier part of the century. Part of the explanation is that many businessmen have now accepted the inevitability (if not the wisdom) of government intervention in the economy to a degree unimaginable in the pre–New Deal era. In light of this development, most economic reformers now concentrate their attention on the question of how to use the regulatory power of government effectively. Many economic issues that were once politically controversial are now treated as technical and practical matters.

Other developments have also contributed to the reduction of tensions between the two traditions. Though income inequality, for example, is still pronounced, per capita and median incomes have risen sharply in the United States, particularly in the two decades following World War II. Moreover, rising levels of affluence generated by the immense productive capacity of the American economy have somewhat ameliorated the problems of poverty and destitution. Government social programs, at least until they were cut by the Reagan administration in the early 1980s, had made considerable progress in reducing, though not entirely eradicating, starvation and gross malnutrition in the United States.

But if tensions between the two traditions have been reduced over the past several decades, they have by no means disappeared. One problem that continues to receive attention is the tendency for the material inequalities of capitalist society to undermine the democratic goals of equal opportunity. Although private enterprise has always in principle valued talent regardless of an individual's social background, talent must be nurtured and developed in order to command its full reward. Obviously, however, children from wealthier families, compared with those from poorer backgrounds, still receive better schooling, broader opportunities for personal development and economic gain, and a more thorough indoctrination into the habits and folkways necessary for success in business and professional life.

The extraordinary size and vigor of modern business corporations pose another kind of challenge to democratic institutions. As the American economy has continued to develop, businesses of modest size have grown into giant enterprises, driving out or absorbing competitors and establishing monopolies, oligopolies, and mammoth multinational corporations whenever they can. Many democrats fear this concentration of power and the disproportionate political and economic influence that goes with it. They view these industrial and commercial behemoths as beyond effective accountability. Such entities often seem too large and mo-

nopolistic to be controlled by consumers registering their preferences in the marketplace, and too formidable in their command
of material resources to be threatened by outside competition. Indeed, some of the largest corporations today are often beyond the
effective reach of even the national government itself. As Charles
Lindblom concludes in his *Politics and Markets:*

> It has been a curious feature of democratic thought that it
> has not faced up to the private corporation as a peculiar or-
> ganization in an ostensible democracy. Enormously large,
> rich in resources, the big corporations . . . command more re-
> sources than do most government units. They can also, over a
> broad range, insist that government meet their demands,
> even if these demands run counter to those of citizens ex-
> pressed through their polyarchal controls. Moreover, they do
> not disqualify themselves from playing the partisan role of a
> citizen—for a corporation is legally a person. And they exer-
> cise unusual veto powers. They are on all these counts dis-
> proportionately powerful . . . The large private corporation
> fits oddly into democratic theory and vision. Indeed, it does
> not fit.[11]

The American political tradition, as we have suggested, distinguishes between issues that are *political* and hence largely subject
to public control, and issues that are *economic* and hence largely
subject to private control. Some democrats contend that this distinction may be inconsistent with the requirements of democracy.
Large business firms, they note, hire and fire, set wages, and control working conditions for millions of workers, and yet effectively
deny workers the right to participate in decision making on these
vital matters. As Robert Dahl comments:

> A large firm is . . . inherently a *political* system because the
> government of the firm exercises great power, including
> coercive power. The government of a firm can have more
> impact on the lives of more people than the government of
> many a town, city, province, state. No one disputes today
> that the government of a city or a state ought to be a public,
> not a private matter. One who supports democratic ideas
> would also hold that people who are compelled to obey pub-
> lic governments ought to control these governments: no tax-
> ation without representation. Should this reasoning not

Table 6–2 (continued)

	Index of democratic values					
	General public			Opinion leaders		
	Low (N = 305)	Middle (N = 329)	High (N = 304)	Low (N = 48)	Middle (N = 171)	High (N = 626)
4. Competition, whether in school, work, or business:						
—is often wasteful and destructive	5	6	14	0	9	17
—leads to better performance and a desire for excellence	87	83	73	94	82	62
—Decline to choose	9	11	14	6	12	21
5. Private ownership of property:						
—has often done mankind more harm than good	3	4	15	0	6	17
—is as important to a good society as freedom	88	82	65	90	80	56
—Decline to choose	9	15	20	10	15	27
6. Public ownership of large industry would be a:						
—good idea	14	22	30	10	11	20
—bad idea	58	42	36	81	64	46
—Decline to choose	28	37	35	8	26	35
7. The profits a company or businessman can earn should be:						
—strictly limited by law to a certain level	13	10	11	5	7	11
—as large as they can fairly earn	74	71	75	86	81	75
—Decline to choose	14	20	15	9	13	15

Sources: questions 1–6, Opinions and Values of Americans survey, 1975–77; question 7, Civil Liberties study, 1978–79.

table, although the differences are in some instances small. Whether the items refer to economic exploitation, the stability of the free enterprise system, the distribution of rewards, the value of competition, private or public ownership of land and industry, or the desirability of limiting profits, those who strongly favor democracy view capitalism more critically than do respondents who are less enthusiastic about democracy.

Having noted this, we should nevertheless also observe that the highly prodemocratic respondents give no indication of being opposed to capitalism as such. Critical though they may be of certain capitalist practices, they profess support for its central ideas.[14] The consistency of this support is, in our opinion, striking. Since the rise of industrial capitalism in the late nineteenth century, the advocates of free enterprise have feared the power of the majority and have tried to find ways to curb it. Judging by present evidence, it would appear that their fears were groundless, since those who favor democracy most fervently are not necessarily hostile to private enterprise. Though democratic reformers over the decades have repeatedly accused business of greed, callousness, and reckless disregard for the well-being of the people, our data reveal only traces of concentrated opposition to the values of capitalism.

The tendency among Americans to accept the principles of capitalist economy does not, however, signify affection for the economically privileged. One can detect in the data of Table 6–3, for

Table 6–3   Support for democratic values and perceptions of the influence of wealth and business

	Index of democratic values					
	General public			Opinion leaders		
	Low (N = 305)	Middle (N = 329)	High (N = 304)	Low (N = 48)	Middle (N = 171)	High (N = 626)
1. Corporations and people with money:						
—really run the country	68	64	72	17	34	50
—have less influence on the politics of this country than many people think	15	15	10	69	36	24
—Decline to choose	16	21	18	15	30	26
2. When it comes to taxes, corporations and wealthy people:						
—don't pay their fair share	75	68	76	29	36	62
—pay their fair share and more	14	14	10	52	36	16
—Decline to choose	11	18	14	19	29	22

Table 6–3   (continued)

	Index of democratic values					
	General public			Opinion leaders		
	Low (N = 305)	Middle (N = 329)	High (N = 304)	Low (N = 48)	Middle (N = 171)	High (N = 626)
3. The laws of this country:						
—mostly favor the rich	41	35	41	8	14	31
—try to benefit most Americans equally	48	51	45	85	68	53
—Decline to choose	12	15	14	6	18	17
4. Both major parties in this country are run for the benefit of the:						
—wealthy and the powerful	33	26	33	10	14	20
—majority	46	44	32	48	42	34
—Decline to choose	22	30	35	42	44	46
5. In the American court system:						
—a poor man usually gets treated worse than a rich man	52	47	65	31	40	70
—almost every citizen can expect a fair trial	40	40	23	60	41	19
—Decline to choose	9	13	12	8	19	11
6. Most newspapers in this country mainly print:						
—the views of the wealthy businessmen who own them	12	8	7	0	3	8
—whatever they think is newsworthy	73	76	78	88	81	78
—Decline to choose	15	16	16	13	16	14

Source: Opinions and Values of Americans survey, 1975–77.

example, signs of resentment toward the advantages enjoyed by corporations and the wealthy. A sizable majority of the mass public believes that corporations and the rich "really run the country," that they do not pay their fair shares of taxes, and that they receive better treatment in the courts than poor people do. A fair number of respondents (though not a majority) also believe that the laws mostly favor the rich.

Among the general population, those who score high on democratic values do not differ on these questions from those who score low. Among the opinion leaders, however, the tendency to view corporations and the wealthy as excessively privileged is clearly related to the strength of their democratic commitment. Substantial differences between those who most strongly favor and those who least strongly favor democratic values turn up on almost every question in the table. The opinion leaders as a whole are generally less hostile to corporate influence and capitalist privilege than is the general public, but because elites are more sensitive to questions of ideology, the most strongly democratic among them exhibit greater suspicion toward the advantages enjoyed by the rich and the powerful than do the less democratic.

Signs of the same resentment toward concentrated capital among those who believe strongly in democracy can also be discerned in their attitudes toward the relationship between business and labor, as shown in Table 6–4. Although few Americans of any major political persuasion embrace the Marxist notion that business and labor are "natural enemies" who have fundamentally opposing interests, they disagree sharply on the proper distribution of power between organized labor and management. Among both the opinion leaders and the general public, the stronger democrats are more likely to believe that workers should have greater influence in making decisions in the workplace, and that strikes are often necessary to improve wages and working conditions. Those less favorable to democratic values tend to hold the contrary view, namely, that decisions regarding industry should be left to management and that strikes are rarely justified.

A similar pattern emerges in Table 6–5, especially among the opinion leaders. Although, as we have seen, nearly all Americans uphold the principle of wage differentials, they are divided on the concrete issue of whether businessmen or workers ought to receive more income, or less, than they do at present. As the data in Table 6–5 indicate, those scoring low on the democracy scale are more likely than the strong democrats to believe that most businessmen deserve the high salaries they receive, and that workers, even including the unskilled, are fairly paid. The differences, once

Table 6-4 Support for democratic values and perceptions of the relationship between business and labor

	Index of democratic values					
	General public			Opinion leaders		
	Low (N = 328)	Middle (N = 283)	High (N = 327)	Low (N = 375)	Middle (N = 199)	High (N = 271)
1. Workers and management:						
—have conflicting interests and are natural enemies	12	13	15	6	3	8
—share the same interests in the long run	65	63	63	88	78	79
—Decline to choose	23	24	22	6	19	13
2. When it comes to making decisions in industry:						
—workers should have more to say than they do now	21	39	45	4	16	40
—the important decisions should be left to management	60	42	34	88	57	32
—Decline to choose	20	20	21	8	26	28
3. The use of strikes to improve wages and working conditions is:						
—often necessary	35	52	68	29	46	71
—almost never justified	46	25	16	50	26	7
—Decline to choose	19	23	16	21	29	22

Source: Opinions and Values of Americans survey, 1975–77.

more, are especially sharp among the opinion leaders—among those, in short, who hold more clearly defined ideological views and apply them more consistently.

Our data thus highlight the existence of important disagreements between stronger and weaker democrats on a wide range of capitalist issues, even though both continue to support the fundamental values of the economic system itself.

But what of the attitudes toward democracy of those who most and least strongly support capitalism? Despite the disagreements between them, are both groups committed to fundamental democratic values? Consider first their attitudes toward the value of

Table 6–5 Support for democratic values and fairness of differential rewards

| | Index of democratic values | | | | | |
| | General public | | | Opinion leaders | | |
	Low (N = 328)	Middle (N = 283)	High (N = 327)	Low (N = 375)	Middle (N = 199)	High (N = 271)
1. Most businessmen:						
—receive more income than they deserve	31	26	35	10	16	26
—do important work and deserve high salaries	42	37	28	67	46	28
—Decline to choose	28	37	38	23	37	46
2. Working people in this country:						
—do not get a fair share of what they produce	32	36	38	2	7	24
—usually earn about what they deserve	51	36	33	79	60	37
—Decline to choose	17	28	29	19	33	39
3. Unskilled workers (such as janitors, dishwashers, and so on) usually receive wages that are:						
—much too low for the dirty work they do	33	38	43	10	13	28
—about right, considering the amount of skill required	53	41	35	79	60	41
—Decline to choose	15	20	22	10	28	31

Source: Opinions and Values of Americans survey, 1975–77.

popular sovereignty. From the earliest days of the Republic, men and women of upper status and wealth have been deeply skeptical of the wisdom of allowing the people to govern themselves. In arguing for a property qualification on suffrage in the 1820s, for example, Chancellor Kent expressed the fear, widespread among the wealthy classes, that "the tendency of universal suffrage, is to jeopardize the right of property, and the principles of liberty. There is a constant tendency in human society . . . in the poor to covet . . . the plunder of the rich; in the debtor to relax or avoid the obligation of contract; in the indolent and profligate, to cast the whole burthens of society upon the industrious and the virtuous."[15]

These apprehensions have persisted in the age of industrial capitalism. The writings of men like Schumpeter and Hayek, as we have seen, contain frequent warnings about the dangers to capitalism posed by an impatient and allegedly antibusiness public. Significantly, however, these twentieth-century writers stop short of challenging the legitimacy of democratic institutions as such. Moreover, our data indicate that among the general public even the strongest advocates of capitalism are, on the whole, as firmly attached to the principle of popular sovereignty as are those whose support for capitalism is more qualified. Table 6–6 shows that the most fervent adherents of private enterprise, like other

Table 6-6   Support for capitalist values versus democratic items: popular sovereignty

	Index of capitalist values					
	General public			Opinion leaders		
(Form A)[a]	Low (N = 254)	Middle (N = 461)	High (N = 311)	Low (N = 144)	Middle (N = 255)	High (N = 202)
(Form B)	(N = 249)	(N = 428)	(N = 290)	(N = 183)	(N = 196)	(N = 177)
1. To be realistic about it, our elected officials:						
—would badly misuse their power if they were not watched and guided by the voters	71	63	75	67	62	66
—know much more than the voters about issues, and should be allowed to make whatever decisions they think best	6	9	10	8	11	12
—Decline to choose	23	28	15	25	28	22
(Form A)						
2. Elections are:						
—one of the best ways to keep elected officials on their toes	63	76	85	84	86	89

Table 6–6   (continued)

	Index of capitalist values					
	General public			Opinion leaders		
(Form A)[a]	Low (N = 254)	Middle (N = 461)	High (N = 311)	Low (N = 144)	Middle (N = 255)	High (N = 202)
(Form B)	(N = 249)	(N = 428)	(N = 290)	(N = 183)	(N = 196)	(N = 177)
—mostly a waste of time and money, since the same people run things anyway	12	6	4	5	1	3
—Decline to choose (Form B)	25	18	11	11	13	9

3. Competitive elections:

—may not be perfect, but no one has yet invented a better way to choose leaders in a free country	71	77	87	92	94	96
—make little sense when you consider how little most voters really know	17	12	9	2	3	3
—Decline to choose (Form B)	13	11	4	6	3	2

4. Who should be allowed to vote?

—All adult citizens, regardless of how ignorant they are	68	68	72	85	74	79
—Only people who know something about the issues	12	9	11	6	7	9
—Decline to choose (Form B)	21	23	18	9	19	12

5. Democracy is a political system which mostly:

—recognizes the special talents of each individual and tries to bring out his or her best qualities	43	45	51	55	64	69

Table 6–6   (continued)

	Index of capitalist values					
	General public			Opinion leaders		
	Low	Middle	High	Low	Middle	High
(Form A)[a]	(N =	((N = 461)	(N = 311)	(N = 144)	(N = 255)	(N = 202)
(Form B)	(N = 249)	(N = 428)		N = 290)	(196)	(N = 177)
—caters to the average person and therefore encourages what is ordinary and second-rate rather than what is excellent	9	8	12	10	6	11
—Decline to choose (Form B)	48	47	37	35	30	20

6. When making new laws the government should pay most attention to the opinions of the:

—average citizens, regardless of how little they know	24	23	16	22	16	18
—people who really know something about the subject	47	50	64	51	59	67
—Decline to choose (Form A)	29	27	19	26	25	15

7. Should people with more intelligence and character have greater influence over the country's decisions than other people?

—No, because every citizen must have an equal right to decide what's best for the country.	49	44	43	49	37	32
—Yes, because they have more to offer and can do more to benefit the society.	33	37	46	37	43	57
—Decline to choose (Form B)	19	19	11	14	20	12

Source: Civil Liberties study, 1979.

a. Data from the Civil Liberties study, reported in this and other tables in this chapter, were drawn from two national samples, which we have designated Form A and Form B. While most questions were asked of both samples, some were asked only of Form A respondents and others only of Form B respondents.

Americans, strongly uphold the values of the electoral process, universal suffrage, and the need for a vigilant public to prevent official abuse of power. They are also inclined to assert that popular democracy tends to bring out the best qualities of each individual. The respondents who are most devoted to capitalism, however, are a bit more likely than other Americans to believe that experts and people of greater "intelligence and character" ought to have more influence over legislation and public policy than others—an idea not wholly consistent with classical democratic theory.

But even though those who differ in their support for capitalism share similar attitudes toward popular sovereignty, they disagree over virtually every other democratic value, beginning with the value of equality. While the strongly procapitalist support egalitarianism in the abstract (like most other Americans, they, too, deny the claim that "some kinds of people are better than others"), they reject specific public policies that aim to promote greater equality far more often than do those who are critical of capitalism (see Table 6–7). Sizable majorities among the strong procapitalists believe that government efforts to bring about racial integration have moved "too fast," that laws guaranteeing equal opportunities for blacks and other minorities "sometimes go too far," and that granting homosexuals equal rights to teach or hold other public service jobs is a bad idea. They also display little enthusiasm for increasing the efforts "to make everyone as equal as possible." Respondents who are more critical of capitalist values, especially among the opinion leaders, choose the egalitarian alternative by a clear majority on each of these issues.

Results from many other questions bearing on egalitarian and other democratic values could be presented, but the findings would not alter the pattern of inferences we have just presented. A more important question, at this point, concerns the interpretation of these findings.

Conclusions

The data presented in this chapter offer clear evidence of both the conflict and harmony between the values of capitalism and de-

Table 6-7 Support for capitalist values and the principle of equality

| | Index of capitalist values | | | | | |
| | General public | | | Opinion leaders | | |
	Low (N = 328)	Middle (N = 283)	High (N = 327)	Low (N = 375)	Middle (N = 199)	High (N = 271)
1. Teaching that some kinds of people are better than others:						
—goes against the American idea of equality	75	73	73	79	76	65
—only recognizes the facts	9	10	16	3	6	17
—Decline to choose	17	17	10	18	18	18
2. The laws guaranteeing equal job opportunities for blacks and other minorities:						
—should be made even stronger	33	15	10	55	35	15
—sometimes go too far	41	66	73	16	37	63
—Decline to choose	27	19	18	29	28	22
3. Government efforts to bring about racial integration have been too:						
—slow	30	18	6	55	37	14
—fast	26	33	54	2	7	28
—Decline to choose	45	50	39	43	57	58
4. Complete equality for homosexuals in teaching and other public service jobs:						
—should be protected by law	42	22	20	63	46	29
—may sound fair but is not really a good idea	34	54	64	17	27	50
—Decline to choose	24	24	17	20	28	14
5. Efforts to make everyone as equal as possible should be:						
—increased	70	57	43	74	60	39
—decreased	5	7	19	1	5	20
—Decline to choose	25	36	39	25	36	41

Source: Opinions and Values of Americans survey, 1975–77.

mocracy. The conflict manifests itself mainly in the form of disagreements over incremental adjustments in existing practice—greater or less regulation of business, higher or lower pay for workers, more power or less power for labor unions. The most democratic of our respondents, especially among the opinion leaders, are critical of certain capitalist institutions and want to modify them, but their criticism stops far short of a preference for communism, socialism, or any other system that presents itself as an alternative to capitalism. Similarly, those who most strongly favor capitalism resist the broadening or extension of democratic rights, especially to new groups and new situations, but they do not oppose, at least in general form, such democratic values as freedom, equality, and popular sovereignty.

Most public debate in America—and, in particular, most debate relating to conflicts between the values of capitalism and democracy—takes place within a relatively restricted segment of the ideological spectrum, as we have shown schematically in Figure 6-1. In some countries, disagreements about the values of capitalism and democracy cover a broad range of ideas and preferences—from communist collectivism to laissez-faire capitalism in the domain of economics, and from totalitarianism to democracy in the political sphere. In the United States, however, most serious public conflict and discussion take place around a range of alternatives that presuppose widespread popular support for the basic values of each tradition. Disagreements about democratic values between those who favor capitalism most and least strongly tend to fall within this relatively narrow segment of the ideological

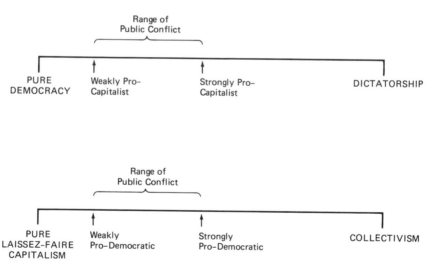

Figure 6-1   Range of public conflict concerning the values of capitalism and democracy.

spectrum. The same holds, *mutatis mutandis,* for those who disagree about capitalist values. Contained within this limited compass, conflict between the two traditions, though genuine and substantial, does not really threaten support for either capitalism or democracy.

One should not, in our opinion, be surprised by the evidence of disharmony between capitalist and democratic values. To expect the two traditions to coexist in perfect harmony is to assume that society's most important values need to be fully compatible with one another. Such an assumption is unrealistic. While most societies aspire to a unified value system, complete unity of belief is impossible to sustain in large and complex societies experiencing rapid change and containing groups that are free to express their diverse viewpoints. To remain viable, a free society requires not uniformity of belief, but countervailing groups and institutions that are able to check each other and to prevent any one from acquiring a monopoly of power over the nation's institutions and ideas.

Although the data we have presented tell us something about the nature and extent of the conflict between the values of capitalism and democracy, they do not fully explain why Americans respond to the conflicts as they do. Why, for example, do some individuals side consistently with one tradition rather than the other? A satisfactory answer to this question, as we shall see, requires a closer examination of the beliefs, motivations, and characteristics that distinguish supporters and critics of the two traditions.

Nor can one fully understand the conflict between capitalist and democratic values without reference to the larger context of ideas in which the two traditions are embedded. For example, a staunch procapitalist might, because of his commitment to laissez-faire, oppose laws that require companies to adopt preferential hiring practices in order to help blacks, women, and other minorities overcome the effects of discrimination. But why, as we have seen, should someone who strongly favors capitalism also be unwilling to permit homosexuals to teach in the schools? It seems unlikely that one could derive this attitude from capitalist doctrine itself. Nor can we explain as yet why strong defenders of capitalism are likely to be less concerned than other Americans about the rights of the accused, the liberation of women, or the protection of citizens from invasion of their privacy. Why, in fact, do they tend to score relatively low on the full range of values in the democratic tradition, even when those values are not manifestly inconsistent with capitalist doctrine? Only by referring to other explanatory factors—such as the role of ideology—can one hope to throw light on these questions. The tendency among strong adherents of capitalism to resist the extension of democratic values appears to be etched into their mental set, part of an ideological perspective on man and society that extends to questions affecting a broad range of social and political issues.

7 Ideology and the American Ethos

No study of American political beliefs and values can safely ignore the influence of political ideology. Politicians and the policies they espouse, for example, are routinely appraised in terms of their ideological orientation. They are usually described as liberal if they seek to advance such ideas as equality, aid to the disadvantaged, tolerance of dissenters, and social reform; and as conservative if they place particular emphasis on order, stability, the needs of business, differential economic rewards, and defense of the status quo. Public opinion is also often discussed in these terms: political analysts will say that the public mood is liberal if it supports such ideas as a stronger government role in economic redistribution or increased spending for social welfare, and conservative if it opposes such measures.

We are concerned with liberalism and conservatism in the present context principally because of their possible influence on support for the values of capitalism and democracy. Yet in raising the question of ideology, we are venturing into a domain with many difficult and presently unresolved intellectual problems, such as the nature and measurement of ideology.[1] Liberalism and conservatism, in addition, are terms that arouse passionate feelings of support and opposition, so that universal agreement about their meaning is difficult to achieve. Nevertheless, an examination of the principal writings of acknowledged spokesmen of conservative and liberal ideologies (for example, Burke, John Adams, Hobhouse, J. S. Mill, Jefferson), as well as surveys we have con-

ducted among members of known liberal and conservative "criterion" groups, discloses numerous beliefs and values that have long
distinguished the rival ideological camps from one another. The
characteristics of liberal and conservative beliefs described in this
chapter are based on this research.

In the analysis that follows we distinguish between the broad
philosophical orientations associated with the two ideologies
(such as attitudes toward social change) and the concrete political
issues on which liberals and conservatives publicly differ (such as
government regulation of the economy). Having made this distinction, we shall attempt to show how the first kind of belief is
related to the second.

Liberalism is distinguished by a marked concern for social
progress and human betterment, especially for the poor and powerless. Since liberals believe that personal happiness and success
depend heavily on institutional arrangements, most liberals are
inveterate reformers—continually looking for ways to improve
the human condition by remodeling the social, economic, and political institutions that, in their view, shape it. Underlying this
pursuit of change, social reform, and benevolence is a faith in the
potential perfectibility of man and his capacity to manage his
own affairs in a responsible and reasoned fashion.

Conservatism, too, is concerned with human betterment, but it
differs from liberalism in its vision of what constitutes the good
society and how it can best be achieved. Because conservatism
takes a more pessimistic view of human nature and its perfectibility, it maintains that most people need strong leaders, firm laws
and institutions, and strict moral codes to keep their appetites
under control. Conservatism also holds that firm adherence to
conventional norms and practices is essential to human well-
being. Thus conservatives tend to resist proposals for relaxing
conventional restraints on behavior and to be skeptical of novel
ideas for large-scale social change, emphasizing instead the need
to defend established institutions against threats to the foundations of social order and stability. They are also inclined to believe
that those who fail in life are the architects of their own misfortune and must, for this reason, bear primary responsibility for
solving their own problems. Hence conservatives are far less likely
than liberals to support movements or causes that have as their

objective the eradication of poverty, better treatment of oppressed minorities, or the alleviation of social distress generally. Such movements, they believe, are misguided and, moreover, will endanger the stability of the social order by disrupting existing institutions—thereby doing more harm than good.

For more than two centuries the ideas and arguments briefly summarized here have furnished the philosophical justifications for liberal and conservative programs in Europe and America and have provided some of the central ideas guiding the two ideological camps in their response to a wide variety of economic, political, and social issues. However, despite the persistence of these important differences between liberals and conservatives, changing social and economic conditions have at times compelled them to alter their positions on certain issues without altering their underlying philosophies. Thus, throughout American history, one encounters new movements of the "left" or "right" that espouse a few new (or relatively new) ideas while remaining faithful to the philosophical cores of their respective traditions. For example, conservatives favored a strong central government when, in the early nineteenth century, government appeared to function as a source of social order, but began to oppose big government when, in the twentieth century, government appeared to function as a stimulus to social reform.

Despite the importance of liberalism and conservatism in American politics, one must bear in mind that many members of the general public know little about liberal and conservative ideologies. Many of them, for example, cannot describe the contents of the Bill of Rights, let alone the writings of Burke, Jefferson, or Hobhouse. They may have definite attitudes on such topics as order, stability, or income redistribution, but they are frequently unable to relate these views to the other ideas associated with each of the ideologies. Some people, therefore, cannot clearly be classified as either liberals or conservatives.

Among elites and the more politically sophisticated members of the general public, however, an individual's ideological orientation can be a powerful explanatory variable. To gain insight into the differences between liberals and conservatives, it is useful to compare the attitudes of people belonging to liberal organizations (such as Americans for Democratic Action) with the attitudes of

Table 7-1   Attitudes of liberal and conservative activists toward order, stability, and social change

	Liberal activists (N = 875)	Conservative activists (N = 551)
1. Replacing traditional policies with new ones that seem attractive but have not been tested by experience is:		
—often necessary for progress	77	19
—usually short-sighted and dangerous	7	61
—Decline to choose	16	20
2. If a society had to choose between (a) and (b), which should it choose:		
—(a) making progress	68	27
—(b) keeping things stable and orderly	8	44
—Decline to choose	24	30
3. People who are always trying to reform things are usually:		
—people who really care about other people	63	18
—busybodies who do more harm than good	5	47
—Decline to choose	32	35
4. Trying to make sweeping reforms in a society as complicated as ours is usually:		
—worth trying, despite the risks	83	38
—much too risky	4	34
—Decline to choose	13	28

Source: Opinions and Values of Americans survey, 1975–77.

those who belong to conservative organizations (for example, American Conservative Union).[2] As shown in Table 7–1, liberal activists are far more likely than conservative activists to favor change and reform. For example, 68 percent of the liberals, compared with only 27 percent of the conservatives, say that if a society had to choose between "making progress" and "keeping things stable and orderly," it should choose the former. Table 7–2 shows that liberals are also more likely than conservatives to exhibit concern for those suffering social distress and material privation. For example, 70 percent of the liberals, but only 30 percent of conservatives, say that if the world food shortage worsens, "we should greatly increase our effort to share our food with the hungry." In addition, 57 percent of the liberal activists, but only 32 percent of the conservative activists, say that "people who

Table 7-2 Relationship between ideology and social benevolence

	Liberal activists (N = 875)	Conservative activists (N = 551)
1. If the world food shortage continues to get worse:		
—we should greatly increase our effort to share our food with the hungry	70	30
—we'll just have to get used to the fact that some people are going to starve	10	34
—Decline to choose	19	35
2. People who want to be liked better should:		
—be given every possible chance to show their worth	57	32
—first try to get rid of their irritating faults	22	54
—Decline to choose	21	14
3. People who get into trouble because they have not saved for the future:		
—are still human and should be helped	85	44
—don't deserve any help	2	24
—Decline to choose	14	32
4. People who are always worrying about the suffering of others:		
—should be admired for their sympathy and generosity	70	43
—are mostly soft-headed and sentimental	4	22
—Decline to choose	26	35
5. If a person has a weak character, he:		
—deserves sympathy more than blame	38	21
—should be treated for what he is—a moral weakling	19	42
—Decline to choose	43	37

Source: Opinions and Values of Americans survey, 1975–77.

want to be liked better should . . . be given every possible chance to show their worth."

Conservatives, of course, claim to be as benevolent toward others as liberals are, and a few of our items reflect this. In their personal lives, moreover, many conservatives show great solicitude for the feelings and needs of their families, friends, and associates. Our data nonetheless make it plain that, in their attitudes toward people who are outside their circles of personal acquaintance, conservatives are, as a group, less likely than liberals to favor action aimed at alleviating social distress. Note, in addition, that the differences in Table 7–2 extend across a variety of contexts, including some in which actions by government or society are necessary to alleviate distress and others in which the emphasis is on personal kindness and sympathy toward the unfortunate. Thus the divisions between liberals and conservatives seem to represent genuine differences in social benevolence rather than differences that reflect attitudes toward extending government activity. The items in the table deal not simply with manifestly political beliefs, but with personal attitudes that are to some extent rooted in individual personality structures.[3]

The data in Tables 7–1 and 7–2 are impressive not only because of the size and consistency of the differences between liberals and conservatives, but because they have been obtained from the members of a number of "criterion" groups that are indisputably engaged in the promotion of liberal or conservative doctrines. Thus they clearly establish the existence of a strong relationship between liberalism or conservatism, on the one hand, and attitudes toward order, stability, change, and social benevolence, on the other. In what ways, however, does this relationship affect the attitudes of liberals and conservatives toward democratic and capitalist values?

Ideology and Democratic Values

Democracy in the late eighteenth century was a bold new idea whose prospects for success, it was thought, depended heavily on the capacity of ordinary citizens to exercise rational self-restraint. Since conservatives tend to resist rapid social change and to doubt the capacity of ordinary people to control their impulses in the absence of strong institutional constraints, it was natural for them to be wary of the rise of democratic ideas and institutions. The excesses of the French Revolution served merely to vindicate fears they had long harbored about the dangers of democracy.

Since the War of Independence had discredited the notion of royal and aristocratic rule in the eyes of most Americans, opposition to popular government was never as strong in the United States as it was in the Old World. Nonetheless, a conservative party, the Federalists, soon formed in the United States to resist the trend toward "too much" democracy. Among other goals, the Federalists wanted to restrict suffrage, to protect the property and economic privileges of the wealthy, and to safeguard the political stability of the new nation by setting limits on freedom of speech and press.

In contrast, eighteenth- and early nineteenth-century liberals (though they were not yet called by that name) took a more positive view of popular sovereignty and democratic self-rule. One reason is that they found popular majorities relatively sympathetic to their goals of social, egalitarian, and humanitarian reform. But beyond this, liberals, with their greater faith in the common man, found it easier to believe that, whatever the issue, "the people" could be relied upon to decide it fairly and intelligently.

The differences between the two perspectives can be illustrated by comparing the views of John Adams and Thomas Jefferson. Each was a signer of the Declaration of Independence, each became president of the United States, and each was a leader of a political party. But their divergent ideological orientations led them to adopt different positions on many issues involving democratic values.

Adams, the more conservative of the two, was an outspoken opponent of measures designed to extend popular control over government. In keeping with his conservative, and hence more pessimistic, view of human nature, he wrote that "to expect self-denial from men, when they have a majority in their favor, and consequently the power to gratify themselves, is to disbelieve all history and universal experience; it is to disbelieve Revelation and the Word of God, which informs us, the heart is deceitful above all things, and desperately wicked."[4] Despite these views, Adams was no monarchist. He believed that republican government was possible, provided strong institutional restraints could be devised to keep unruly human appetites under control. To this end he favored a system of checks and balances under which power would be widely dispersed among different levels and branches of government. As he wrote in a letter chastising Jefferson for his faith in popular assemblies: "Checks and Ballances, Jefferson, however you and your Party despise them, are our only Security, for the progress of Mind, as well as Security of Body. Every Species of these Christians would persecute Deists, as soon as either Sect would persecute another, if it had unchecked and unbalanced Power. Nay, the Deists would persecute Christians, and Atheists would persecute Deists, with as unrelenting Cruelty, as any Christians would persecute them or one another. Know thyself, human Nature!"[5]

Jefferson's faith in popular rule and democratic government grew partly out of his more optimistic assessment of human nature. As he once explained, "We believed . . . that man was a rational animal, endowed by nature with rights, and with an innate sense of justice; and that he could be restrained from wrong and protected in right by moderate powers. The cherishment of the people then was our principle, the fear and distrust of them that of the other [that is, Adams'] party."[6] And he wrote at another point, "I am not one of those who fears the people."[7]

Differences between liberals and conservatives, however, extend beyond their views of human nature and popular sovereignty to other democratic values. On questions of free expression, for example, conservatives are far more likely than liberals to fear that unconventional behavior or the dissemination of unorthodox ideas may occasion excesses and subvert the social and political order. Thus they are inclined to set narrower limits on freedom of expression.

Strong disagreements between the rival ideological camps also turn upon issues relating to equality. Believing that many people are essentially weak, conservatives tend to regard strength of character as rare and therefore worthy of particular reward. Hence they feel that people who, by hard work, greater ability, or other appropriate demonstrations of superiority, amass large amounts of wealth or influence should be entitled to keep and enjoy these benefits.

Liberals, by contrast, dislike most forms of inequality. Since they regard people as essentially good (or at least capable of improvement) and virtue as widely dispersed throughout the population, they believe that material and political benefits ought to be broadly distributed as well. If glaring inequalities exist, liberals contend that they can usually be traced to the corrupting influence of unjust institutions rather than to human nature. Whereas conservatives point to the poverty and lack of achievement of the lower classes as evidence of character flaws, liberals advocate institutional reforms to remove what they regard as the real sources of inequality.

The differences between the liberal and conservative perspectives on equality and freedom are clearly illustrated in the writings of Adams and Jefferson. Both recognized that individuals differ in their innate capacities, and both endorsed the principle of equal rights and opportunities. Yet, within these limits, their views differed sharply. Adams' writings contain numerous discussions of inequality—lengthy and lavishly detailed descriptions of the kinds of inequality that naturally exist among people, and the futility of trying to ameliorate them:

> I have seen, in the Hospital of Foundlings, the "Enfans Trouvés," at Paris, fifty babes in one room—all under four days old, all in cradles alike, all nursed and attended alike, all dressed alike, all equally neat. I went from one end to the other of the whole row and attentively observed all their countenances. And I never saw a greater variety or more striking inequalities in the streets of Paris or London. Some had every sign of grief, sorrow, and despair; others had joy and gayety in their faces. Some were sinking in the arms of death; others looked as if they might live to fourscore. Some were as ugly and others as beautiful, as children or adults ever are; these were stupid; those sensible. These were all born to equal rights, but to very different fortunes, to very different success and influence in life . . .
>
> That all men are born to equal rights is true . . . But to teach that all men are born with equal powers and faculties, to equal influence in society, to equal property and advantages through life, is as gross a fraud, as glaring an imposition on the credulity of the people as ever was practised by monks, by Druids, by Brahmins, by priests of the immortal Lama, or by the self-styled philosophers of the French revolution. For honor's sake . . . for truth and virtue's sake, let American philosophers and politicians despise it.[8]

If Adams was prone to insist upon—and even to relish—the inevitability of certain forms of inequality, Jefferson was inclined to emphasize as far as possible the ways in which all people were alike. For example, the famous phrase from the Declaration of Independence—"All men are created equal"—was Jefferson's. Jefferson insisted that all people, regardless of station in life or degree of education, were equally competent to judge issues of morality and human character. "State a moral case to a plowman and a professor," he once wrote. "The former will decide it as well and often better than the latter because he has not been led astray by artificial rules."[9] Jefferson, furthermore, labored throughout his career to reduce inequalities by making education widely available. Indeed, he cherished his role in founding a public university in Virginia as one of his proudest achievements.

In the matter of freedom of expression, Adams, though professing high regard for freedom of speech and press, helped to formulate and eventually signed into law the Sedition Act of 1798, one of the most sweeping antilibertarian measures ever adopted in the United States. Some commentators regard the Sedition Act as an attempt not only to insulate governing officials from criticism, but to destroy the right of political opposition as such.[10]

On becoming president in 1801, Jefferson pardoned those who had been arrested under the Sedition Act. He had long been identified with libertarian views; for example, he wrote the Statute of Virginia for Religious Freedom, an extended and eloquent argument for unhindered freedom of religion. Jefferson was confident of the beneficent effects of freedom of worship and freedom of expression because, as he explained, "Truth is great and will prevail if left to herself . . . she is the proper and sufficient antagonist to error and has nothing to fear from the conflict unless by human interposition disarmed of her natural weapons, free argument and debate."[11] Along with Madison and other more liberal Founding Fathers, Jefferson also helped to generate the pressure that led to the adoption of the Bill of Rights in 1791.

None of this is meant to suggest that liberals are invariably democratic in their outlook or that conservatism is an antidemocratic ideology. The point is, rather, that the philosophical dispositions at the heart of the two ideologies make it easier for liberals than for conservatives to embrace certain democratic values.

In order to test our argument, we have developed three new attitude scales. The first, a social change scale, measures a respondent's concern for order and stability against his receptivity to change and reform. The items in this scale cover such matters as the wisdom of "replacing traditional policies with new ones that seem attractive but have not been tested by experience," the value of "laws and institutions which have existed for a long time," and the possible risks in "trying to make sweeping changes in a society as complicated as ours." The attitudes measured by the social change scale constitute, as we shall see, one of the most theoretically important variables included in our survey.[12] The second new measure, a social benevolence scale, assesses a respondent's solicitude for people who are suffering some form of social distress. It includes items asking about "kindness toward those who have failed in life," the sharing of America's resources with the poorer nations of the world, and sympathy toward "people who have not been well-treated by society."[13] A third new measure, a "faith in human nature" scale, assesses a respondent's attitudes toward the strength or weakness of human character. For example, one of the items in the scale asks respondents whether, in the absence of "strong laws and strict moral codes," most people would "give in to every selfish desire" or "learn to control their behavior."[14]

To assign scores on these measures, we have summated each person's responses to all items included in the scale. Those scoring among the top third of the mass distribution on the scale have been classified as "high" on the attitude being measured; those scoring among the middle third have been designated "moderate"; and those scoring among the bottom third have been labeled "low."[15] The scales, then, measure *relative* rather than absolute levels of support for, say, social change.

Table 7-3 shows that all three measures of ideological orientation are strongly correlated with support for democratic values. Respondents who espouse liberal views—that is, who are favorably disposed toward change, express an optimistic view of human nature, and show particular solicitude for the disadvantaged—are, on the average, more likely to exhibit strong support for democratic values than are those who hold the conservative view. The correlations are, as one would expect, strongest among ideological activists, but they are large and statistically significant among the opinion leaders and the general public as well. For example, among opinion leaders scoring high on social benevolence, 88 percent score high on democracy, while among those scoring low on benevolence, only 41 percent score high on democracy.

Many Americans, as we suggested earlier, are unaware of the philosophical principles associated with liberalism and conserva-

Table 7-3 Influence of ideological orientation on support for democratic values (percentage scoring high on democratic values)

Type of respondent	Social change			Social benevolence			Faith in human nature		
	Low	Middle	High	Low	Middle	High	Low	Middle	High
General public	18 (N = 343)	27 (N = 266)	53 (N = 329)	23 (N = 318)	30 (N = 340)	47 (N = 280)	13 (N = 218)	32 (N = 535)	57 (N = 185)
Opinion leaders	42 (N = 161)	71 (N = 192)	87 (N = 482)	41 (N = 138)	68 (N = 244)	88 (N = 463)	39 (N = 119)	73 (N = 454)	93 (N = 272)
Ideological activists	17 (N = 513)	63 (N = 220)	93 (N = 693)	26 (N = 456)	61 (N = 381)	89 (N = 589)	14 (N = 369)	63 (N = 573)	96 (N = 484)

Source: Opinions and Values of Americans survey, 1975–77.

tism.[16] Our data show, however, that elites and the more politically sophisticated members of the general public are aware of these principles and can accurately characterize their own ideological tendencies.* Thus Table 7–4 shows that people who describe themselves as liberals or strong liberals score much higher on the social change, social benevolence, and human nature scales than do people who label themselves conservatives or strong conservatives. This table also shows that liberals are much more likely to score high on the democracy scale than are conservatives.[17]

One can gain a better understanding of the nature of these differences by examining the responses of liberals and conservatives to specific democratic issues. Consider the value of equality. Although both conservatives and liberals profess support for such established egalitarian norms as equal opportunity and equal rights for minorities,[18] it is clear from Table 7–5 that conservatives are much less enthusiastic about egalitarian values than are liberals. For example, conservatives, and especially strong conservatives, are far more likely to say that "like fine race horses, some classes of people are just naturally better than others"; that private individuals who wish to discriminate against blacks "should have a right" to do so; that both the low salaries of unskilled workers and the high salaries of businessmen are equitable; and that laws guaranteeing equal rights for homosexuals are a bad idea. On almost all such issues, a large majority of liberals take the egalitarian position. Similar differences between the two ideological groups turn up on questions concerning the intelligence of various racial groups, the rights of children, the proper role of women in society, and the amount of respect that should be accorded people of high status.

Disagreements between liberals and conservatives tend to be

* Among members of the general public scoring above the fiftieth percentile on our measure of political sophistication, a large majority (89 percent) knew that liberals tend to favor "more rapid change and reform"; 94 percent of the influentials also knew that liberals tend to favor reform; however, only 48 percent of the less sophisticated members of the general public could supply this elementary information about liberal doctrines. In view of these findings, our analysis in the remainder of this chapter will focus on the attitudes of respondents who are most likely to understand the meanings of liberalism and conservatism—that is, we will focus on the opinions of elites and of members of the public scoring in the top half of the distribution on our measure of political sophistication.

Table 7-4 Relationship among ideological self-designation, ideological disposition, and support for democratic values

	General public[a]					Opinion leaders					Ideological activists				
	Strong lib.[b] (N=22)	Lib. (N=85)	Middle of road (N=139)	Con. (N=168)	Strong con. (N=29)	Strong lib. (N=109)	Lib. (N=318)	Middle of road (N=237)	Con. (N=133)	Strong con. (N=15)	Strong lib. (N=304)	Lib. (N=374)	Middle of road (N=141)	Con. (N=261)	Strong con. (N=237)
Social change scale															
Low	0	13	35	55	79	1	5	23	53	73	1	8	32	76	88
Middle	9	15	34	26	10	7	20	31	32	13	8	21	30	17	8
High	91	72	31	19	10	92	75	46	15	13	91	72	38	8	4
Social benevolence scale															
Low	9	18	31	41	59	6	9	16	36	60	6	12	32	54	73
Middle	46	33	36	38	24	23	28	29	34	40	22	29	32	31	21
High	46	49	33	21	17	72	63	55	30	0	72	59	36	15	7
Faith in human nature scale															
Low	0	17	19	34	62	4	6	18	32	53	0	7	27	51	64
Middle	36	53	62	58	35	35	51	63	63	33	27	50	55	44	34
High	64	31	19	8	3	62	43	19	5	13	72	44	18	5	2
Democratic values scale															
Low	0	5	22	36	79	0	1	3	20	33	0	1	13	53	59
Middle	9	20	39	40	17	4	11	25	42	53	2	8	30	31	27
High	91	75	40	24	3	96	88	72	38	13	98	91	57	16	14

Source: Opinions and Values of Americans survey, 1975–77.
a. Includes only those respondents who scored in the upper half of the distribution on the political sophistication scale (see text footnote, p. 201).
b. Ideology in this table is determined by self-designation (see note 17).

sharpest on new or emerging issues. Liberals, as a rule, favor the extension of egalitarian values to new domains and issues; conservatives, and especially strong conservatives, are reluctant to disturb existing or traditional inequalities.

Important ideological differences also show up on matters relating to freedom of expression and the rights of due process. Although the great majority of conservatives endorse such general values as free speech, a free press, and protection from arbitrary authority, they are much more likely than liberals to believe that these values can be carried "too far." Table 7–6 shows that, especially among the general public, strong conservatives are reluctant to let "crackpots" speak out in public, or to permit radicals to work in the media. They are also more willing than liberals to allow authorities to "break the rules" in order to catch criminals. What criminals, "crackpots," and radicals have in common is that each group represents, in its own way, a destabilizing and nonconforming influence. Since conservatives are more apprehensive than liberals about the maintenance of order and conventionality, they are also more inclined than liberals to suppress ideas or practices that threaten these values—even if such actions violate the rights and protections to which Americans are ordinarily entitled.

This line of argument raises an interesting question: How might liberals respond if a group seriously threatened *their* values—if the group were not merely pernicious in a general way, but (like the Nazis, for example) clearly dedicated to the destruction of liberal values as such? Presumably, in cases of this kind, the differences between the tolerance scores of liberals and conservatives should be somewhat diminished.

The data represented in Table 7–7 offer some support for this expectation. Although liberals are far more tolerant than conservatives when the target groups are ideologically neutral or oriented to the left, they are, in certain cases, only moderately more tolerant than conservatives when the target groups are on the right. Among community influentials, for example, 82 percent of the strong liberals, but only 39 percent of the strong conservatives, uphold the right of atheists to ridicule God—a difference of 43 percentage points between the two ideological groups. But on a roughly parallel item concerning the right of a humor magazine

Table 7-5   Effect of ideology on support for the value of equality[a]

	General public[b]					Community influentials				
	Strong lib.[c]	Lib.	Middle of road	Con.	Strong con.	Strong lib.	Lib.	Middle of road	Con.	Strong con.
1. Which of these opinions do you think is more correct?										
—All people would be about the same if they were treated equally.	72	63	47	32	16	49	51	31	31	21
—Like fine race horses, some classes of people are just naturally better than others.	6	14	29	41	58	9	15	34	31	50
(Form B)										
2. People who discriminate against minority groups in such matters as jobs and housing should:										
—be fined or sued for damages	63	52	35	24	16	89	70	46	32	7
—have a right in a free country to do as they please in such matters	0	12	22	38	45	0	4	13	28	48
(Form A)										
3. For the most part, local ordinances that guarantee equal rights to homosexuals in such matters as jobs and housing:										
—uphold the American idea of human rights for all	91	85	61	45	28	94	85	68	40	22
—damage American moral standards	0	10	24	43	58	3	6	18	43	57
(Total sample)										

4. Most businessmen:

—receive more income than they deserve	56	39	36	26	16	58	24	18	11	8
—do important work and deserve high salaries	28	33	29	38	47	9	39	46	58	63

(Form B)

5. Unskilled workers (such as janitors, dishwashers, and so on) usually receive wages that are:

—much too low for the dirty work they do	56	34	38	30	16	59	40	26	24	8
—about right, considering the amount of skill required	33	43	40	48	79	21	39	48	59	84

(Form B)

Source: Civil Liberties study, 1978–79.

a. The number of cases falling within each cell of this table are as follows. For Form A items among the general public, the N's are 18, 95, 162, 199, and 34; for strong liberals, liberals, middle-of-the-roaders, conservatives, and strong conservatives, respectively; among the community influentials, the Form A N's are 47, 128, 178, 198, and 27. For Form B items among the general public, the N's are 17, 95, 143, 195, and 24; among the influentials, the Form B N's are 44, 143, 156, 176, and 25. The N's for the total sample may be calculated by appropriate addition of these figures; for example, among the general public, there are 35 (17 + 18) strong liberals.

b. Includes only those respondents who scored in the upper half of the distribution on the political sophistication index (see text footnote, p. 201).

c. Ideology in this table is determined by self-designation (see note 17).

Table 7-6 Effect of ideology on support for the values of freedom and due process of law

	General public[a]					Opinion leaders				
	Strong lib.[b] (N=22)	Lib. (N=85)	Middle of road (N=139)	Con. (N=166)	Strong con. (N=29)	Strong lib. (N=105)	Lib. (N=308)	Middle of road (N=232)	Con. (N=127)	Strong con. (N=15)
1. The employment of radicals by newspapers and television:										
—is their right as Americans	96	78	58	44	14	88	83	71	59	53
—should be forbidden	6	8	21	29	66	1	2	3	9	20
2. "Crackpot" ideas:										
—have as much right to be heard as sensible ideas	96	80	60	58	45	87	82	81	76	87
—sometimes have to be censored for the public good	5	14	30	29	48	6	9	9	17	7

3. In enforcing the law, the authorities:

—should stick to the rules if they want other people to respect the law	91	67	65	60	59	93	86	76	59	80
—sometimes have to break the rules in order to bring criminals to justice	9	20	27	28	34	4	6	13	23	20

4. In dealing with crime, the most important consideration is to:

—protect the rights of the accused	50	52	40	33	35	62	53	36	35	7
—stop crime even if we have to violate the rights of the accused	9	10	17	22	45	3	5	8	21	53

Source: Opinions and Values of Americans survey, 1975–77.

a. Includes only those respondents who scored in the upper half of the distribution on the political sophistication index (see text footnote, p. 201).

b. Ideology in this table is determined by self-designation (see note 17).

Table 7-7 Effect of ideology on tolerance of left-wing and right-wing target groups

	General public[a]					Community influentials				
	Strong lib.[b] (N=34)	Lib. (N=183)	Middle of road (N=286)	Con. (N=368)	Strong con. (N=50)	Strong lib. (N=89)	Lib. (N=271)	Middle of road (N=336)	Con. (N=372)	Strong con. (N=52)
1. The freedom of atheists to make fun of God and religion should:										
—be legally protected no matter who might be offended	68	57	32	30	40	82	66	52	38	39
—not be allowed in a public place where religious groups gather	9	26	47	52	42	14	21	27	43	39
2. A humor magazine which ridicules or makes fun of blacks, women, or other minority groups should:										
—have the same right as any other magazine to print what it wants	88	78	68	64	76	84	78	72	71	68
—lose its mailing privileges	3	8	17	18	12	7	13	13	14	14
3. If a political group known for its violent political activities wants to picket the White House, it should be:										
—granted police protection like any other group	53	44	35	30	32	73	58	40	35	25
—prevented from doing so because it might endanger the president	24	34	46	54	58	14	25	36	46	62

4. When groups like the Nazis or other extreme groups require police protection at their rallies and marches, the community should:

—supply and pay for whatever police protection is needed	59	40	27	21	26	72	61	40	33	22
—prohibit such groups from holding rallies because of the costs and dangers involved	9	32	50	55	58	12	20	31	42	59

5. Which of these comes closer to your own view?

—The government has no right to decide what should or should not be published.	77	57	37	23	40	74	62	40	32	29
—To protect its moral values, a society sometimes has to forbid certain things from being published.	6	34	49	63	52	12	24	48	58	60

6. A group that wants to buy advertising space in a newspaper to advocate war against another country should:

—have as much right to buy advertising space as a group that favors peace	49	44	35	30	40	73	48	47	38	48
—be turned down by the newspaper	24	43	47	55	44	14	33	39	48	40

Table 7-7   (continued)

	General public[a]					Community influentials				
	Strong lib.[b] (N=34)	Lib. (N=183)	Middle of road (N=286)	Con. (N=368)	Strong con. (N=50)	Strong lib. (N=89)	Lib. (N=271)	Middle of road (N=336)	Con. (N=372)	Strong con. (N=52)
7. Refusing to hire a professor because of his unusual political beliefs:										
—is never justified	53	30	18	10	44	49	31	16	7	6
—may be necessary if his views are really extreme	21	46	67	81	90	26	50	69	85	85
8. Refusing to hire a professor because he believes certain races are inferior:										
—cannot be justified	35	40	31	26	22	54	38	29	26	37
—may be necessary if his views are really extreme	44	42	57	61	62	32	45	51	59	48

Source: Civil Liberties study, 1978–79.

a. Includes only those respondents who scored in the upper half of the distribution on the political sophistication index (see text footnote, p. 201).

b. Ideology in this table is determined by self-designation (see note 17).

to ridicule blacks, women, or other minorities, 84 percent of the strong liberals and 68 percent of the strong conservatives are tolerant—a difference of only 16 percentage points.

Altogether, our OVS and Civil Liberties surveys contain approximately 100 tolerance items in which the target groups are either on the left or (in a majority of cases) ideologically neutral in orientation, and in every one of these cases liberals were more tolerant than conservatives, usually by large margins. Liberals also scored higher on 11 of the 13 tolerance items in the two surveys in which the target group has a right-wing coloration. Thus, for a wide variety of unorthodox groups and activities—left-wing, ideologically neutral, or even right-wing in their orientation—liberals proved, with only a few exceptions, substantially more tolerant than conservatives.[19]

One can gain further insight into the relationship between ideology and support for democratic values by examining attitudes toward popular sovereignty and democratic self-rule. Eighteenth- and nineteenth-century liberals, as we saw earlier, were more disposed than conservatives to believe that the masses were capable of rational public conduct and self-restraint. They were, in addition, confident that popular majorities would be sympathetic to the kinds of reforms that liberals favored. Hence liberals became the champions of universal suffrage and direct popular elections, while conservatives tended to favor property and literacy qualifications that would effectively disenfranchise many working-class citizens and racial minorities.

Ideological divisions over popular sovereignty, however, have been modified by events of the twentieth century. The election of fascist and other authoritarian governments in Europe and elsewhere in the 1920s and 1930s demonstrated that voters are capable of making disastrous misjudgments when frightened by social conditions or misled by demagogues. Events thus seemed to vindicate the old conservative fears about the dangers of democracy in general and universal adult suffrage in particular—and to vindicate them in a way that made a deep impression on liberals. As S. M. Lipset has observed: "The gradual realization that extremist and intolerant movements in modern society are more likely to be based on the lower classes than on the middle and upper classes has posed a tragic dilemma for those intellectuals of the democratic left who once believed the proletariat necessarily to be a force for liberty, racial equality and social progress."[20]

In the United States, too, popular majorities have on many occasions exhibited strong support for antidemocratic candidates and movements. In the South, for example, openly racist and demagogic candidates were for many decades routinely returned to office by overwhelming majorities.[21] More recent experience in states that allow citizens to vote directly on ballot initiatives has again shown that, given the opportunity, popular majorities often favor measures designed to restrict civil rights and other values associated with the democratic tradition.[22]

For all these reasons, twentieth-century liberals can no longer be certain that popular majorities will always respond favorably to liberal or democratic reform measures. Conservatives, on the other hand, have less reason to fear popular rule than they once did. Two centuries of experience with popular government in the United States have made democracy seem less risky than it appeared to be during the early days of the Republic, and rising levels of education and affluence among the mass electorate have further relieved conservative anxieties about the ability of voters to behave reasonably and responsibly. Conservatives have also been encouraged by what they perceive to be widespread public support for conservative views on such issues as abortion, busing, affirmative action, and gay rights. Then, too, political controversy in the United States (as in other advanced industrial democracies) no longer tends as sharply as in the past to pit a wealthy minority against a much less affluent majority. Under these circumstances, conservatives have found it easier to accept the principles of popular consent and majority rule.

The patterns of support for popular sovereignty among contemporary liberals and conservatives show the effects of these changed outlooks. As can be seen in Table 7–8, both liberals and conservatives have accepted the fundamental principles of popular sovereignty and competitive elections. Neither group, however, seems eager to permit average citizens, "regardless of how little they know," to exert much influence on day-to-day policy-making. Nor, as other data show, is either ideological camp strongly persuaded that "the majority of voters . . . use their votes wisely most of the time."

Table 7–8 Relationship between ideology and support for the principle of popular sovereignty[a]

	General public[b]					Community influentials				
	Strong lib.[c]	Lib.	Middle of road	Con.	Strong con.	Strong lib.	Lib.	Middle of road	Con.	Strong con.
1. Competitive elections:										
—may not be perfect, but no one has yet invented a better way to choose leaders in a free country	88	88	91	90	90	98	94	94	95	100
—make little sense when you consider how little most voters really know	6	6	5	5	11	0	3	3	2	0
(Form B)										
2. To be realistic about it, our elected officials:										
—would badly misuse their power if they weren't watched and guided by the voters	75	72	68	75	84	66	70	62	63	78
—know much more than the voters about issues, and should be allowed to make whatever decisions they think best	6	5	8	9	3	9	6	13	14	0
(Form A)										

Table 7-8 (continued)

	General public[b]					Community influentials				
	Strong lib.[c]	Lib.	Middle of road	Con.	Strong con.	Strong lib.	Lib.	Middle of road	Con.	Strong con.
3. When making new laws, the government should pay most attention to the opinions of:										
—average citizens, regardless of how little they know	19	26	25	17	10	15	21	17	20	7
—the people who really know something about the subject (Form A)	38	59	49	61	58	53	52	62	69	52

Source: Civil Liberties study, 1978–79.

a. For N's in this table, see Table 7–5, note a.

b. Includes only those respondents who scored in the upper half of the distribution on the political sophistication index (text footnote, p. 201).

c. Ideology in this table is determined by self-designation (see note 17).

Important and illuminating differences between the two ideological camps nonetheless exist. When questions of universal suffrage and the right of antidemocratic groups to compete in elections are at issue, liberals, in keeping with their political heritage, are more likely than conservatives to uphold the value of popular sovereignty. Yet, in cases in which a popular majority attempts to violate the rights of an unpopular group, liberals tend to uphold freedom and individual rights. Table 7–9 shows, for example, that among the community influentials 93 percent of strong liberals, but only 44 percent of strong conservatives, say that the majority has no right to forbid "a mass protest march for some unpopular cause." By an even greater margin, liberals are more likely than conservatives to deny that the majority has a right to make homosexuality a crime. Faced with a conflict between majority rule and minority rights, liberals usually favor the latter.

These results suggest that the attitudes of liberals and conservatives toward popular sovereignty reflect, to some extent, the context in which the issue arises. Conservatives, though historically wary of popular rule and still more inclined than liberals to deny the franchise to the politically uninformed, champion popular sovereignty when the majority of voters favor conventional conduct or the maintenance of social order. Liberals are inclined to uphold popular sovereignty—unless the majority attempts to violate the rights of the minority.

Ideology, in sum, has a clear impact on support for democratic values. Whether measured in terms of broad intellectual and personal dispositions, such as attitudes toward order, stability, and change, or by a respondent's self-designation, liberalism is associated with strong support for democratic values, including a desire to extend those values to new and possibly controversial domains. Conservatism, though accepting the principal tenets of the democratic creed, is reluctant to disturb traditional inequalities or to extend the values of freedom and due process beyond familiar boundaries.

Ideology and Capitalism

Many of the oldest and most bitterly disputed disagreements between liberals and conservatives center on such economic issues as

Table 7-9   Effect of ideology on support for majority rule and the rights of certain groups[a]

	General public[b]					Community influentials				
	Strong lib.[c]	Lib.	Middle of road	Con.	Strong con.	Strong lib.	Lib.	Middle of road	Con.	Strong con.
1. Who should be allowed to vote?										
—All adult citizens, regardless of how ignorant they are.	83	81	68	72	63	91	85	81	77	58
—Only people who know something about the issues.	11	3	6	11	26	4	5	8	9	8
(Form B)										
2. Should demonstrators be allowed to hold a mass protest march for some unpopular cause?										
—Yes, even if most people in the community don't want it.	85	77	56	47	50	93	86	74	56	44
—No, not if the majority is against it.	9	14	24	32	36	2	7	12	29	35
(Total sample)										
3. Suppose the majority gets a law passed making homosexuality a crime. Should homosexuals be fined or arrested?										
—No, because a person's sexual preference is a private matter, beyond the majority's wishes.	97	74	62	40	38	89	77	54	37	33
—Yes, because the voting majority has the right to decide the kind of society it wants.	0	10	18	33	34	3	8	21	37	39
(Total sample)										

4. If the majority in a referendum votes to stop publication of newspapers that preach race hatred:

—such newspapers should be closed down	27	24	41	37	38	11	18	21	28	23
—no one, not even the majority of voters, should have the right to close down a newspaper	59	59	42	43	50	82	72	59	54	60

(Total sample)

5. Suppose a majority of voters elected a congressman who advocates the use of violence against certain minorities. Should he be allowed to take office?

—Yes, because we have to stand by what the majority decides.	27	28	30	32	40	36	32	40	44	42
—No, because such a person is unfit to hold congressional office.	56	51	56	54	38	36	50	43	37	42

(Total sample)

6. If the majority votes in a referendum to ban the public expression of certain opinions, should the majority opinion be followed?

—No, because free speech is a more fundamental right than majority rule	88	74	60	55	64	90	82	69	53	50
—Yes, because no group has a greater right than the majority to decide which opinions can or cannot be expressed	6	13	19	24	16	3	9	13	24	21

(Total sample)

Source: Civil Liberties study, 1978–79.

a. For N's in this table, see Table 7–5, note a.

b. Includes only those respondents who scored in the upper half of the distribution on the political sophistication index (see text footnote, p. 201).

c. Ideology is determined in this table by self-designation (see note 17).

the distribution of wealth in society, the amount of taxes to be paid by the rich, and control over the use of property. A generally reliable rule of thumb in such disputes is that liberals usually take the side of the poor and working classes, while conservatives tend to take the side of the more established and propertied classes.

In the democratic and egalitarian culture of the United States, conservatives do not, as a rule, openly defend privilege, inequality, or entrenched wealth per se. Instead, they argue that the wealthy classes have *earned* the material advantages they enjoy, and that every society must observe such "just distinctions" if it is to survive. Even when conservatives concede that the acquisition of wealth has in some cases resulted from family inheritance rather than individual initiative and merit, they are still likely to oppose heavy inheritance taxes or other devices for redistributing wealth. In these cases, they contend that such measures destroy the incentive to work hard, take risks, save, and build a business enterprise in order to leave a legacy for one's family.

Liberals and conservatives differ, then, in certain of their attitudes toward capitalism—though not in a straightforward or obvious way. In the eighteenth century, when capitalism was a relatively novel economic system that promised to enlarge individual freedom and equality, liberals were for the most part favorably disposed toward free enterprise, while conservatives, especially in Europe, wanted to maintain a greater measure of state control over economic affairs. With the rise of large-scale economic enterprise in the nineteenth century, it seemed to many liberals that, far from promoting freedom and equality, laissez-faire capitalism had become an impediment to these values. As a result, liberals became more critical of unfettered capitalism, while conservatives, for reasons we will discuss, grew more favorable.

The shift in the attitudes of liberals toward capitalism occurred during the same period in which the conflicts between capitalism and democracy were becoming more intense. The two developments were closely related. Faced with what seemed to them a conflict between the values of personal freedom and equality on the one hand, and the values of property and unfettered enterprise on the other, liberals opted for the former. In doing so, they acknowledged that democratic values were more fundamental to the liberal creed than were capitalist values.

Given the close association between liberalism and social benevolence, this preference is scarcely surprising. Benevolence, of
course, is an honorific term, and one must be careful not to as-
cribe it only to conduct one prizes while denying it to conduct one
dislikes. As employed here, it refers to those forms of behavior that
reflect a heightened sensitivity to human rights, solicitude for the
oppressed and the suffering, and an active desire to relieve social
distress.

Social benevolence, thus defined, has an obvious affinity with
democratic values. A concern for human worth and well-being
provides the motivating force for many of the values and practices
associated with democracy. Devotion to social and political
equality, political and religious freedom, fair laws and law enforcement procedures, the right to privacy, the freedom to hold
and express unorthodox opinions, and the right of citizens to be
governed by rules of their own choosing—all are reflections of a
benevolent impulse to protect people at all levels of society from
arbitrary and despotic rule. It is difficult, however, for liberals to
find any comparable concern for social benevolence among the
principles and values that animate capitalism. Those who manage and speak for the laissez-faire economy stress that it functions most efficiently when it adheres strictly to the laws of economic competition and free exchange, avoiding insofar as possible
the intrusion of altruistic sentiments into the business process.
Capitalist enterprises exist to maximize private profits, not
human welfare; any social good they may provide is incidental to
their overriding goal, which is to achieve the largest possible return on capital investments.

Thus, in both the theory and practice of capitalism, considerations of sentiment and humanitarian service rarely enter into the
decision-making process. Businessmen are required, of course, to
obey the civil and criminal laws of society and to comply with
government regulations, but beyond this they are free to pursue
corporate ends without paying heed to who is helped or hurt by
their actions. Few indeed are the business managers or boards of
directors who would be prepared to terminate profitable activities
for reasons of altruism; only occasionally do they undertake vol-
untary programs for the alleviation of human distress, or turn
their energies away from the primary task of increasing profits.

This is not to say that capitalism is in principle opposed to humanitarian aims or the advancement of human welfare. Some capitalist entrepreneurs are renowned for their extensive private philanthropies. A few corporations sponsor cultural programs on television, or volunteer some of their personnel to assist in philanthropic activities directly. Management, however, usually justifies these apparent departures from normal business practice as useful for building "goodwill" in the community—as activities from which the company, and the private enterprise system as a whole, will ultimately benefit.

The defenders of capitalism are likely to argue that private enterprise serves humanity best by performing the economic functions it was designed to perform. They view the pursuit of profit as, above all, a stimulus to high productivity and hence to the satisfaction of society's wants. The devotion to profit is thus seen as benevolent in its outcomes, if not in its explicit intent. By adhering to rational and impersonal procedures and by focusing on the market and the competition for gain, capitalists believe they have set in motion mechanisms through which economic productivity and growth—and hence the "wealth of the nation" itself—will be maximized. Humanity, they argue, is thus far better served than it would be by other economic arrangements, such as socialism, which profess to serve mankind consciously and directly but which generally prove to be stagnant and comparatively unproductive. Of all the economic systems (so the argument goes), pure capitalism offers by far the most bountiful opportunities for individual effort and prosperity. It affords the greatest freedom, the best use of resources, and the most equitable distribution of rewards in relation to an individual's skill and the value of his contribution. Its concern for human welfare is thus implicit in its nature. In its efforts to protect property, encourage initiative and achievement, and promote economic growth, capitalism pursues goals that are not only economically useful but also advance the welfare of mankind.

These are strong arguments, and they no doubt help to account for the widespread acceptance of capitalism by the American public. They may also explain why many liberal reformers favored free enterprise in the late eighteenth and early nineteenth centuries. And even though liberal enthusiasm for capitalism waned with the rise of large-scale industrial capitalism, the liberal shift away from laissez-faire did not occur quickly or easily. A generation of liberals that had been reared on the ideas of Paine, Jefferson, and Jackson found it difficult to believe that a bigger and more active central government, or limitations on the uses of private property, could possibly promote progressive or humanitarian goals. As the tensions between the imperatives of economic rationality and social benevolence heightened, however, liberals finally turned away from the principles of laissez-faire.

The turnabout in liberal attitudes toward unregulated capitalism furnishes an opportunity to observe the role of opinion elites in shaping a modern ideology. The new creed, as the historian Charles Forcey has argued, "had its first real beginnings in the minds of certain publicists and politicians of the Progressive era."[23] Foremost among these were Walter Lippmann, Walter Weyl, Theodore Roosevelt, and perhaps most important, Herbert Croly. In his influential book *The Promise of American Life* (1909), Croly set out to reshape certain aspects of American liberalism. The ideals of Jefferson and Paine on the role of government in society, he argued, were shortsighted and outdated; only a strong central government could foster the conditions necessary to achieve genuine freedom and equality for the mass of ordinary Americans. Croly went on to found an influential new journal, *The New Republic,* which became a principal organ for disseminating the new liberal creed to other opinion leaders and to the more politically sophisticated liberals in the mass public. Buttressed and augmented by the work of other liberal reformers, including such English writers as J. S. Mill, L. T. Hobhouse, and John Maynard Keynes, the new liberalism became the dominant reform ideology in America, especially with the advent of the New Deal.

As liberals became increasingly critical of unfettered capitalism, conservatives gradually emerged as the champions of laissez-faire. Capitalism appealed to conservative sensibilities in several important ways. For example, the system of social stratification and differential rewards under modern industrial capitalism is consistent with conservative notions of how a just society ought to be organized. In creating and maintaining a powerful financial and industrial class, capitalism fulfills what conservatives regard as society's essential need for strong and meritorious leaders. Capitalism also emphasizes the need for everyone either to work hard or to suffer material loss—thus providing the strong incentives that conservatives believe are necessary for developing self-discipline and the restraint of appetites. Then, too, capitalist institutions, such as private property, have become vital features of social stability and the established order in America. Since conservatives especially fear instability and are strongly averse to schemes and theories for reconstituting society, they are reluctant to experiment with alternative economic systems, or even to attempt major changes in the present system; such changes would involve more risk than conservatives are willing to countenance. For these and other reasons, capitalism seems to them far preferable to the radically egalitarian, collectivist, and still experimental systems that represent themselves as the principal alternatives to private enterprise.

Our data strongly bear out these observations. Table 7–10 shows that respondents who score high on social change, social benevolence, and faith in human nature, compared with those who score low on these measures, are much more likely to be critical of capitalist values. For example, among the opinion leaders who are most favorably disposed to social change, only 13 percent score high on capitalist values; by contrast, among the opinion leaders who are most opposed to social change, the proportion scoring high on capitalist values is 70 percent.

Sharp as these differences are, they do not show that liberals are unequivocally opposed to private enterprise. Most liberals would readily concede that compared to the state-controlled economies of the communist nations, capitalism provides far more individual freedom and a fair measure of equality. Many liberals also admit—though often with a notable lack of enthusiasm—that in purely economic terms, capitalism seems to outperform all other economic systems.

Liberals are nonetheless impatient with the shortcomings of capitalism—its inability to assure everyone an equal chance to develop his or her talents, its chronic business cycles and depressions, its seemingly permanent residue of unemployment, and its failure to provide all citizens with a decent standard of living. As Paul Samuelson, a renowned liberal economist, has observed: "These days, good is not good enough. Why be satisfied with rela-

Table 7–10 Influence of ideological orientation on support for capitalist values (percentage scoring high on capitalist values)

Type of respondent	Social change			Social benevolence			Faith in human nature		
	Low	Middle	High	Low	Middle	High	Low	Middle	High
General public	48 (N = 343)	29 (N = 266)	18 (N = 329)	39 (N = 318)	32 (N = 340)	23 (N = 280)	53 (N = 218)	31 (N = 535)	9 (N = 185)
Opinion leaders	70 (N = 161)	37 (N = 192)	13 (N = 482)	57 (N = 138)	35 (N = 244)	18 (N = 463)	65 (N = 119)	32 (N = 454)	10 (N = 272)
Ideological activists	84 (N = 513)	39 (N = 220)	10 (N = 693)	76 (N = 456)	38 (N = 381)	15 (N = 589)	87 (N = 369)	41 (N = 573)	5 (N = 484)

Source: Opinions and Values of Americans survey, 1975–77.

tive inequalities? Why permit any hunger in the affluent society? Why not an all-out war on poverty? So declare the critics of the existing order in increasing numbers."[24] In pressing for economic reforms, liberals have insisted that they do not wish to uproot capitalism but to alleviate its more egregious shortcomings. Many conservatives and businessmen, however, have never fully accepted this claim, accusing liberals of trying to wreck the capitalist system by requiring it to adopt regulations and practices more compatible with socialism than with private enterprise.

Our data afford an opportunity to examine this conservative accusation. Examining first the attitudes of liberals and conservatives (rather than those who call themselves "strong liberals" or "strong conservatives"), we can see in Table 7–11 that the rival ideological groups do differ, and in the expected direction, in their attitudes toward capitalist principles. It is equally clear, however, that, like the conservatives, most liberals exhibit attitudes that are essentially compatible with capitalist values. By sizable majorities, they affirm the importance of the free enterprise system, private property, competition, and wages based on achievement rather than need.

Those who label themselves strong liberals, however, are somewhat more critical of capitalism than are the majority of liberals. This may account for the impression among some conservatives that liberals are, as a group, hostile to capitalism. Note, however, that the strong liberals constitute only a minority of the liberal camp, and that, despite their lesser enthusiasm for capitalist principles and practices, they can scarcely be considered "enemies" of capitalism. A plurality among them concedes, for example, that the private enterprise system is "generally fair and efficient," while only a small fraction believe that the system "mostly leads to poverty and widespread depression." Strong liberals likewise tend to reject the socialist doctrine of equality of economic reward, holding instead (by sizable pluralities) that people should be paid according to "how hard they work." By the same token, few liberals of any degree of conviction attach much credence to the Marxist claim that the private enterprise system survives by "keeping the poor down," or that "the main features of Communism," if adopted here, would do much to improve the conditions of

Table 7-11 Liberal and conservative attitudes toward fundamental capitalist values[a]

	General public[b]					Community influentials				
	Strong lib.[c]	Lib.	Middle of road	Con.	Strong con.	Strong lib.	Lib.	Middle of road	Con.	Strong con.
1. In your opinion, is the free enterprise system necessary for free government to survive?										
—Probably not.	28	11	5	3	6	53	23	6	2	4
—For the most part, yes. (Form A)	61	82	91	93	94	40	74	89	94	93
2. Private ownership of property:										
—has often done mankind more harm than good	12	6	3	3	4	41	14	4	2	0
—is as important to a good society as freedom (Form B)	77	81	93	95	83	23	64	81	90	96
3. Giving everybody about the same income regardless of the type of work they do would:										
—be a fairer way to distribute the country's wealth than the present system	35	6	2	0	4	25	9	0	0	0
—destroy the desire to work hard and do a better job (Form B)	47	80	92	94	88	43	73	92	96	100

Table 7-11 (continued)

	General public[b]					Community influentials				
	Strong lib.[c]	Lib.	Middle of road	Con.	Strong con.	Strong lib.	Lib.	Middle of road	Con.	Strong con.
4. Which would be fairer—to pay people wages according to:										
—their economic needs	24	4	2	2	0	16	10	1	1	0
—how hard they work (Form B)	47	68	82	83	88	35	59	71	87	96
5. If adopted here, the main features of Communism would:										
—greatly benefit the average person	25	4	3	0	0	14	4	2	2	0
—make things worse for most Americans (Form B)	38	77	87	94	96	54	76	83	94	100
6. The free enterprise system:										
—survives by keeping the poor down	6	6	2	1	8	27	11	2	1	0
—gives everyone a fair chance (Form B)	12	56	76	79	75	9	44	63	82	80

7. Competition, whether in school, work, or business:

—is often wasteful and destructive	38	12	8	3	0	36	16	8	2	0
—leads to better performance and a desire for excellence	24	79	83	92	92	50	61	78	92	93
	(N=22)	(N=84)	(N=137)	(N=168)	(N=29)	(N=109)	(N=318)	(N=237)	(N=133)	(N=15)

8. Under a fair economic system:

—all people would earn about the same	5	10	4	2	0	13	4	3	2	0
—people with more ability would earn higher salaries	73	73	82	81	100	56	74	80	92	93
	(N=22)	(N=84)	(N=137)	(N=168)	(N=29)	(N=109)	(N=318)	(N=237)	(N=133)	(N=15)

Sources: questions 1–6, Civil Liberties study, 1978–79; questions 7 and 8, Opinions and Values of Americans survey, 1975–77.

a. For N's in questions 1–6, see Table 7–5, note a.

b. Includes only those respondents who scored in the upper half of the distribution on the political sophistication index (see text footnote, p. 201).

c. Ideology is determined in this table by self-designation (see note 17).

American life. Thus strong liberals exhibit little interest in socialism or any other doctrines that propose to replace capitalism.

Examination of the two items in Table 7–12 offers an interesting insight into the nature of liberal attitudes toward capitalism. Only a minority of liberals agree with the familiar capitalist claim that "when businesses are allowed to make as much money as they can, everyone profits in the long run." But this does not mean that liberals—even strong liberals—want to impose tight limits on business profits. As the final item in Table 7–12 indicates, a plurality still believes that businessmen should be able to earn as much profit as they fairly can.

Given the data reported in Table 7–13, one can assume that if liberals were entirely free to enact their preferences, they would adopt more stringent government regulations over the uses of property, reduce the influence of corporations on national life, and make other alterations in the operation of capitalism. But free enterprise capitalism, as these findings suggest, would continue to exist even under a strong liberal regime, though in somewhat modified form. Since liberals must function in a political system in which other, more conservative, ideological outlooks also have influence, they would scarcely be able to alter the system in any fundamental way, even if they wished to. Only on those issues that represent marginal or incremental reforms—for example, government regulation of business—are liberals sufficiently united among themselves to be able to enact significant changes in the conduct of the free enterprise system.

Summary and Conclusions

Historians have long disagreed about the prevalence of ideological conflict in American history. In the 1920s V. L. Parrington argued that American history has always been characterized by deep ideological divisions:

> From the first we have been divided into two main parties. Names and battle cries and strategies have often changed repeatedly, but the broad party division has remained. On one side has been the party of the current aristocracy—of church, of gentry, of merchant, of slave holder, or manufacturer— and on the other the party of the commonality—of farmer,

Table 7-12 Ambivalence of liberals toward capitalist values[a]

	General public[b]					Community influentials				
	Strong lib.[c]	Lib.	Middle of road	Con.	Strong con.	Strong lib.	Lib.	Middle of road	Con.	Strong con.
1. When businesses are allowed to make as much money as they can:										
—workers and the poor are bound to get less	46	30	25	11	14	62	26	12	8	6
—everyone profits in the long run	17	38	46	57	69	10	35	52	67	77
(Total sample)										
2. The profits a company or businessman can earn should be:										
—strictly limited by law to a certain level	22	17	9	6	3	32	10	6	4	4
—as large as they can fairly earn	50	68	78	83	85	45	71	81	92	89
(Form A)										

Source: Civil Liberties study, 1978–79.

a. For N's in this table, see Table 7–5, note a.

b. Includes only those respondents who scored in the upper half of the distribution on the political sophistication index (see text footnote, p. 201).

c. Ideology is determined in this table by self-designation (see note 17).

Table 7-13　Liberal and conservative attitudes toward reform of capitalist institutions[a]

	General public[b]					Community influentials				
	Strong lib.[c]	Lib.	Middle of road	Con.	Strong con.	Strong lib.	Lib.	Middle of road	Con.	Strong con.
1. Government regulation of business:										
—is necessary to keep industry from becoming too powerful	69	53	52	36	31	82	57	43	27	8
—usually does more harm than good	23	22	28	43	57	2	19	31	55	82
(Total sample)										
2. Unskilled workers (such as janitors, dishwashers, and so on) usually receive wages that are:										
—much too low for the dirty work they do	59	36	38	28	13	59	40	26	24	8
—about right, considering the amount of skill required	29	39	39	51	83	21	39	48	59	84
(Form B)										
3. The way property is used should mainly be decided by the:										
—community, since the earth belongs to everybody	35	29	28	21	19	56	35	27	18	8
—individuals who own it	56	53	55	62	60	24	50	50	64	71
(Total sample)										

4. Public ownership of large industry would be a:

—good idea	48	33	24	10	8	43	16	11	11	0
—bad idea	10	38	53	75	81	18	46	63	78	93
	(N=22)	(N=85)	(N=169)	(N=168)	(N=29)	(N=109)	(N=318)	(N=237)	(N=133)	(N=15)

5. Corporations and people with money:

—really run this country	86	77	69	47	54	73	55	32	23	33
—have less influence on the politics of this country than many people think	5	8	13	31	35	2	16	45	52	53
	(N=22)	(N=85)	(N=169)	(N=168)	(N=29)	(N=109)	(N=318)	(N=237)	(N=133)	(N=15)

Sources: questions 1–3: Civil Liberties study, 1978–79; questions 4 and 5, Opinions and Values of Americans survey, 1975–77.

a. For N's in questions 1–3, see Table 7–5, note a.

b. Includes only those respondents who scored in the upper half of the distribution on the political sophistication index (see text footnote, p. 201).

c. Ideology is determined in this table by self-designation (see note 17).

villager, small tradesman, mechanic, proletariat. The one has persistently sought to check and limit the popular power, to keep the control of the government in the hands of the few in order to serve special interests, whereas the other has sought to augment the popular power, to make government more responsive to the will of the majority, to further the democratic rather than the republican ideal—let one discover this and new light is shed on our cultural tendencies.[25]

While Parrington and other "progressive historians" have underscored the existence of ideological conflict in American history, a newer school of historiography, that of the so-called consensus historians, began in the 1950s to emphasize the values that Americans have traditionally held in common. For example, Daniel Boorstin, a leading member of the consensus school, has argued that Americans never experienced sharp ideological conflict because their beliefs and values had been shaped by their common experiences in the New World.[26]

More recently, Richard Hofstadter has contended that the accounts of both the progressive historians and the consensus historians have merit. American history, he claims, has been characterized by both ideological conflict and a broad underlying consensus.

> Consensus history has a certain validity, as I see it, in that no society can function at all unless there are certain very broad premises, moral and constitutional, on which the overwhelming majority of its politically active citizens can agree at any time ... However, the consensus point of view is limited in that it is only an assertion about the frame of the configuration of history and not about what goes on in the picture ... Americans may not have quarreled over profound ideological matters, as they are formulated in the history of political thought, but they quarreled consistently over issues that had real pith and moment ... William James used to say that there is not much difference between one man and another but that the little difference there is is of great importance. The same is true of the political conflicts that we find in the history even of states that are permeated by a strong feeling of consensus.[27]

Our data support Hofstadter's views. Such ideological conflict as exists in America is confined within a broad framework of almost universal public support for the basic values of capitalism and democracy. Today, as in the past, one encounters in America few fascists, monarchists, communists, or other radicals of the far left or far right. Even democratic socialism has attracted few adherents in the United States. Yet our data also show that an individual's ideological tendencies clearly affect his attitudes toward capitalism and democracy. People who are convinced of the need for social change, who are strongly motivated to alleviate distress, and who take an optimistic view of human nature tend, for reasons we have explained, to be enthusiastic about democracy and wary of capitalism. Liberal efforts to reform the private enterprise system, and to extend the values of the democratic tradition to new domains, have been among the principal driving forces of American politics. In contrast, people who value order and stability, who are tough-minded about the prospects for alleviating social distress, and who take an essentially pessimistic view of human nature tend to be strongly procapitalist and cautiously democratic. The efforts of conservatives to prevent what they regard as democratic excesses, and to defend the private enterprise system from its critics, have obviously influenced the speed of social and economic reform in the United States.

We are not claiming, of course, that ideology has been the only important force in American politics. Various other factors—economic interests, ethnic cleavages, pressures from abroad, technological changes, among many others—have converged to shape the options from which Americans must choose. Ideology, nevertheless, often influences which of the options people select.

Among the most important choices Americans face, as we saw in the last chapter, are those between the competing values of capitalism and democracy. Asked to decide between preserving a laissez-faire economy and enacting measures that promise greater social and economic equality, conservatives emphasize capitalist values while liberals emphasize democratic values. Although both liberals and conservatives accept the basic values of the two traditions, each group emphasizes those parts of the ethos most compatible with its own philosophical disposition.

8 Social Learning and the Acquisition of Political Norms

One of the contentions of this book is that the public's attitudes toward capitalism and democracy are, to a great extent, shaped by the traditional ideologies and values of the political culture, as articulated by its opinion leaders. When most opinion leaders agree on a given issue, the more politically sophisticated members of the general public tend to learn and adopt the elite norm as their own. When they disagree, however, the members of the public who are politically aware begin to divide in ways that mirror the disagreements among the opinion leaders. In short, the more attention citizens pay to public affairs, the more faithfully will their opinions tend to reflect the beliefs that prevail among the elites. Although we might wish that the opinions held by the elites in a democracy had largely been shaped by the public, the available evidence suggests that the contrary is more often the case. The average citizen is free to choose among various elite-sponsored programs and ideologies, but he is not likely to participate actively in their formulation.

The opinion leaders who play the leading roles in articulating the values of the political culture are usually individuals or groups who specialize in the issue areas they attempt to influence. Obvious examples include economists, legal scholars, educators, foreign policy specialists, and various science and policy ex-

---

This chapter was written in collaboration with Dennis Chong.

perts, both in and outside of government. By virtue of their training, expertise, and active involvement, they are more likely than other citizens to propose new ideas and to have their ideas taken seriously by the attentive members of the public and by other elites. Of course, many of the respondents who turn up in our elite samples do not play leading roles in creating and promulgating the norms of the political culture. Most of them, however, function as repositories of mainstream opinions and values, as consumers and critics of political ideas and policies, and as carriers who transmit the values of the political culture to the general public.[1]

In this chapter we are mainly concerned with the process by which citizens acquire their values from the elite political culture, a process commonly known as social learning. As we noted earlier, social learning involves three steps: *exposure* to political communications that embody the norms, *comprehension* of the messages contained in these communications, and *acceptance* (or internalization) of the norms. In the discussion that follows we shall test hypotheses relating to each of these steps. In so doing, we hope to increase our understanding of why it is that some Americans systematically support capitalist and democratic values and others do not—why, in other words, some people embrace the prevailing values while others fail to do so or even appear to reject them.

Clear and Contested Norms

Most of the elite political discourse in the United States tends either explicitly or implictly to promote the general values of capitalism and democracy. Consider, for example, the role of the nation's news media in affirming democratic beliefs. The press, radio, and television routinely report on elections in ways which leave no doubt that the winner has the right to take office and govern and that the loser (even if he happens to be the incumbent president) does not. The media cover political controversies in ways which suggest that frank discussion of public issues, including sharp criticism of public officials, is not only legitimate but healthy. They expose instances of racial or sexual discrimination or arbitrary behavior by authorities in ways which make it plain that such actions violate the norms of acceptable conduct.

The media play an equally important role in affirming the values of capitalism. They routinely report news of business activities, including stock prices on Wall Street, the value of gold on the international market, and the amounts of corporate earnings. Major business innovations or mergers are treated as news, as are instances of major business failures. Implicit in such reports is the assumption not only that investment, economic competition, and profit making are legitimate activities, but that business is essential to the nation's well-being. In contrast, the media give little serious attention to anticapitalist ideas—for example, the idea that everyone ought to enjoy the same income or that government ought to own and control the nation's industries.

So much of the political discourse in the United States consists of partisan debate and disagreement that it is easy to overlook the broad areas of consensus that lie beneath the surface. Consider even so explosive an issue as racial discrimination. The Supreme Court has repeatedly condemned *de jure* segregation; Congress has passed numerous laws upholding the principle of racial equality; and every president who has held office in the past four decades has put himself on record as opposing overt discrimination against minorities. Even George Wallace, whose 1968 presidential campaign obviously was intended to appeal to opponents of racial equality, eschewed overt expressions of bigotry. As Lipset and Raab observe, "George Wallace personally avoided explicit racist talk." They also cite a study by the American Jewish Committee which found that "there was surprisingly no national circulation of anti-Negro material; this despite enthusiastic support given to Wallace by the racist White Citizens Councils and the Klan."[2]

Wallace could afford to keep race an implicit rather than an explicit theme of his campaign because ever since the famous barring-the-schoolhouse-door incident of 1962, his views were widely known. It is not customary, however, for politicians to keep their main campaign themes muffled and veiled from public view. That a candidate as outspoken as Wallace felt compelled to do so is evidence of the power of the present consensus against public expressions of racism. One may question, of course, whether many of the avowed segregationists of the recent past have been fully converted to the principle of racial equality. For present purposes, however, their private convictions are less important than what they assert in public. It is, after all, the public discourses of elites (not their private reservations) to which the average citizen is exposed.

These observations are central to our claims about the learning of political values. If, as we maintain, elite discourse in the United States tends on balance to support the basic values of capitalism and democracy, we should expect that, other things being equal, the people who are most heavily exposed to public affairs will exhibit greater support for these values than do people who are less heavily exposed.

Having noted that most elite discourse in the United States tends to promote the basic values of capitalism and democracy, we must also recognize that the elites—politicians, economic commentators, publicists, ideological activists—frequently disagree about the application of these values to concrete situations. For example, although many opinion leaders favor capitalism in its traditional laissez-faire form, the modern liberal critique of unfettered capitalism also enjoys considerable standing in the elite political culture. By the fourth quarter of the twentieth century, the liberal alternative to pure capitalism had won the support of many professional economists and countless other social commentators; it had become institutionalized in the political programs of the Democratic party; and it had begun to serve as the rationale for an ever-widening range of government regulations and social legislation designed to correct "abuses" in the performance of capitalism and, in some measure, to reallocate wealth. Welfare capitalism, as articulated by modern liberals, thus stands as an important, culturally legitimated alternative to the traditional notion of laissez-faire capitalism.

Differences have also developed around the democratic tradition, but to a lesser extent. Few opinion leaders of any ideological persuasion have made serious assaults on traditional democratic ideas and practices. Occasionally, however—and mainly among some groups of conservatives—one encounters protests that civil liberties have been extended too far at the expense of law, order, and stability; that the growing emphasis on equality has jeopardized the recognition of individual differences in contribution and worth; or that due process has been adhered to so inflexibly that justice miscarries and the guilty too often go free. More recently, influential conservative and religiously motivated movements have aimed to reinstitute prayer in the public schools, ban abortion, and limit the rights of homosexuals in matters of jobs and housing.

One of the areas that has generated intense disagreement among opinion leaders centers on the proper role of the federal government in promoting civil rights. Notwithstanding the apparent consensus among the elites that racial discrimination is morally indefensible, many opinion leaders argue that such policies as affirmative action, racial hiring quotas, and school busing go "too far." These policies, they claim, are forms of "reverse discrimination" against school children and other members of the white majority who have done nothing wrong. Other opinion leaders, however, maintain that unless the government takes an active role in promoting racial equality—through affirmative action, for example—private and *de facto* discrimination cannot be corrected and will persist for decades into the future. In light of these sharp divisions among the opinion leaders, the exposure of ordinary citizens to elite political discourse cannot be expected to increase public support for federal programs that give preference to the claims of minorities. Such exposure, in fact, might engender as much opposition to these policies as support for them.

Our basic argument might now be summarized as follows. When opinion leaders largely agree on a particular norm—when, in other words, elites hold up a "clear" or "uncontested" norm— we should find that most members of the public who pay close attention to public affairs will tend to learn and embrace that norm; when, on the other hand, opinion leaders clearly disagree about the values to be honored, exposure to elite political discourse will engender public attitudes that reflect the divisions existing among the elites.

To test these expectations, we created scales designed to assess public attitudes toward clear and uncontested norms, and other scales to assess attitudes toward contested norms. From the large pool of democracy items in our civil liberties survey, we selected nine that seemed to exemplify our notion of a clear democratic norm. These items tap attitudes toward a variety of democratic ideas that are fundamental to the American political system and are almost universally endorsed by political elites, such as popular sovereignty, the right of political opposition, freedom of speech, and racial equality. In our scale of contested democratic norms we included items concerning the right of the press to report information classified as secret by the government, the rights of homosexuals, and affirmative action, among others. (See Appendix III for lists of clear and contested norms.)

From the pool of capitalism items in our OVS survey,[3] we also created a scale of clear capitalist norms and another scale of contested capitalist norms. For example, an item asking whether the land of America should be left in private hands or "turned over to the people" was considered to reflect a clear norm because nearly all American opinion leaders currently support the principle of private ownership of property. By contrast, questions about the regulation of business and the appropriate uses of private property were believed to reflect contested norms because they represent issues on which opinion elites are sharply divided.

The results obtained from the use of these indices strongly confirmed our initial expectations. As Table 8-1 indicates, exposure to the elite political culture—whether measured by an individual's level of political knowledge, participation, or education—is significantly correlated with support for both clear democratic and clear capitalist norms. When the norms are contested, however, exposure to the elite culture has no substantial effect on levels of popular support.[4]

To be certain that these findings were free of confounding or spurious influences, we ran regressions in which we imposed si-

Table 8-1   Effect of exposure to public affairs on support for clear and contested norms of capitalism and democracy

Type of norm	Measures of exposure		
	Information	Participation	Education
Clear democratic norms[a]	0.36[b]	0.17	0.28
Contested democratic norms	0.02	−0.09	0.08
Clear capitalist norms	0.37	0.26	0.19
Contested capitalist norms	0.02	0.05	0.00

Sources: Data on democratic norms are from the Civil Liberties Survey, 1978–79; data on capitalist norms are from the Opinions and Values of Americans survey, 1975–77.
  a. For information on the construction of these measures, see Appendix III.
  b. Cell entries are Pearson correlation coefficients.

multaneous statistical controls for respondents' age, income, religiosity, race, sex, and attitudes toward order and stability. The results confirmed our initial conclusion that as exposure to public affairs increases, support for the *clear* norms of capitalism and democracy becomes greater;[5] such exposure, however, has little effect on support for the *contested* norms of either tradition.

The main contention here has been that opinion leaders play a critical role in defining the political norms that the more politically sophisticated and alert members of the general public learn and adopt as their own. A recent initiative campaign in California on the rights of homosexuals furnishes a particularly striking illustration of this process. The California campaign, centered on a ballot initiative proposed by State Assemblyman John Briggs, would have permitted school officials to dismiss or refuse to hire any teacher or school official who was found to engage in or to promote homosexual conduct. When the campaign on the initiative began in the summer of 1978, the polls showed that a substantial majority of the public in both California and the nation favored a prohibition on the right of homosexuals to teach in the public schools. As the campaign progressed, however, many of the state's prominent opinion leaders, as well as some notable out-of-state leaders, spoke out against the Briggs Initiative. Among the declared opponents of the measure were President Jimmy Carter, former California Governor Ronald Reagan, Governor Jerry Brown, Howard Jarvis (the leader of a recent tax revolt), influential state legislators, and many of the state's prominent religious leaders.

The state's largest newspaper, the *Los Angeles Times,* set the tone of the anti-Briggs campaign. The initiative, the editors wrote, was "political yahooism at its nastiest." If passed, the measure would represent "as flagrant a grant of power to the state to interfere with the rights of privacy, free speech and free association, and as broad a license for subjecting citizens to malicious harassment, as we are likely to see in a democracy . . . We urge citizens to reject 'the Briggs initiative' with the contempt it deserves."[6]

In the face of such overwhelming opposition among the elites, public opinion in California shifted markedly, and the initiative was soundly defeated in the fall election. Thus what remained in most of the nation a contested democratic norm became, among

California elites at least, a relatively uncontested one that appears to have had a marked effect on the opinions held by the attentive public.

If we are correct in these inferences, we should find that in California (where gay rights had now emerged as a relatively clear norm), political sophistication was significantly associated among the mass public with support for homosexual rights, while in the nation as a whole (where the norms on this issue were still contested), sophistication was only weakly associated with support for such rights. Fortunately, we are in a position to test these expectations. In addition to conducting our nationwide study of attitudes toward civil liberties in the summer of 1978, we also surveyed the California electorate shortly after the Briggs campaign had been completed. Since most of the questions used in the two surveys were identical, we have comparable measures of attitudes toward the rights of homosexuals for both California and the nation.

These surveys bear out our expectations. In the country as a whole, the level of political sophistication was only weakly associated with support for gay rights. This relationship, moreover, vanished once we imposed statistical controls for such variables as age, degree of religiosity, and ideological tendency. Yet, among Californians who had just witnessed the public debate over the Briggs Initiative, support for homosexual rights increased with sophistication, and this relationship remained significant even after we introduced statistical controls to take account of the influence of extraneous factors.[7]

Two other surveys of the California electorate offer further corroboration of these findings. In the first, conducted early in August of 1978, the relationship between an individual's level of education and his support for gay rights was modest. But a second statewide survey, taken after the Briggs campaign was well under way, showed that better-educated Californians—those most likely to have been exposed to the elite discussions of the Briggs Initiative—had become substantially more favorable toward gay rights. Poorly educated Californians, by contrast, had scarcely changed their attitudes at all.[8]

We have developed one additional and, to our minds, decisive test of the arguments we have been advancing. We had expected that when the norms of capitalism or democracy are clear, greater exposure to public affairs should lead individuals, whether they score high or low on such measures as social change, to express greater support for those norms. When, however, the norms are contested, greater exposure should lead the two groups to diverge: people favoring social change should gravitate toward the position taken by liberal opinion leaders, while those who stress the need for order and stability should gravitate toward the position taken by conservative opinion leaders. These expectations are borne out by the graphs in Figure 8–1 and the regression coefficients in Table 8–2.[9]

Some researchers question whether the politically sophisticated or better educated are, in general, more likely than the unsophisticated to support the norms of racial and political tolerance.[10] Our data show that the sophisticated are indeed more tolerant—but mainly when they are responding to norms that are relatively clear and uncontested among the elite. When, however, they are responding to norms that are contested, increases in political information (or education) lead some respondents (for example, liberals) to become more tolerant, and others (for example, conservatives) to become less tolerant.[11]

Although we have used social change as our measure of ideological orientation, other measures provide comparable results.[12] For example, Figure 8–2 and Table 8–3 show that people who differ in the strength of their religious convictions react differently to elite debates over such morally sensitive and contested issues as abortion, homosexuality, and pornography. Among people who describe themselves as "not religious" or only "fairly religious," increases in political sophistication lead to greater tolerance on such moral issues. Among people who describe themselves as "very religious," however, increases in sophistication lead, if anything, to less tolerance on contested moral issues.

Thus, when the norms of capitalism or democracy are clear and uncontested, most Americans, liberals as well as conservatives, usually accept them—and the more politically sophisticated they are, the more likely they are to do so. When the norms are contested, however, increases in exposure to public affairs give rise to greater divergence of opinion among the general public.

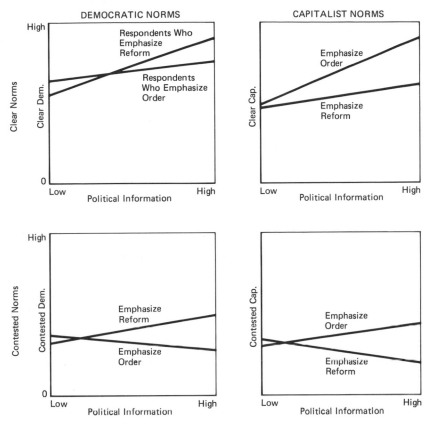

Figure 8-1   Effect of political information and ideology on support for clear
and contested norms. The lines in the figure represent slopes
derived from a regression analysis that also controlled for re
spondents' age, income, race, and sex. The democracy and capitalism measures have been standardized so that a score of zero
is the lowest possible score on a given measure, and a score of
"high" is the highest possible score on that measure. The difference between a score of low information and a score of high information is approximately four standard deviations. *Sources:*
Data on democratic norms: Civil Liberties study, 1978–79; data
on capitalist norms: Opinions and Values of Americans survey,
1975–77.

Table 8-2 Regression coefficients for the effect of political information and ideology on support for clear and contested norms[a]

Variable	Clear democracy[b] (Range: 0–18)	Contested democracy[b] (Range: 0–18)	Clear capitalism[c] (Range: 0–10)	Contested capitalism[c] (Range: 0–10)
Information (Range: CL, 21–36; OVS, 19–39)	0.244 (0.04)[e]	−0.015 (0.06)	0.108 (0.03)	−0.044 (0.03)
Information × Liberal[d]	0.176 (0.06)	0.21 (0.07)	−0.031 (0.03)	−0.009 (0.04)
Information × Conservative	−0.075 (0.06)	−0.06 (0.07)	0.062 (0.03)	0.119 (0.04)
Adjusted R for equation	0.41	0.45	0.54	0.32

a. Each regression permitted separate dummy intercepts for prochange and antichange respondents, as well as measures for age, race, sex, and income.
b. Civil Liberties study, 1978–79.
c. Opinions and Values of Americans survey, 1975–77.
d. The ideology measure is our "change and reform" variable. The baseline category is a score of "middle" on this variable.
e. Numbers in parentheses are standard errors.

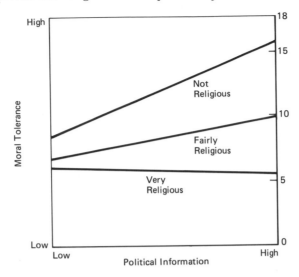

Figure 8-2   Effect of religiosity and political information on moral tolerance. The lines in the figure represent slopes derived from a regression analysis that also controlled for respondents' age,
income, race, and sex. The moral tolerance scale contains nine
items pertaining to homosexuality, abortion, and pornography.
It has a range from 0 to 18, a standard deviation of 4.97, and
an alpha reliability of 0.81. The difference between a score of
low information and a score of high information is approximately four standard deviations. *Source:* Civil Liberties study,
1978–79.

Patterns of Support for Capitalism and Democracy

The American political tradition is often described by political
analysts as a liberal tradition. By this they mean that it embodies
the principal values of nineteenth-century liberalism, a European
reform ideology stressing individual freedom, equality, popular
sovereignty, and progress, along with private property, competition, and laissez-faire. In the preceding section we discussed some
of the ways in which Americans acquire their attitudes toward the
specific democratic and capitalist norms of the nineteenth-century liberal culture. We also showed how disagreements among
contemporary liberal and conservative opinion leaders can affect
the learning of these norms. We turn now to an analysis of how
individuals learn to organize their political attitudes into conventionally recognized belief patterns.[13]

Table 8-3   Regression coefficients for the effect of political information and religiosity on support for moral tolerance[a]

Variable	Moral tolerance (Range: 0–18)
Information[b] (Range: 21–36)	0.36 (0.06)[c]
Information × Not Religious	0.100 (0.13)
Information × Fairly Religious	−0.17 (0.07)
Information × Very Religious	−0.42 (0.08)

Source: Civil Liberties study, 1978–79.

a. The regressions permitted separate dummy intercepts for each religious subgroup, as well as measures for age, race, sex, and income.

b. The baseline category is "somewhat religious."

c. Numbers in parentheses are standard errors.

Although most individuals probably acquire their political attitudes one at a time, they often learn these attitudes from elite sources that transmit "packages" of ideologically coherent ideas. Obvious sources of such ideologically consistent packages include party leaders, newspaper columnists, journals of political opinion, and reference group leaders (for example, chamber of commerce officials, civil rights leaders). Though individuals in a democracy normally encounter a wide variety of opinion leaders, the more politically astute citizens usually learn to identify some elites as having views consistent with their own developing ideological predispositions. From exposure to these congenial elite sources over a period of time, individuals gradually acquire the elements of a recognized ideology or belief pattern.

While much of this argument may be familiar to students of political socialization, we take note of it here because it has important implications for our analysis. If, as we believe, members of the general public tend to acquire their attitudes toward capitalism and democracy from the elite political culture, our observations suggest that they may end up learning them in at least three different combinations: the nineteenth-century liberal pattern described by Louis Hartz and others as the prevailing American tendency (strong support for the values of both traditions); the welfare state liberal pattern (strong support for democracy and qualified support for capitalism); or the pattern favored by many strong conservatives (strong support for capitalism and qualified support for certain democratic values). Each of these three patterns involves strong support for the values of at least one of the principal traditions of the American ethos; each qualifies as a belief system in the sense that it represents a coherent social philosophy; and each can claim significant support among such legitimating agencies of the political culture as the press, political institutions, and the universities. To the extent, therefore, that an individual's attitudes correspond to one of these three combinations, we may say that his attitudes are consistent with a culturally sanctioned pattern of support for the values of capitalism and democracy.

One other belief pattern, however, is obviously possible—the combination of low support for the values of both capitalism and democracy. This belief pattern differs from the other three in that it enjoys little acceptance in the political culture. No widely respected political movement is identified with it; no important philosopher has sought to justify its principal tenets; and (with the possible exception of minuscule movements on the far left or far right) none of the usual sources that disseminate political values seek to inculcate it. On the contrary, the adherents of this pattern of antiregime beliefs are often derided as "rednecks," "authoritarians," "yahoos," or "extremists." Although groups expressing this combination of beliefs have occasionally surfaced in American politics—the short-lived appearance of George Wallace's American Independent Party is an example—their views are rejected by the vast majority of American opinion leaders and enjoy little, if any, legitimacy. For want of a better term, we have described this as the antiregime belief pattern.

These observations lead to several readily testable propositions. If, as we have maintained, support for political values is the result of social learning, we should find that adherence to the antiregime value cluster (low on democracy, low on capitalism) is concentrated among the most politically inert and least sophisticated strata of society—that is, those who have had the fewest opportunities to learn the prevailing norms. Among those who are more politically active and aware, on the other hand, most should reject the antiregime pattern and embrace one of the three culturally sanctioned alternatives.

Scatterplots showing data on the joint distribution of attitudes

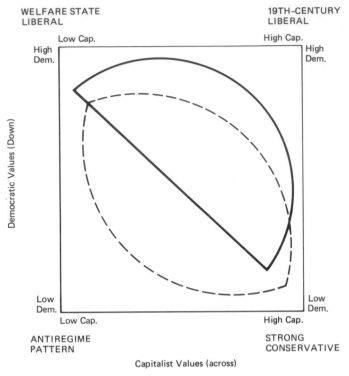

Figure 8–3   Schematic representation of the distribution of mass and elite
attitudes toward capitalism and democracy (solid line represents opinion leaders; dashed line represents the general public).
Source: Based on Opinions and Values of Americans Survey,
1975–77.

toward capitalism and democracy clearly confirm these expectations. To simplify the presentation, we have provided a schematic
diagram that summarizes the central tendencies of these scatterplots. In Figure 8–3, the distribution of scores among the opinion
leaders assumes the shape of a half-moon, which contains scarcely
any respondents who score low on the values of both capitalism
and democracy. Among the general public, however, the distribution of scores assumes the shape of a football, containing a
large number of respondents who score low on the values of both
traditions. Thus few members of the elite, but a substantial number of the general public, embrace the belief pattern we have labeled antiregime. Note, too, that nearly all opinion leaders,
relative to the general public, score moderate or high in their sup-

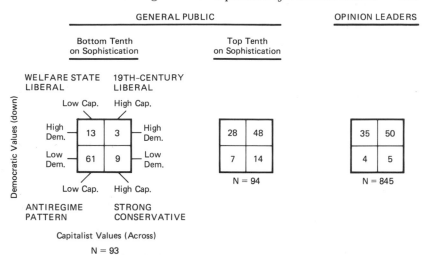

Figure 8–4 Patterns of support for the values of capitalism and democracy among the elites and the general public (corner percentaging). Labels shown in the first set of quadrants apply to all the others. *Source:* Opinions and Values of Americans survey, 1975–77.

port for democratic values. Thus disagreements among elites arise mainly from the differences in their orientations toward capitalism. These disagreements, although often intense, occur within a subspace defined by relatively high levels of overall support for democratic values.

Visual patterns of the kind represented in Figure 8–3 can also be summarized in tabular form.* For example, Figure 8–4 shows

* Any procedure for representing the scatterplots in tabular form is to some degree arbitrary. We began by trichotomizing scores on the capitalism and democracy scales, using the thirty-third and sixty-seventh percentiles of the mass distribution as the cutting points. We next classified respondents as follows: respondents scoring in the top third on the values of one tradition *and* high or moderate on the values of the other were counted as nineteenth-century liberals; those scoring high on democracy and low on capitalism were counted as strong welfare state liberals; those scoring low on democracy and high on capitalism were counted as strong conservatives; and finally, those scoring low on the values of one tradition and low or moderate on the values of the other were counted as falling within the antiregime cell. Respondents scoring in the middle third of both scales have been excluded from the analysis as ambiguous cases, unclassifiable for our purposes. This method of classification was designed to highlight the tendencies that exist in the data. The asymmetrical grouping of cells reflects our judgment that those who fall into cells off the main liberal-conservative diagonal hold positions other than strong liberalism or strong conservatism.

that respondents in the mass sample who are low on political sophistication gravitate toward the low-low quadrant, while the more sophisticated respondents more often fall into the high-high category. Some 61 percent of those who score in the bottom tenth of the sophistication scale turn up in the antiregime cell, compared with only 7 percent of the most sophisticated respondents in the mass public and 4 percent of the opinion leaders. Similarly, only 25 percent of the politically unsophisticated but 90 percent of the opinion leaders and the sophisticated respondents adopt one of the three belief patterns that indicate strong support for either capitalism or democracy or both. Thus, as political sophistication increases, one discerns a strong tendency to reject the antiregime pattern and to embrace one of the three traditional patterns.

Similar results were obtained from an analysis of the 1958 PAB survey of the American public and party influentials (that is, delegates to the national party conventions). Figure 8–5 shows that the modal tendency of less educated Americans in the late 1950s was to score low on an index of business values and low on a mea-

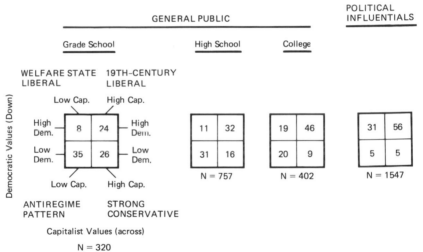

Figure 8–5   Patterns of support for the values of capitalism and democracy among the elites and the general public in the 1950s (corner percentaging). Labels shown in the first set of quadrants apply to all the others. Political influentials (that is, political convention delegates) have been screened for education. *Source:* Political Affiliations and Beliefs study, 1958.

sure that combined procedural rights and tolerance. Most political influentials, on the other hand, scored moderate to high on both measures.[14]

The belief patterns common among the most and least politically sophisticated strata of society thus seem to have changed little between the 1950s and 1970s. In view of the differences between the two decades and the turbulent period that separates them, this fact is itself noteworthy. But equally impressive is the powerful influence of the traditional American norms. Only among the politically unsophisticated do we find significant support for the antiregime pattern. Despite their personal idiosyncrasies, individuals who are sophisticated enough to understand the traditional patterns of political belief in American life are highly likely to embrace one of them.

Our analysis so far has made no effort to ascertain which of the three culturally sanctioned belief patterns—welfare liberalism, nineteenth-century liberalism, or strong conservatism—enjoys the strongest standing in the elite political culture. Our data, however, show that the strong conservative pattern is the least popular of the three. For cxample, among elites in both the OVS and PAB studies, welfare liberals outnumber strong conservatives by a very wide margin.[15] Moreover, Figure 8–6 shows that this tendency turns up within each of our five OVS elite subsamples.

The explanation for this finding is, we believe, clear. Since at least the New Deal, liberal politicians and publicists have been relatively uninhibited in their denunciations of business abuses and in their demands for programmatic alterations in the conduct of the private enterprise system. Having been exposed to such criticisms, sophisticated liberals in the general public and in our elite samples often express skeptical attitudes toward many traditional capitalist values.

Political controversies over democratic values are, in most cases, comparatively restrained. Even when conservatives have reservations about particular democratic norms—such as free speech for dissenters, or strict legal protections for the rights of the accused—many of them are reluctant to attack democratic norms openly. One can, to be sure, cite exceptions to this tendency, such as Joseph McCarthy's strident assault on freedom of expression in the 1950s. However, the very notoriety generated by McCarthy

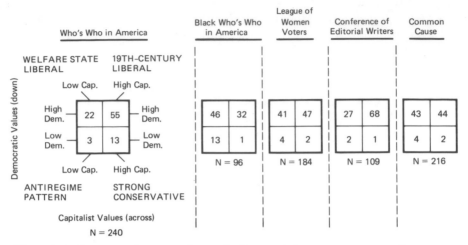

Figure 8–6   Patterns of support for capitalism and democracy among elite subgroups (corner percentaging). Labels shown in the first set of quadrants apply to all the others. *Source:* Opinions and Values of Americans survey, 1975–77.

underscores the infrequency of blatantly antidemocratic actions or expressions of opinion in American politics. The honorific status of democratic values makes it not only difficult but politically risky to attack policies carried out in the name of these values. As a result, conservatives rarely criticize specific democratic norms that they dislike as vehemently as liberals criticize specific capitalist norms that *they* dislike.[16] (In the language of our earlier discussion, most democratic norms tend to be relatively clear and uncontested, while capitalist norms are more often contested.)

Our data reflect this asymmetry in the political culture. Many more opinion leaders and sophisticated members of the public score high on democracy and low on capitalism (the welfare state liberal pattern) than score low on democracy and high on capitalism (the strong conservative pattern).

Social and Psychological Influences on the Learning of Norms

Despite its importance, political sophistication is only one of several factors influencing support for the values of the two traditions. Other possible influences include respondents' personality dispositions, ideological orientations, and such social characteristics as economic status, age, and place of residence. Since we cannot, within the compass of this book, examine all such variables, we shall concentrate on those that help to illuminate the general process by which people learn to support fundamental political and economic values.

We begin with place of residence as a possible influence on *exposure* to political norms. People who live in large metropolitan areas are typically close to the cultural mainstream. Although some urban residents are, to be sure, poorly educated or immobilized by poverty, most are nevertheless exposed to a broad flow of social and political communications that serve as carriers of society's dominant values. People who live in rural or small-town settings, by contrast, are more removed from the central sources of opinion and culture. Communication about national political and economic norms is less frequent in these settings, and the concerns of the existing media tend to be narrower and more parochial then they are in the cities. One has reason to expect, therefore, that support for the values of the American political culture will be weaker in rural than in urban areas.

Table 8–4 confirms this expectation.[17] Although the differences are not large, people in the smaller and more isolated communities are indeed more likely than residents of the urban areas to score low on the values of both capitalism and democracy. As one might expect, people living in small communities are also more likely than urban residents to score low on political sophistication. Controlling for political sophistication, however, produces an interesting result (Table 8–5): urban and rural differences on capitalism and democracy continue to turn up only among the un-

Table 8–4   Frequency of antiregime belief pattern by place of residence

Belief pattern	Rural or farm	Small town	Small city	Large city or its suburbs
Antiregime pattern: low on capitalism, low on democracy	37[a] (N = 188)	31 (N = 271)	24 (N = 182)	22 (N = 288)

Source: Opinions and Values of Americans survey, 1975–77.

a. Cell entries are percentage in each cell who score in the antiregime category.

Table 8–5 Frequency of antiregime belief pattern by sophistication and place of residence

Level of sophistication	Rural or farm	Small town	Small city	Large city or its suburbs
Low	58[a]	51	41	39
Middle	24	30	29	22
High	12	9	7	12

Source: Opinions and Values of Americans survey, 1975–77.

a. Cell entries are percentage in each cell who score in the antiregime category; N = 938.

sophisticated. Among the unsophisticated in the rural population, 58 percent score in the low-low (or antiregime) category as compared with 39 percent of the unsophisticated in the cities. Among the sophisticated, however, differences in the antiregime scores of urban and rural residents disappear. A sophisticated respondent, in other words, is unlikely to score in the low-low category whether he lives in the country or in the city. As this example illustrates, political sophistication can enable individuals to overcome influences that function as barriers to social learning among the less sophisticated.

Physical distance from the centers of social and political communication, therefore, is for some segments of the population an impediment to the learning of social norms. One can, however, also identify certain psychological impediments that, even in urban centers, prevent some individuals from comprehending the norms they encounter. One such impediment is psychological inflexibility. To show the effects of this disposition, we included in our survey a measure that assesses a respondent's willingness to keep an open mind and avoid premature conclusions, to entertain partial explanations and alternative points of view, and to adjust his own opinions as he encounters new information. As we said of this psychological trait on an earlier occasion: "Inflexibility reduces one's capacity to accommodate to diversity and contingency, and limits one's ability to perceive uniformities that may underlie diversity. Faced by complex stimuli from the social world, inflexible people are easily overwhelmed. Their anxiety is aroused, [and] they become confused."[18] Although people who are highly inflexible may wish to conform to society's norms,

Table 8-6   Influence of inflexibility on the acquisition of political information among the mass public

Level of political information	Psychological inflexibility				
	Low (N = 174)	Medium-low (N = 151)	Middle (N = 182)	Medium-high (N = 260)	High (N = 171)
Low	23	27	27	36	50
Middle	36	36	40	36	30
High	41	37	34	28	21

Source: Opinions and Values of Americans survey, 1975–77.

their personality characteristics may make it difficult for them to do so. Bewildered by the disparate social influences they encounter, they are often unable to tell what is expected of them or to discern what society's norms are. Even simple factual information often eludes them. As can be seen in Table 8–6, 50 percent of those scoring high on inflexibility score low on our measure of political information, compared to only 23 percent of those who are low on inflexibility.[19]

Although inflexibility hinders learning, its effects are not entirely debilitating; they can often be overcome by formal education, active involvement in public affairs, or other compensatory influences. Evidence of the compensatory effect of schooling, for example, is shown in Figure 8–7, where we see that increases in formal education serve to close the gap in political knowledge between flexible and inflexible respondents. The largest differences in political knowledge between the two personality types occur at the lowest levels of education. Among the most highly educated, however, the differences separating the two vanish. In the language of social learning theory, these results indicate that psychological inflexibility hampers the ability of the culturally impoverished to comprehend the dominant values of the political culture, whereas it has little effect on the learning capacities of those who have been more extensively exposed to public affairs.

If we are correct in this observation, we should find that people who are psychologically inflexible will score low more often than other Americans in their support for the values of both capitalism and democracy. The totals reported in Table 8–7 show that this is indeed the case. This psychological impediment to social learn-

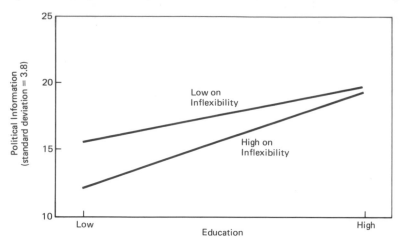

Figure 8-7   Influence of inflexibility on the acquisition of political information among different education groups. The plotted lines represent levels of political information among different education
groups for people who are high on the inflexibility scale and for
people who score low. The data have been obtained from a regression analysis that included statistical controls for respondents' age, sex, place of residence, income, and attitudes toward
change and reform. *Source:* Opinions and Values of Americans
survey, 1975–77.

ing, however, exerts its greatest influence on those whose capacity
for learning the norms is already weakest, namely, the politically
unsophisticated. These results, of course, parallel our finding on
the effects of place of residence.

So far, our discussion of belief patterns has shown that factors
that increase exposure to or comprehension of the values of the
political culture also increase the likelihood of accepting one of
the three culturally legitimated belief patterns. But people obviously differ in their preferences among the three patterns. Some
politically sophisticated respondents gravitate toward the norms
of welfare state liberalism; others verge toward the nineteenth-
century liberal pattern; still others favor the strong conservative
belief pattern. To account for these differences in preference, it is
necessary to focus on those factors that influence *acceptance* of political values.

One such factor, as we have seen, is ideological orientation.
People who exhibit a strong concern for social reform tend to be

Table 8–7   Frequency of antiregime belief pattern by sophistication and psychological disposition[a]

Level of sophistication	Inflexibility[b]		
	Low	Middle	High
Low	37	49	56
Middle	22	26	29
High	10	10	12
Total	21	28	36

Source: Opinions and Values of Americans survey, 1975–77.
a. N = 938.
b. Cell entries are percentage in each cell holding antiregime belief patterns.

enthusiastic democrats and wary capitalists, while people who emphasize order and stability exhibit the contrary tendencies. With this in mind, we can press our analysis a step further by showing what happens to people with different ideological predispositions as they acquire greater political awareness. Figure 8–8 shows that the politically unsophisticated tend to score in the antiregime category whether they preponderantly resist or lean toward change and reform. Even among the unsophisticated, however, the prochange respondents tend to favor the welfare state position over the strong conservative position, whereas the reverse is true for the antichange respondents. As sophistication increases, these tendencies become more pronounced. Among those in the mass public who score high on sophistication, 46 percent of the prochange respondents are welfare state liberals and only 4 percent are strong conservatives; among those who resist change, only 5 percent are welfare state liberals and 30 percent exhibit the strong conservative pattern.

Among opinion leaders the pattern is slightly altered: those favoring change and reform prefer the welfare state position, but those who oppose change and reform are, by a very wide margin, nineteenth-century liberals.* What this seems to reflect is the predominantly prodemocratic nature of the American political cul-

* The reader should bear in mind that for an individual to score as a nineteenth-century liberal, he must score high on the values of one tradition and moderate or high on the values of the other. Hence, for example, some members of the elite who have been classified as nineteenth-century liberals have scored high on capitalism and only moderate on democracy. (See footnote to p. 249.)

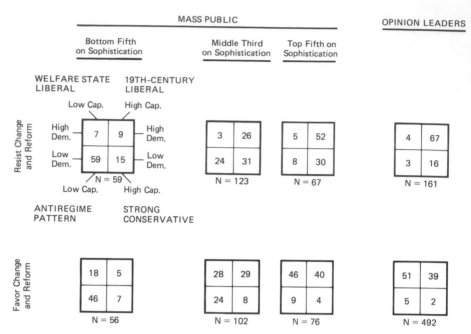

Figure 8–8   Effect of attitude toward change on support for the values of capitalism and democracy (corner percentaging). Labels shown in the first set of quadrants apply to all the others. *Source:* Opinions and Values of Americans survey, 1975–77.

ture. Although people strongly opposed to change and reform are clearly less enthusiastic about some democratic values than are those who favor change, they must nevertheless accommodate to a political culture that affords little legitimacy to antidemocratic sentiments. Hence elite conservatives, though strongly supporting capitalism, also score moderate to high on democratic values and thus fall into the nineteenth-century liberal cell rather than the strong conservative category.

The Structure of Political Belief

In examining the patterns of popular support for the two traditions, we have focused on the substance of the public's attitudes toward capitalism and democracy—whether, for example, they favor or oppose freedom of speech, racial equality, the profit system, and so forth. To understand the two traditions adequately, however, citizens must also comprehend the organizing principles that tie the values together into coherent systems of belief.

The distinction we are making is between the *content* and the *structure* of one's attitudes. For example, a person might favor the profit system, economic competition, and the inviolability of property rights (that is, he might have absorbed some of the content of capitalist values) and yet may fail to understand how these values are linked to one another. Effective social learning can be said to have occurred only when one has both absorbed the values of a given set of beliefs and also grasped the organizing principles—or structure—that hold those beliefs together.

In his seminal paper entitled "The Nature of Belief Systems in Mass Publics,"[20] Philip Converse concluded that many members of the general public lack the political awareness to grasp the organizing principles that underlie traditional belief systems such as liberalism and conservatism (and, we might add, capitalism and democracy). Hence many of the political opinions held by large numbers of the mass public tend to be labile and to shift back and forth between competing ideological principles.

The meaning of attitude structure or coherence can be illustrated by considering the notion as it applies to capitalist doctrines. No strictly logical considerations can explain why someone who believes in the sanctity of private property should also believe in business competition, unlimited private profits, and sharply stratified pay differentials. These ideas, however, have been intimately linked for at least two centuries as part of the capitalist creed. Hence, insofar as an individual organizes his beliefs with respect to the principles of capitalism, he ought to exhibit fairly consistent support for (or opposition to) such values as private property, competition, and the profit system.

The point is illustrated in Table 8–8, which shows the relationship between respondents' attitudes toward private property and their attitudes toward the profit system. The less sophisticated members of the general public obviously exhibit little consistency in their responses to these two sets of issues. Among the unsophisticated respondents, in fact, individuals who favor the profit system are scarcely more likely to endorse the rights of property owners than are individuals who are skeptical of the profit system.

Table 8–8   Attitude consistency among ideological activists and members of the general public

	Bottom third of the general public on sophistication		Ideological activists	
Attitude toward property rights[a]	Unfavorable to profit system[b] (N = 98)	Favorable to profit system (N = 70)	Unfavorable to profit system (N = 313)	Favorable to profit system (N = 479)
Unfavorable	27	17	76	11
Favorable	74	83	24	89

Source: Opinions and Values of Americans survey, 1975–77.

a. The exact question was: "The way property is used should mainly be decided: (a) by the community, since the earth belongs to everyone; (b) by the individuals who own it." Respondents scoring "neither" or "undecided" on either question have been omitted from this table.

b. The exact question was: "When businesses are allowed to make as much money as they can: (a) workers and the poor are bound to get less; (b) everyone profits in the long run."

By contrast, the ideological activists are highly consistent in their answers to the two questions. Among those who favor the profit system, 89 percent take a strongly traditional view of property rights as well. But among those who are less sympathetic toward the profit system, only 24 percent strongly favor traditional property rights. Expressed differently, the gamma score (which indicates the degree of attitude structure) is far higher among the ideological activists (0.93) than it is among the less sophisticated members of the general public (0.27).

The tendencies illustrated in Table 8–8 hold for most issues relating to capitalism and democracy. As people become more politically aware and active, they are more likely to respond to the values of the two traditions in a principled and ideologically coherent manner. Further evidence of this tendency is shown in Table 8–9. In their responses to a representative selection of issues drawn from capitalist and democratic belief systems, opinion leaders and ideological activists exhibit much higher levels of attitude consistency than do members of the general public. Within the mass public, moreover, politically sophisticated citizens are far more consistent than the unsophisticated. Thus the data conform to our claim that the greater an individual's opportunity for social learning, the higher are his overall levels of attitude structure.[21]

We saw earlier in this chapter that unsophisticated respondents tend to score relatively low on support for both capitalism

Table 8-9   Average interitem gammas for a representative sample of items relating to capitalism and democracy

	General public			Elites	
	Low soph. (N = 309)	Middle soph. (N = 310)	High soph. (N = 310)	Opinion leaders (N = 845)	Ideological elite (N = 1,426)
Democratic values	0.37[a]	0.45	0.62	0.55	0.80
Capitalist values	0.23	0.46	0.71	0.69	0.88

Source: Opinions and Values of Americans survey, 1975–77.

a. Cell entries represent average interitem gammas for the domain and subpopulation indicated.

and democracy. The present findings raise an interesting question about this conclusion: to what extent can one say that these respondents are actually rejecting democratic and capitalist values rather than simply failing to understand them?

Most of the evidence suggests a failure of understanding. The unsophisticated are more likely to make sweeping antidemocratic or anticapitalist statements than are other Americans, but given the inconsistencies reflected in the attitudes they express, it is difficult to believe that they are consciously rejecting capitalism and democracy out of conviction or principle. Indeed, we have seen that their political thought is only weakly influenced by systematic or structured ideological principles of *any* kind. We believe it safer to infer, therefore, that their low overall levels of support for capitalist and democratic values and their poorly developed belief systems stem largely from a failure to have learned the prevailing norms—in effect, a failure of social learning.

Various characteristics of the antiregime respondents lend weight to this inference. They are, for example, poorly educated; they exhibit low levels of political knowledge; they participate minimally in the political system, often functioning outside the mainstream of the political culture; and they are likely to possess personality characteristics such as psychological inflexibility that inhibit social interaction. All these attributes impede social learning and reduce a person's ability to discern what society values. It is scarcely surprising, therefore, that people who possess these characteristics tend to exhibit low levels of support for the values of capitalism or democracy.

Some of the unsophisticated, of course, doubtless have strong opinions on particular subjects relating to these belief systems. If one could devise an "objective" measure of intensity of conviction, one might discover that their attitudes—particularly on matters of racial or political tolerance—are as deeply felt as those of the more sophisticated. It is also possible that the unsophisticated have a roughly serviceable view of the way in which certain features of capitalism and democracy work—they might, for example, know which political party is more egalitarian, or why a private business enterprise needs to make profits. But it is highly unlikely that their views on topics of this kind are tied together as part of a well-developed and historically sanctioned belief system.

Summary

We have examined in this chapter the process of political acculturation, the process by which people acquire their political beliefs and ideologies. Our basic argument can be briefly summarized: most individuals possess general orientations toward such matters as order, stability, and social benevolence—orientations that are, to begin with, independent of their political participation. As people gain more knowledge and become more involved in public affairs, two things occur. First, they learn to see relationships between their developing ideological orientations, on the one side, and the different issue positions being debated in elite circles, on the other. Second, they become aware of the cultural norms that exist on many democratic and capitalist issues— or, to put it differently, they learn which attitudes are regarded as politically "respectable" (especially among the opinion elites) and which are not.

These two processes jointly shape an individual's attitudes toward the norms of the political culture. When the elite norms are clear and relatively uncontested, increases in political awareness lead most Americans, regardless of their ideological tendencies, to conform to them. When the norms are contested, individuals adopt, from the range of alternatives being argued among the opinion leaders, those attitudes that best reflect their own ideological tendencies.

While much of our analysis in this chapter has focused on the learning of specific clear and contested norms, we have also examined the *patterns* of popular support for various norms relating to capitalism and democracy. Opinion leaders, we observed, tend to disseminate political norms as parts of ideologically integrated "packages." As a result of exposure to these packages over a period of time, most politically sophisticated Americans end up forming attitudes that conform to one of three well-recognized ideological patterns—the welfare state liberal pattern, the nineteenth-century liberal pattern, or the strong conservative pattern. Only among the least sophisticated members of the public do we encounter large numbers of people who have failed to learn one of the conventionally recognized belief patterns.

9 The Future of Capitalist Democracy in the United States

Perhaps no development since the industrial revolution has had a more far-reaching influence on the character of American political and economic life than the growth of the welfare state. Every step in its development, however, has generated intense controversy. For well over half a century, Americans have debated the proper role of government in guaranteeing to its citizens such necessities as food, shelter, and medical care; in promoting the rights of women, racial minorities, and other historically deprived groups; and in overseeing the performance of the economy so that a fair measure of prosperity might be achieved for all.

For our purposes, the debates over the welfare state are important because they draw strongly on the values of the American ethos, casting the conflicting perspectives of capitalism and democracy into sharp relief. The conservative defenders of capitalism contend that government, in trying to guarantee the welfare of its citizens, will undermine self-reliance and individual initiative, stifle the private economy, and destroy such cherished American values as competition and the desire for achievement. Liberals and social reformers, however, argue with equal conviction that the promise of American democracy cannot be realized without the assistance of the welfare state. How, they ask, can a genuine democracy be achieved when powerful private interests dominate the society and millions of citizens lack the necessities for a decent and fulfilling life?

The outcome of the debate over the welfare state will be affected by many factors, including the performance of the capitalist economy and the relative strength of opposing interest groups. But traditional values will obviously play an important role as well. As we shall see, the debate over the welfare state is in essence a debate over which strand of the ethos, the democratic or the capitalist, should be given priority. As such, it is a debate over the future of capitalist democracy in the United States.

But however this debate is decided, it is already clear that the United States has taken major steps toward the creation of a modern welfare state. The federal government has become active in countless areas of human endeavor. It tries, for example, to ensure that the rights of all citizens are protected and their well-being fostered. It is held responsible for the alleviation of problems that were once left almost entirely to the private sector, including hunger, poverty, illness, unemployment, and discrimination. It plays a major role in regulating the economy, protecting the environment, managing the nation's resources, and performing a great many other functions formerly left to private initiative.

In taking on these responsibilities, the United States has developed a set of economic and political arrangements that might be described as "welfare capitalism." Even though the economy remains in the hands of private owners and entrepreneurs who are largely motivated by a desire for profit, the government not only regulates various aspects of the private economy but diverts a significant portion of the nation's wealth to help assure the comfort, health, and happiness of all citizens. The federal government, in short, is the single most influential participant in the economic, social, and political life of the nation.

In this chapter we will argue that the impetus toward welfare capitalism stems in great part from the democratic and egalitarian aspects of the ethos. Yet other elements in the American creed—in particular, traditional notions of individualism, self-help, minimal government, and economic independence from government—have functioned as a counterforce to the growth of the welfare state and to the principle of government responsibility for individual well-being. We believe that the forms taken by the American welfare state and the attitudes Americans exhibit toward it can be accounted for only if these disparate cultural influences are given adequate consideration.

Individualism, Self-Help, and the Welfare State

Few beliefs were more deeply entrenched in the political culture of the early Republic than the conviction that government ought to play a minimal role in the conduct of human affairs. Although the Founders fashioned a federal government with power to rule the entire nation, few of them wanted it to dominate economic or political life. The national government was, at the beginning, an isolated clutch of offices and institutions located far from the commercial and social centers of culture. As such, it was often ignored by the citizens of the new Republic, while it, in turn, had only "negligible engagement in the lives of the people."[1] The branches and agencies that composed the new government, moreover, were designed to check each other—to slow rather than to speed the enactment of public policies. The atmosphere in which the central government functioned was one of widespread distrust of political power, a distrust that was deeply ingrained in both the electorate and its leaders by the colonists' experience with British rule and by their awareness of the tendencies toward absolutism that marked the governments of most other nations of the world. Scarcely anyone in these circumstances tried to argue that the federal government had an obligation to guarantee the welfare of individual citizens. To the contrary, Americans were committed to the belief that each individual was obligated to get ahead on his own.

The American belief in individual responsibility was reinforced from another source—namely, comparisons made by American observers of the conditions existing in Europe and the United States. Throughout the eighteenth and early nineteenth centuries, Americans tended to view Europeans as submissive, lethargic, and ignorant, while they saw themselves as vigorous, enterprising, and self-reliant. For the most part they attributed their superior traits to the influence of America's free institutions, which fostered individual independence and the desire for achievement. The typical inhabitant of the Old World, they believed, was trapped in a web of legal and customary controls that effectively subjugated him to the will of self-aggrandizing overlords, made him dependent, and deprived him of any incentive to display initiative and imagination. In these circumstances, they thought, men lost their ambition to achieve, their capacity for hard work, and their desire for excellence. "Dependence," as Jefferson wrote, "begets subservience and venality" and opens the way to political corruption.[2] Americans, by contrast, saw themselves as subservient neither to overlord nor to custom, but as answerable mainly to themselves. They believed that such independence was invigorating, and that it infused the citizenry with a strong sense of self-respect and civic responsibility.

These ideas became articles of faith in the young Republic. They enjoyed an honorific status ordinarily reserved for proven scientific theories: make a person independent of government (or any other master) and responsible for his own welfare, and he will become energetic, enterprising, and virtuous; make him dependent and he will become dull, lethargic, unproductive, and shiftless.

The country's strong Protestant tradition reinforced these ideas. In contrast to Catholic theology, which maintained that the individual needed the continual support and guidance of the Church and its sacraments to achieve salvation, most Protestant denominations stressed that each individual must find his own way to heaven. Protestantism thus helped to accustom Americans to the belief that each person must bear responsibility for his own fate.

Taken together, these ideas largely determined early American attitudes toward the proper role of the state in providing for the welfare of its citizens. Each individual was expected to be self-reliant and to get ahead with little or no help from government or any other social institution. This expectation held even in the face of personal failure or material privation, since any outside assistance might engender habits of dependence that would destroy an individual's incentive to care for himself.

These beliefs, as we shall see, are still common in the United States, especially among conservatives and other opponents of welfare capitalism. In the early days of the country's history, however, they appear to have been accepted by almost everyone, including those who were actively involved in efforts toward social and humanitarian reform. Even among those most concerned with the alleviation of pauperism, the prevailing view was that public charity discouraged individual self-help. Such reformers believed that society could be improved only by the moral regeneration of the individual, who should be rescued from pernicious habits of religious indifference, sloth, and intemperance.[3]

Though originating in pre-industrial America, these ideas appealed strongly to the rising industrialists of the later nineteenth century and helped to shape their response to problems attending the growth of a massive working class in an increasingly urban and industrial society. Andrew Carnegie, for example, who was noted not only for his great wealth but for his philanthropy, argued that charitable activities must be carefully tailored to encourage people to overcome the personal deficiencies which, he believed, were the real source of their problems:

> One of the serious obstacles to the improvement of our race is indiscriminate charity. It were better for mankind that the millions of the rich were thrown into the sea than so spent as to encourage the slothful, the drunken, the unworthy.
>
> In bestowing charity, the main consideration should be to help those who will help themselves; to assist, but rarely or never to do all . . . the best means of benefitting the community is to place within its reach the ladders upon which the aspiring can arise—free libraries, parks, and means of recreation, by which men are helped in body and mind.[4]

The traditional view of philanthropy, however, has come under attack. Many reformers, intellectuals, and social workers, then as now, argued that direct relief of the symptoms of poverty—through government programs if necessary—is more useful than exhortations to self-help and moral improvement. Public confidence in economic individualism, especially the notion that the poor are responsible for their own misfortune, also declined, and has continued to decline. As we saw in an earlier chapter, for example, only about a third of the American public now accepts the notion that the poor are poor because "they are lazy and lack self-discipline," and even fewer (24 percent) believe that poverty is caused by the failure of the poor "to try hard enough to get ahead."

What led to this change in outlook? In addressing this question, one should bear in mind that the term *individualism* does not mean today exactly what it meant in the early nineteenth century. In the earlier period, individualism and its associated values were invoked mainly to justify the American experiment in democratic freedom and equality. The relative prosperity of the United States compared to that of European nations served, in addition, to buttress the case for individualism. By the end of the nineteenth century, however, the highly visible poverty of the urban working classes made America seem suddenly less prosperous than it had before. In addition, the traditional doctrines of individualism were to some extent preempted by Social Darwinists, who employed them to justify the increasingly sharp social and economic stratifications then developing. The more individualism came to be identified with the inequities of industrial capitalism, the more it suffered in popular esteem.

The traditional notion of individualism was also challenged by the new social scientific thought, especially in sociology, economics, and psychology. Whereas early American individualism had stressed the uniqueness of individuals and their independence from one another and from society at large, many of the leading social scientists in the late nineteenth century began to describe social reality rather differently. Society, they maintained, was an interlocking system of values and social influences that shaped not only social interaction, but human nature itself. In this view, people are largely the products of their environment. They are, to be sure, responsible moral agents, but their personalities, ambitions, and abilities are shaped in large part by the society in which they live. Social scientists also held that social systems and institutions are subject to human understanding and hence to rational control. In keeping with these beliefs, the pioneering American sociologist Lester Ward called for "the scientific control of . . . social forces by the collective mind of society."[5]

This perspective on man and society was in turn seized upon by progressive social critics in order to justify new types of reform and new kinds of government responsibility. If, they argued, people are largely the product of their environment, their poverty signifies not so much the failure of individuals as the failure of society itself—a failure which obliges the members of society, acting through their government, to enact changes that would end poverty. Hence American progressives of the early twentieth century—people like John Dewey, Herbert Croly, Walter Lippmann, and Thorstein Veblen—contended that major reforms were necessary to solve the problems spawned by industrialism. As Dewey wrote: "We may desire abolition of war, industrial justice, greater equality of opportunity for all. But no amount of preaching . . . will accomplish the results. There must be change in objective arrangements and institutions. We must work on the environment, not merely on the hearts of men."[6] In what was then perceived as a radical set of recommendations, the reformers called for such measures as minimum wages, consumer safety standards, old-age pensions, greater emphasis on public education, and a marked increase in state regulation of business. A modern industrialized society, they argued, has an obligation to intervene in the private economy whenever such action is necessary to correct abuses or relieve social distress.

Despite such challenges from liberals, socialists, and other progressives, the older ideas of individualism and self-reliance retained much of their vitality and even today are frequently invoked to justify opposition to welfare capitalism. Dwight D. Eisenhower, for example, speaking as a Republican and a conservative, drew on the values of the individualist tradition when he maintained in 1964 that "in far too many ways we are . . . moving toward federal domination over almost every phase of our economy . . . This may give to some an immediate sense of material well-being and personal security. But it is dangerous to our future . . . what is stolen by paternalistic government is that precious compound of initiative, independence, and self-respect that distinguishes a man from an automaton, a person from a number, productive and competitive enterprise from a regimented people."[7]

The enduring appeal of the traditional values of independence and self-reliance is suggested by the data reported in Table 9–1. In the early 1940s, for example, a majority (59 percent) of the American public rejected the idea that government should try to provide minimum levels of security from "cradle to grave," while only 20 percent unequivocally favored this idea. As late as the 1970s most Americans were still saying that the poor should "help themselves" and that the government should "just let each person get ahead on his own" rather than guaranteeing everyone a job and a good standard of living. Even if a person is elderly or impoverished, many Americans continue to be-

Table 9-1   General attitudes toward welfare state ideology

	General public
1. Do you think a "cradle to grave" program of minimum security for all people in the United States is:	
—impossible and undesirable	44
—economically possible but undesirable	15
—desirable but impossible	21
—economically possible and desirable	20

2. After a person has worked until he is 65, it is proper for the community to support him.

—Agree	30
—Disagree	70
	(N = 1,484)

3. Some people feel that the government in Washington should see to it that every person has a job and a good standard of living . . . Others think the government should just let each person get ahead on his own . . . And, of course, other people have opinions somewhere in between.

—government guarantee jobs	21
—neutral	23
—individual on his own	53
—other	3

	CL	OVS
4. In order to improve their condition, the poor should:		
—receive special government help	25	22
—help themselves	49	53
—Decline to choose	26	25
	(N = 938)	(N = 1,995)

Sources. question 1, *Fortune Magazine,* 1943, cited in *Public Opinion, 1935–1956,* ed. Hadley Cantril (Princeton, N.J.: Princeton University Press, 1951), p. 362; question 2, Political Affiliations and Beliefs study, 1958; question 3, University of Michigan, National Election study, 1978; question 4, Opinions and Values of Americans survey, 1975–77; Civil Liberties study, 1978–79.

lieve that responsibility for his welfare rests principally with him and not with the government.

The persistence of these traditional beliefs is remarkable in light of the American government's involvement in numerous large-scale programs intended to ensure a minimum standard of well-being for all its citizens. Even more striking, however, is that despite some philosophical reservations, Americans exhibit strong support for many specific social assistance programs. A series of survey questions beginning in the 1930s shows that Americans favor government assistance when people cannot find jobs, have no visible means of subsistence, or seriously need help (see Table 9–2).

The disjunction between the philosophical dispositions of many Americans and their beliefs about specific social welfare programs is clearly evident from the data presented in Table 9–3. At a time in the 1950s when the federal government was becoming heavily

Table 9–2   General attitudes toward welfare state programs

	General public
1. Are you in favor of government old-age pensions for needy people?	
—Yes	89
—No	11
2. Should the federal government provide free medical care for those unable to pay?	
—Yes, it should	79
—No, it should not	21
3. Do you think our government should or should not provide for all people who have no other means of subsistence?	
—Yes, it should	69
—No, it should not	24
—Other	7
4. When people can't find any jobs, would you be in favor of the government putting them on the payroll and finding work for them such as helping out in hospitals or cleaning parks, or would you be against this idea?	
—Favor	89
—Oppose	8
—Decline to choose	3
5. The federal government has a deep responsibility for seeing that the poor are taken care of, that no one goes hungry, and that every person achieves a minimum standard of living.	
—Agree	68
—Disagree	27
—Other	5

Sources: questions 1–3, Gallup, cited in *Public Opinion, 1937–1946,* ed. Hadley Cantril (Princeton, N.J.: Princeton University Press, 1951), pp. 541, 439, 258; questions 4 and 5, Gallup, cited in Hazel Erskine, "The Polls: Government Role in Welfare," *Public Opinion Quarterly,* 39 (Summer 1975), pp. 266, 259.

Table 9–3   Contrasting attitudes toward general welfare principles and specific welfare programs

	General public
1. Everyone should have a good house even if the government has to build it for him.	
—Agree	28
—Disagree	72
	(N = 1,484)
2. [Should we spend more or less on] slum clearance and public housing?	
—More	79
—Same	14
—Less	7
	(N = 1,484)
3. Who should bear the main responsibility for taking care of our senior citizens?	
—The community	35
—The elderly themselves and their families	38
—Decline to choose	28
	(N = 938)
4. As far as you personally are concerned, do you feel it very important, only somewhat important, or not at all important for Congress to . . . help the poor, the elderly, and others hard hit by inflation?	
—Very important	82
—Somewhat important	15
—Not at all important	2
—Not sure	1

Sources: questions 1 and 2, Political Affiliations and Beliefs study, 1958; question 3, Opinions and Values of Americans survey, 1975–77; question 4, Harris, 1974, cited in Hazel Erskine, "The Polls: The Government Role in Welfare," *Public Opinion Quarterly,* 39 (Summer 1975), p. 260.

involved in large-scale housing programs, 79 percent of Americans thought it should be spending even more money on "slum clearance and public housing," an additional 14 percent were satisfied with the present level of spending, and only 7 percent wanted current spending reduced. When the same respondents, however, were asked whether they agreed with the assertion that "everyone should have a good house even if the government has to build it," 72 percent disagreed. A similar finding turns up in data collected in the mid-1970s. The vast majority—97 percent of those polled in a Harris survey—considered it important for government to "help the poor, the elderly, and others hard hit by inflation." But when a comparable national sample in our 1975–77 survey was asked whether the individual or the community bore "the main responsibility" for taking care of the elderly, only a third of the public said that the community was responsible.

Americans, it seems, want their government to contribute to the well-being of the poor, the elderly, and other needy people. But they also believe, as Carnegie said, that the purpose of such contributions should be "to assist, but rarely or never to do all." Hence they tend to deny that society bears the primary responsibility for individual welfare, or that it ought to provide lifetime security for all of its members. Americans are, in short, willing to have society assist people who are in distress, but do not believe it has a duty to provide assistance permanently.

Popular attitudes toward public assistance and the welfare state are also affected by traditional American values about the importance of hard work. In keeping with the Protestant ethic, Americans have been inclined to believe that the moral worth of an individual can be judged by how diligently and skillfully he works. A man or woman who exhibits the discipline necessary for a life of sustained and productive toil is likely to be perceived not only as a good citizen but as one upon whom God will bestow His favor. Reinforced by Social Darwinism, the Protestant emphasis on hard work as a mark of an individual's character has led some Americans to object to the welfare state on the ground that it sustains people without requiring them to work. As Richard Hofstadter observed:

> One of the keys to the controversy of our time over the merits or defects of the "welfare state" is the fact that the very idea affronts the traditions of a great many men and women who were raised if not upon the specific tenets of Social Darwinism, at least upon the moral imperatives that it expressed. The growing divorcement of the economic process from considerations that can be used to discipline human character, and, still worse, our increasing philosophical and practical acceptance of that divorcement, is a source of real torment to the stern minority among us for whom the older economic ethic still has a great deal of meaning.[8]

A comparison of the results reported in Tables 9–4 and 9–5 shows how traditional work values have influenced popular atti-

Table 9–4 Attitudes toward government-assisted income maintenance—without work requirement

	General public
1. It has been proposed that instead of relief and welfare payments, the government should guarantee every family a minimum annual income. Do you favor or oppose this idea?	
—Yes, favor	19
—No, oppose	67
—Depends, no opinion	14
2. Some people have said that instead of providing welfare and relief payments, the federal government should guarantee every American family a minimum yearly income of about $3,000. Would you personally favor or oppose such an income guarantee?	
—Yes, favor	30
—No, oppose	61
—Depends, no opinion	9

3. As you may know, there is talk about giving every family an income of at least $3,200 a year, which would be the amount for a family of four. If the family earns less than this, the government would make up the difference. Would you favor or oppose such a plan?

	May 1968	December 1968
—Favor	36	32
—Oppose	58	62
—Other	6	6

Sources: questions 1 and 3, Gallup, cited in Hazel Erskine, "The Polls: Government Role in Welfare," *Public Opinion Quarterly*, 39 (Summer 1975), pp. 268–269, 270; question 2, Opinion Research Corporation/Gallup, 1969, p. 270.

tudes toward welfare measures. When asked whether the federal government should simply give money to needy people, Americans usually say that it should not. However, if the proposal for welfare contains a strong reference to work or its associated values, opinion reverses sharply. By margins that are sometimes very large, Americans support welfare programs that require recipients to perform useful work in order to receive aid.

The long-standing attachment of Americans to the values of self-reliance and individual responsibility is reflected in the character of the American welfare state itself. While some West European nations try to guarantee every citizen "cradle-to-grave" security, America's largest and most widely accepted income maintenance program, Social Security, is justified as a self-supporting program of social insurance. Other important economic pro-

Table 9–5   Attitudes toward government-assisted income maintenance—with work requirement

	General public

1. It is proposed that the federal government set up youth camps—such as the CCC camps of the 1930s—for young men who want to learn a trade and earn a little money by outdoor work. Do you think this is a good idea or a poor idea?

—Good idea	89
—Poor idea	6
—No opinion	5

2. It is suggested that large firms, those employing more than twenty persons, be required to hire a certain small percentage of persons who are now on welfare. In return, the government would pay three-quarters of the salary of these persons for the first year. Companies that hire persons from the welfare roles would give them work available and at the going wage for these jobs. If they refuse to accept this work, they would lose their welfare payments. Would you like to have the government adopt this plan?

—Yes	67
—No	27
—No opinion	6

3. People were asked whether they favored or opposed "the Nixon welfare plan—which would give every family on welfare $1,600 a year with a provision that anyone able to work either enter a job training program or get a job."

—Yes, favor	79
—No, oppose	13
—Depends, no opinion	8

4. Here's how the proposed Nixon welfare program would work for a family of four where the head of the family is willing and able to work. The least a family could receive is $1,600 a year plus food stamps. As the family earned more of their own money, welfare payments would be gradually reduced, and when the family reached $3,920, welfare payments would stop. Does this sound like a good idea or a poor idea?

—Yes, favor	57
—No, oppose	33
—Depends, no opinion	10

Sources: questions 1 and 2, *The Gallup Poll, 1935–1971* (New York: Random House, 1972), pp. 1838, 2312; question 3, Harris for *Life,* 1969, cited in Hazel Erskine, "The Polls: Government Role in Welfare," *Public Opinion Quarterly,* 39 (Summer 1975), p. 270; question 4, Minnesota Poll, 1970, cited in Erskine, "The Polls," pp. 270–271.

grams, including medical care for the aged, unemployment payments, and disability benefits, are likewise organized as insurance programs. The "insurance" label, moreover, is a meaningful one. Those who fail to pay into such programs when they are working—that is, fail, in effect, to purchase insurance—are usually ineligible for benefits. To be sure, other welfare programs exist to provide aid to the destitute, the handicapped, and others unable to purchase social insurance. But the recipients of these forms of welfare cannot claim their benefits as earned entitlements; hence they are frequently stigmatized as idlers or charity cases in a way that recipients of insurance payments are not.

As we have seen, American ideas about self-reliance and independence from government were formed in an era in which most of the population lived in the countryside. The continued vitality of these ideals under the conditions of modern industrial capitalism is a testament to the power of ideas not only to survive under new and unforeseen conditions, but to shape a nation's response to novel problems as they arise. To appreciate fully the nature of this influence, it is necessary to understand how conflicts between capitalism and democracy have influenced the form of the welfare state as it has emerged in the United States.

Capitalism, Democracy, and the Welfare State

The theory of laissez-faire holds that if the private enterprise system is allowed to function according to pure market principles of free exchange and unfettered competition, it will maximize the nation's wealth and provide the highest possible standard of living for all who are willing and able to work. To those who speak for pure capitalism, therefore, any interference with the free exchange of labor, raw materials, or other elements of commerce can only impede the efficient functioning of the economy. This stands, of course, in direct contrast to the views held by the defenders of welfare capitalism, who argue that free enterprise is in many respects inefficient and unfair, and that the state has a positive duty to intervene in the private economy whenever it is necessary to correct serious economic faults.

Opposition to the welfare state was perhaps most pungently expressed by William Graham Sumner, a prominent nineteenth-century sociologist and leading spokesman for the values of both the Protestant ethic and Social Darwinism:

> It would be hard to find a single instance of a direct assault by positive effort upon poverty ... which has not either failed or ... entailed other evils greater than the one it removed. The only two things which really tell on the welfare of man ... are hard work and self-denial (in technical language, labor and capital), and these tell most when they are brought to bear directly upon the effort to earn an honest living, to accumulate capital, and to bring up a family of children to be industrious and self-denying in their turn. I repeat that this is the way to work for the welfare of man on earth.[9]

As a Social Darwinist, Sumner believed that life is a competitive struggle for existence in which the naturally superior triumph while the weak perish. To interfere with this struggle as it occurs within a laissez-faire economy would not only dampen the enthusiasm, the incentives, and the efficiency of the strong, but would also sustain (contrary to the principles of nature) the least productive members of society.

While Sumner, like most Social Darwinists, thus professed to care about the welfare of mankind, he was mainly concerned with the "fit" and the strong. Toward the poor, the unsuccessful, and the "unfit," he was essentially callous. "The fact that a man is here," he once told a congressional committee investigating the problem of economic depression, "is no guarantee that other people shall keep him alive and sustain him."[10]

Modern proponents of pure capitalism still draw on certain Social Darwinist arguments to justify their opposition to the welfare state. For example, they often object that under the welfare state the affluent and successful are heavily taxed for the benefit of the indolent poor and unsuccessful. This, in effect, penalizes those who have worked hard, disciplined themselves, sacrificed, taken risks, and demonstrated character and initiative. They also complain that, in a welfare state, too many people are rewarded for failure rather than success. A system of welfare capitalism offers, on the one side, too few incentives for inventiveness and enterprise; and on the other, too much encouragement for such undesirable traits as sloth and profligacy. Economic resources, credit, and other forms of capital, as well as labor, are thus deflected from their optimal flow into channels that are economically wasteful and morally questionable. Although the proponents of pure capitalism agree that, in some cases, the poor may need special help, they insist that private charity is nearly always preferable to state-run welfare programs. As Andrew Carnegie once wrote, "Thus is the problem of Rich and Poor to be solved. The laws of accumulation will be left free; the laws of distribution free. Individualism will continue, but the millionaire will be but a trustee for the poor; intrusted for a season with a great part of the increased wealth of the community, but administering it for the community far better than it could or would have done for itself."[11]

While arguments against the welfare state develop mainly out of the values associated with laissez-faire capitalism, arguments in favor of the welfare state largely stem from the values of the democratic tradition. Democratic doctrine holds, for example, that since every person must be considered equally worthy and inviolable in certain respects, no one can be allowed to suffer exploitation, mistreatment, or other social and economic injustice. All are entitled to live in dignity and to enjoy a fair share of society's benefits. Although democratic theory does not explicitly require that the community guarantee the prosperity of every individual, it is a natural extension of the democratic concern for human well-being and equality to contend that all individuals should be assured the material necessities for a decent and fulfilling life.

Although the proponents of traditional capitalism argue that the free enterprise system, by virtue of its productivity and the play of the free market, promotes prosperity and human well-being more effectively than any type of welfare state, its critics dispute this claim on several grounds. They question, for example, whether the severe material inequalities associated with capitalism are necessary to the effective operation of the economic system. As the economist F. W. Taussig wrote shortly after the turn of the century: "No stretch of psychological analysis concerning the spur of ambition, the spice of constant emulation, the staleness and flatness of uniformity, can prevail against the universal conviction that the maximum of human happiness is not promoted by great, glaring, permanent, inequality."[12]

Democratic critics of unchecked capitalism also question the claim that private enterprise works best in the absence of government "interference." When the economy is gripped by depression, when inflation or unemployment causes serious economic distress, when business monopolies command exorbitant prices for their goods, when shoddy or unsafe products flood the market, or when natural resources are wastefully exploited, many democratic critics begin to look to government to correct what they regard as serious flaws in the free enterprise system. They are unwilling to stand by and do nothing in the hope that the natural forces of the free market will eventually resolve such difficulties.

Faced with the conflicting perspectives of capitalism and democracy toward the welfare state, liberals and conservatives make choices that reflect their underlying philosophical orientations. Liberals, who stress the need for social benevolence and reforms that benefit the disadvantaged, are more likely to argue that the welfare state is necessary for the full realization of democratic values. Conservatives, because of their dislike of programmatic social change, their skepticism about the effects of reforms motivated by social benevolence, and their greater tolerance of economic inequalities, are inclined to oppose the welfare state. Adherence to traditional capitalist principles, they maintain, offers the best hope for advancing human happiness.

In order to test the arguments we have developed, we constructed an index of support for welfare state principles and programs. This measure contains questions about government-sponsored medical care, aid to the needy, public housing for the destitute, school lunch programs, and the like. Table 9–6 shows that support for such welfare programs is, as we expected, much stronger among those scoring high on democratic values than among those scoring low. Among our sample of opinion leaders, for example, 80 percent of those scoring high on democracy, compared to 17 percent of those scoring low on democracy, exhibit strong support for welfare state programs. Respondents who strongly support traditional capitalist values (property, unlimited profit, competition, and so forth) are, as expected, far more likely to oppose welfare state programs than are people who are more skeptical about capitalist values. As one would expect, support for welfare state programs is far stronger

Table 9-6 Sources of public support for welfare state programs and principles (percentage who score high on welfare state scale)[a]

	Democratic values		Capitalist values		Ideology[b]		Change and reform		Social benevolence	
	High	Low	High	Low	Lib.	Con.	Favor	Oppose	High	Low
General public	56	12	6	65	66	9	56	19	59	17
	(N = 300)	(N = 306)	(N = 310)	(N = 297)	(N = 107)	(N = 197)	(N = 343)	(N = 329)	(N = 280)	(N = 318)
Opinion leaders	80	17	28	95	90	19	90	28	85	32
	(N = 629)	(N = 48)	(N = 249)	(N = 326)	(N = 427)	(N = 138)	(N = 492)	(N = 161)	(N = 463)	(N = 138)

Source: Opinions and Values Survey, 1975–77.

a. Cell entries are percentage who score in the upper third of the mass distribution of the welfare state measure.

b. Ideology is measured by means of self-designation and includes both liberals and strong liberals. Among the general public, only respondents scoring in the upper half of the political sophistication measure are included in the comparison between self-identified liberals and conservatives. (See Chapter 7 for a discussion of the measurement of ideology.)

among self-identified liberals and among those emphasizing change, social reform, and social benevolence than it is among people who describe themselves as conservatives, who emphasize the need for social order and stability, or who score low on our measure of social benevolence. While the relationships among these several attitude measures are usually stronger for elites than for members of the general public, they remain substantial in both samples.

Tables 9–7 and 9–8 provide further evidence that the various principles and programs of the welfare state draw their greatest support from people who are most strongly committed to democratic values, and experience their greatest opposition from those who most strongly favor capitalist values. For example, Table 9–8 demonstrates that most strong democrats favor state support for medical care, public housing, college scholarships, and school lunches for needy children. The strongly procapitalist respondents are far less enthusiastic about, or even opposed to, such measures.

As these data confirm, the welfare state, like laissez-faire capitalism, remains deeply controversial. Not only have some social welfare programs failed to achieve their objectives, but huge federal budget deficits, the threat of insolvency in the Social Security system, and an erratic economy have led conservatives and the advocates of laissez-faire to renew their long-standing claims that the modern mixed economy is inherently inefficient and unworkable. The election of Ronald Reagan to the presidency intensified this controversy. As the most frankly conservative chief executive in more than half a century, he launched a far-reaching effort to scale back the social welfare functions of the federal government and to reinstate the traditional values of self-help and laissez-faire capitalism. While liberals and the defenders of welfare capitalism have claimed that all Americans have a right to economic security and the essentials of a decent life, the Reagan administration cut into almost every program intended to meet this need. In the words of David Stockman, Reagan's chief budget officer: "The idea that's been established over the past ten years that almost every service that someone might need in life ought to be provided, financed by the government as a matter of basic right, is wrong . . . we reject that notion."[13]

Table 9–7 Attitudes toward welfare state principles among strong democrats and strong capitalists[a]

	General public		Influentials	
	Strong dem. (N = 159)	Strong cap. (N = 143)	Strong dem. (N = 337)	Strong cap. (N = 42)
1. In general, government grows bigger as it provides more services. If you had to choose, which would you rather see?				
—More government services	37	8	41	2
—Smaller goverment	37	73	27	95
—Decline to choose	26	19	32	3
2. In order to improve their conditions, the poor should:				
—receive special government help	45	7	62	5
—help themselves	24	80	5	71
—Decline to choose	32	13	33	24
3. If some people are born poor, the community should:				
—help them to become equal with others	68	40	73	26
—simply accept the fact that not everyone can make it	7	31	4	41
—Decline to choose	25	30	23	33
4. In trying to help needy people to improve their lives, the government has:				
—not done enough	61	8	71	9
—done more than it should already	5	69	1	71
—Decline to choose	34	24	29	19
5. Money spent by the government to relieve poverty is:				
—a worthwhile investment	56	20	66	21
—mostly a waste	22	59	9	52
—Decline to choose	22	21	25	26
6. Who should bear the main responsibility for taking care of our senior citizens?				
—The community	61	18	52	7
—The elderly themselves and their families	15	62	16	76
—Decline to choose	24	20	32	17

Table 9–7   (continued)

	General public		Influentials	
	Strong dem. (N = 159)	Strong cap. (N = 143)	Strong dem. (N = 337)	Strong cap. (N = 42)
7. In matters of jobs and standards of living, the government should:				
—see to it that everyone has a job and a decent standard of living	62	20	65	7
—let each person get ahead on his own	11	57	2	64
—Decline to choose	27	22	33	29

Source: Opinions and Values of Americans survey, 1975–77.

a. "Strong democrats" are those scoring high on our measure of democratic values and low on the capitalism scale. "Strong capitalists" exhibit the reverse pattern.

Given the existence of such sharply articulated divisions among political elites on issues relating to the welfare state, one would expect to find similar divisions among the more politically attentive members of the general public. Figure 9–1 confirms this expectation. Among respondents who emphasize the need for change and reform, increases in political awareness lead to greater support for the welfare state. But among those who stress the need for social order and stability, greater awareness leads to greater resistance to the welfare state. This, of course, confirms our earlier observation that when political elites are deeply divided over public policies, the more politically sophisticated members of the general public tend to be deeply divided as well.

Our discussion of the welfare state has illustrated several of the principal themes of this book.

1. The values of capitalism and democracy, as the principal components of the nation's political culture, exert a major influence on the course of American politics by making some ideas and programs seem attractive and legitimate, and others seem objectionable and undesirable. As the historical evidence on the growth of the welfare state in the United States attests, the nation's traditions of self-reliance, economic individualism, and hos-

Table 9-8   Attitudes toward specific welfare state programs among strong democrats and strong capitalists[a]

	General public		Influentials	
	Strong dem. (N = 159)	Strong cap. (N = 143)	Strong dem. (N = 337)	Strong cap. (N = 42)
1. Providing medical care for everyone at public expense would:				
—greatly improve the health of the nation	66	14	68	7
—reduce the general quality of medical care	9	59	5	71
—Decline to choose	25	27	27	21
2. If some people can't afford good housing:				
—the government should provide it	35	1	45	7
—they should work harder and save, until they can afford it	15	82	4	71
—Decline to choose	50	17	51	22
3. Spending tax money to provide a college education for those who can't afford it is a:				
—good idea	80	34	83	26
—bad idea	2	34	1	38
—Decline to choose	18	32	16	36
4. By providing a good lunch for underprivileged children in schools, the government:				
—is only doing what is right	82	55	91	55
—starts children off with the bad habit of taking government handouts	2	29	1	19
—Decline to choose	16	16	9	26

Source: Opinions and Values of Americans survey, 1975–77.

a. "Strong democrats" are those scoring high on our measure of democratic values and low on the capitalism scale. "Strong capitalists" exhibit the reverse pattern.

tility toward government are generally inhospitable to the idea of the welfare state and appear to have slowed its rise. The influence of these traditions is also reflected in our opinion data, which show that most Americans still deny fundamental state responsi-

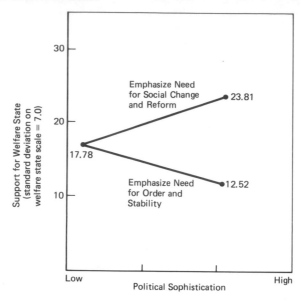

Figure 9-1   Effect of political sophistication and attitudes toward change
on support for the welfare state. The lines in the figure represent slopes derived from a regression analysis that controlled for
respondents' age, income, sex, and place of residence. The data
are calculated from the responses of our national general population sample. *Sources:* Opinions and Values of Americans survey, 1975–77.

bility for individual welfare; although they favor many specific
welfare programs, they exhibit greatest support for those programs that can be made at least minimally consistent with the
traditional values of individualism.

2. The values of the American ethos frequently conflict with
each other and lead to opposing policy prescriptions. Thus we
have observed that the capitalist and democratic traditions offer
conflicting perspectives on the welfare state—the former obviously hostile to it, the latter receptive. Public opinion data confirm our conclusion that citizens who are most strongly attached
to the values of the capitalist tradition are most opposed to welfare programs, while those most strongly committed to democratic values tend to favor them.

3. Elites play a vital role in organizing and articulating the
conflicting tendencies of the two traditions, and help to shape the

attitudes of the general public toward these values. As we have shown, the sharply opposing positions on welfare capitalism held by the nation's political elites are reflected in deep ideological cleavages on welfare state issues among the more politically so phisticated members of the general public.

Influence of the Ethos on Public Opinion and Public Policy

In the late eighteenth and early nineteenth centuries the United States was celebrated among the nations of the world for its wide-spread distribution of wealth and the relative affluence of its citizens. Today, however, several modern nations—for example, Sweden, Denmark, Israel, Japan—appear to have achieved a broader distribution of social and economic benefits than the United States. They have done this by adopting a more extensive set of welfare state programs than the United States has so far been willing to enact.

One should not conclude from this, however, that Americans are no longer as strongly committed as they once were to the ideals of equality and individual well-being; if anything, their belief in equality appears to have grown stronger. If, relative to certain other nations, the United States seems less effective than it once was in assuring the well-being of every individual, the reason can be traced to changing economic conditions rather than to changing values. As long as the primary obstacles to material progress and widespread prosperity in Europe and elsewhere were the vestiges of mercantilism, aristocratic rule, and traditional restrictions on social mobility, the American commitment to individual freedom, economic achievement, and small government led to successes unmatched by other nations. But in adhering to these same values under the conditions of industrial capitalism, the United States, though still remarkably enterprising and prosperous, has lost its former reputation as a nation preeminent in its ability to reduce poverty and provide a decent standard of living for all.

Americans have also continued to espouse libertarian values, but with more favorable results. From its inception the United States has been distinguished by its commitment to individual rights, such as freedom of speech, press, and assembly, the right of privacy, and due process of law. In remaining loyal to *these* values, America has retained its preeminence as one of the freest nations in the world.

If, as these observations suggest, a nation's traditional values exert a major influence on the kinds of public policies its people will favor, the question arises: how, exactly, do values affect public opinion? The empirical data suggest some answers. Consider, for example, the matter of social welfare. Americans, as we have seen, are by no means unconcerned about the needs of the poor: when they are asked in neutral language whether the government ought to help people in distress, they tend to answer in the affirmative. But when they are reminded of ideological considerations relating to individualism and self-reliance, their support for such measures declines markedly. Here one can clearly see the influence that values have on expressions of support for particular social policies.

One may object, of course, that if Americans really wanted to aid the poor, they would disregard ideological considerations and simply help them. But this objection overlooks the critical question of how people decide on acceptable means to a desirable end. In a country with a strong tradition of individualism and self-reliance, many people will conclude that the poor can best be helped by encouraging them to help themselves.

For some people, no doubt, the individualistic ethic merely serves as a rationalization for doing what they would like to do anyway. Yet many Americans are genuinely uncertain about how far a society ought to go in supporting social welfare programs. On the one hand, they may want to be generous and humane; yet they also know that many social welfare programs are costly, expand the size of government, and require sacrifices by taxpayers. Some also fear that such programs may harm people by making them more dependent. Faced with such dilemmas, many Americans look for guidance to the values of the ethos, some of which, as we have seen, are inhospitable to the welfare state.

Because they have the power to shape public opinions, the values of the ethos are frequently invoked by politicians to promote the adoption of policies they favor. Indeed, the conduct of politics often consists of conscious efforts by elites to mobilize public opinion on behalf of particular policies by linking those policies to such values as private property, small government, freedom, or equality. For example, a proposal to deregulate business will have greater appeal if it is described as "getting government off the backs of the American people" than if it is described as a policy to give big business a freer hand. By the same token, a proposed constitutional amendment to outlaw discrimination against women will seem more attractive if it is described as an "Equal Rights Amendment" rather than as a "Women's Liberation Amendment."

Any effort to explain how political values influence public opinion must recognize that public opinion is often diffuse and labile. Many Americans give little sustained thought to political affairs, and, as a result, their expressed attitudes are often influenced by whether a question invokes a traditional value. We have seen, for example, that Americans are more likely to oppose racial discrimination if they have been reminded that such discrimination is at variance with the values of the ethos.

Appeals to cherished values can affect not only public opinion but the political process itself. The record of the Reagan administration offers a case in point. Pursuing conservative goals, Reagan focused on an effort to scale back the social welfare functions of the federal government. He won congressional approval for major cuts in the food stamp program, medical care for the needy, school lunch programs for underprivileged children, public housing, and legal services for the poor—in short, nearly the full range of federal programs aimed at guaranteeing a minimum standard of living to the needy. He also reduced government regulation of business, lowered taxes (especially for business), and scaled back the federal government's role in protecting the environment and promoting safe working conditions in industry.

In proposing—and to some extent accomplishing—these changes in policy, Reagan appealed to some of the most honored values in the American ethos, including the country's traditional hostility toward government, its emphasis on self-reliance, competition, and individualism, and its belief in free enterprise capitalism. Reagan's political victories, to be sure, were not won simply because he invoked these values. The values, however, lent an aura of legitimacy and high purpose to a program that might otherwise have failed to inspire much enthusiasm and that seemed, to many of its critics, insensitive to human suffering.

The Reagan administration also sought to reverse many of the egalitarian policies of its predecessors. In this sphere, it had a record of mixed success that reveals a great deal. On the issues of affirmative action and busing to achieve racial integration in the schools, it sharply reversed existing federal policy—appealing in the former case to the traditional values of individual merit, equal opportunity, and fair competition, and in the latter to the right of neighborhoods to local control over their schools. Both affirmative action and busing were also deplored as forms of reverse discrimination. Yet the Reagan administration was much more cautious on issues closer to the traditional meaning of equal rights and opportunities. Reagan appointed a scattering of blacks, women, and other minorities to positions of responsibility and, in an important symbolic gesture, appointed the first woman justice to the Supreme Court. And although at first reluctant to do so, Reagan endorsed the extension of the Voting Rights Act and expressed support for a new fair housing law.

In a striking exception to the tendency to profess support for the more traditional norms of equal rights, the Reagan administration tried to restore federal tax exemptions to schools that openly refused admission to blacks. The public outcry against this decision, however, was so strong that the administration was soon forced to retreat. Clearly the American ethos no longer offers legitimate grounds for open discrimination against racial minorities, and the violation of this consensus is likely to be politically costly.

Concluding Observations

In the course of this book we have seen that the ideals to which the nation's Founders appealed—values such as freedom, equality, individualism, and private property—are, for the most part, still prized by Americans and their opinion leaders. Yet, despite this continuity, dramatic changes have occurred in the norms through which these general values have been translated into everyday practice. Suffrage, for example, once largely limited to white males who owned property, has been extended to include all adults, of both genders and of every race and religion; the right to speak, publish, and worship freely has been greatly expanded and strengthened; and the notion of equality has been extended to encompass women, blacks, and other dispossessed minorities as well as the poor.

Changes in the norms of capitalism have been equally dramatic: Americans have increasingly favored a form of capitalism in which the economy is subject to government regulation. Numerous laws now cover such matters as industrial and banking practice, labor relations, the hiring of minorities, the safety of manufactured products, protection against environmental damage, minimum wages and pension programs, and in some cases even the prices a business enterprise may charge for its products or services. The laissez-faire economy of the nineteenth century, in short, has given way to a more regulated economy in which business and government share responsibility for many key economic decisions.

These and related changes have transformed the federal government from an institution primarily concerned with domestic order and national security into a complex network of agencies that seeks to regulate the economy, protect the rights of the citizenry, and provide assistance to those unable to care for themselves. These changes in the practices of capitalism and democracy, however, have not developed in a steady stream. Rather, the nation has seemed, at least in this century, to swing from periods in which the values of capitalism are emphasized to other periods in which democratic values are stressed. The 1920s and 1950s, for example, were decades in which business values were dominant and matters of social and political equality excited relatively little public interest. During the decade of the 1930s, by contrast, unrestrained capitalism was on the defensive as Franklin D. Roosevelt and the New Deal pressed for greater popular control of the economy and a more equal distribution of the nation's wealth. Capitalism was again on the defensive in the 1960s and early 1970s, as public concern for such democratic values as the right of dissent, due process, and racial and sexual equality assumed a dominant position in the nation's politics. The early 1980s seemed to herald another swing toward capitalism, with the conservative administration of Ronald Reagan claiming to have received a popular mandate to revive individual initiative, reduce government regulation of the economy, reinforce the "work ethic," and promote business productivity by cutting taxes.[14]

These swings in the national mood reflect a strain that lies at the heart of the American ethos. While most Americans favor a competitive, private economy in which the most enterprising and industrious individuals receive the greatest income, they also want a democratic society in which everyone can earn a decent living and has an equal chance to realize his or her full human potential. Since these two sets of values often conflict with each other in practice, the mood of the country may shift from one era to another as the values of one tradition or the other predominate. In one period the nation may be shocked by society's failure to fulfill the democratic promise of American life for the poor, the unemployed, and other disadvantaged groups, and may accelerate its efforts to rectify this failure; in the next period, however, many people may complain that the nation has gone too far in pursuing these goals and may advocate a shift back toward a more conservative, laissez-faire, and procapitalist course.

There appears, however, to be a marked asymmetry in these swings: movements in the procapitalist direction have increasingly turned out to be little more than holding actions, efforts that have only temporarily halted a long-term trend toward government efforts to assist the needy, broader individual liberties, and greater popular control over the economy. Thus the gains made by the Coolidge, Hoover, and Eisenhower administrations on behalf of free enterprise capitalism in the 1920s and 1950s were largely undone by the liberal Democratic administrations that followed. National swings in the prodemocratic direction, by contrast, have tended to produce enduring changes in American life. Thus the Nixon and Ford administrations, despite their conservatism, showed little inclination to return to the policies of racial segregation or overt sexual discrimination that had prevailed in earlier decades. Nor, on balance, did they slow the movement toward social and economic equality implicit in the welfare state. And even though the Reagan administration succeeded in reversing certain policies relating to civil rights and the welfare state, it is doubtful that these reversals can be made permanent. By Reagan's third year in office, there were signs that the push to trim welfare spending and cut back federal regulation of the economy had run its course and that the pendulum had begun to swing back. The administration, for example, was unable to win congressional approval for further cutbacks in domestic spending, and was even being forced to accept the partial restoration of funds in some welfare programs.

The long-term result of this asymmetry is that norms relating to such democratic values as freedom of expression, due process of law, and equality of rights and opportunities are now more firmly entrenched and substantially broader in scope than they were in the nineteenth century, while the norms relating to the values of capitalism are more qualified and circumscribed. This is not to say that capitalist values have lost their standing in American public opinion; we have seen that this is clearly not the case. But in almost every sphere of economic enterprise, the regulation of business has grown far more extensive than it was in the past.

What this suggests is that the democratic tradition is more securely rooted in the nation's political culture than is the capitalist tradition. As further evidence for this claim, we might cite long-term changes in the arguments by which each tradition attempts to justify itself to the public. For example, the industrial tycoons of an earlier era claimed a virtually unlimited right to do whatever they wished with *their* property, *their* factories, *their* capital— and even *their* employees. As entrepreneurs, they declared their right to pursue profit in whatever manner they wished, and to force weaker competitors into submission. The public's needs or wishes were scarcely considered. The capitalists of that day felt no need to appeal to values outside the capitalist tradition itself; private enterprise and the associated values of property, competition, initiative, and hard work were their own justification. Today, however, businessmen express markedly different attitudes. Although they still claim to possess certain entrepreneurial rights, they no longer thunder about them as they once did. Indeed, the public defense of capitalism, for example, boasts that the system aims above all to serve the interests of the people. Businessmen condemn government regulation less because it interferes with their inalienable right to use their property as they wish, than because it allegedly leads to higher prices and wasteful inefficiencies that (they contend) the public ultimately pays for. In opposing high taxes on business profits, they no longer rest their argument solely on the claim that such taxes are unjust, but contend that low taxes will foster individual initiative and promote capital formation, thus leading to greater prosperity for all.

Some of these arguments, to be sure, are not new. The emphasis now given them, however, is far greater than in the past and testifies to the inability of modern capitalists to present themselves in the heroic postures so often assumed by their predecessors. Their reliance on democratic rhetoric reflects a realistic appreciation of the kinds of appeals that are most likely to succeed in the political arena. The proponents of democracy, on the other hand, rarely if ever appeal to values outside the democratic tradition itself. They assume that freedom, equality, and popular sovereignty are, in America at least, recognized as values that require no higher justification.

As a further indication of the stronger and more secure standing of the democratic tradition, one might compare the range of public debate over issues relating to capitalism with the range of debate over issues relating to democracy. With respect to capitalism, one can, of course, readily find respected public figures who advocate a return to laissez-faire. Elsewhere among the elites one encounters numerous people who, though accepting capitalism as an economic system, are highly critical of many of its features and want to modify them. Here and there among the elites, one can even find strong liberals and socialists who favor the public ownership of large industries, a greater role for workers in managing factories, and a major redistribution of wealth. Thus economic debate in the United States, though mainly occurring within relatively limited boundaries, ranges from support for laissez-faire to support for welfare capitalism or even a mixed economy with marked socialist features.

The range of elite debates over democracy is distinctly narrower. Except for a handful of political extremists, one finds few if any opinion leaders who openly oppose such values as freedom or equality or who advocate any form of authoritarian rule. No political parties of any standing in the United States advocate a one-party system, the abolition of elections, a government-controlled press, or the prohibition of dissent. Conservatives and liberals differ over the degree to which democratic values ought to be extended, but neither camp challenges the definitive features of democracy itself.

Data from our public opinion surveys offer further evidence on the relative standing of the two traditions. Table 9–9 shows that our opinion leaders—the principal repositories of the ethos—score higher than the general public in their support for democratic values, but not for capitalist values. Approximately 74 percent of the opinion leaders in our Opinions and Values study registered high scores on the scale of democratic values, compared with only 33 percent of the general population. On the capitalism scale, however, the scores of the opinion leaders were no higher than those of the general public. The same pattern of elite-mass differences turns up in our Civil Liberties study.

Is it possible, however, that the summaries of elite opinion reported in Table 9–9 conceal important differences among various elite subgroups? Table 9–10 enables us to evaluate this question by disaggregating our Civil Liberties elite samples into seven subgroups. Inspection of the data makes it plain that although elite subgroups vary considerably in their attitudes toward capitalism and democracy, certain uniformities exist. All seven elite subgroups score substantially ahead of the general public in support for both democratic values and the values of the welfare state. By contrast, differences between elite and mass support for capital-

Table 9–9 Support for capitalism, democracy, and the welfare state among elites and the general public[a]

	Democracy	Capitalism	Welfare state
General public[b] (N = 938)	33	32	34
Opinion leaders[b] (N = 845)	74	30	69
General public[c] (N = 1,019)	33	30	37
Community influentials[c] (N = 856)	65	34	53

a. Cell entries are percentage of each sample scoring high on each scale.
b. Opinions and Values of Americans survey, 1975–77.
c. Civil Liberties study, 1978–79.

Table 9–10 Support for capitalism, democracy and the welfare state among elite subgroups[a]

	General public (N = 1,019)	Lawyers and judges (N = 255)	Clergy (N = 61)	College professors and administrators (N = 65)	Editors and reporters (N = 58)	Elementary teachers and administrators (N = 107)	Officers of private organizations (N = 49)	Public officials (N = 47)	Total community influentials (N = 856)
Democracy	33	85	51	83	84	54	63	47	65
Capitalism	30	34	34	23	31	24	41	32	34
Welfare capitalism	37	50	60	62	52	50	54	53	53

Source: Civil Liberties study, 1978–79.

a. Cell entries are percentage of each subgroup scoring high on each scale.

ism are small and inconsequential. The same tendencies show up among the five elite subgroups in the OVS study. Among a broad range of politically active and influential Americans, then, the values of democracy and the welfare state enjoy greater support (at least by comparison with the attitudes of the mass public) than do capitalist values. Insofar as elites influence the course of the nation's development, they are likely to guide it toward a fuller realization of democratic values and—very likely—a more fully developed welfare state.

Other evidence suggggesting the stronger relative standing of democratic values is reported in Table 9–11, where we see that young people are substantially more likely than their elders to register strong support for both democracy and the welfare state. They are also much less likely than their elders to support capitalism in its laissez-faire form. If the attitudes expressed by young people persist as they advance in age, the gradual replacement of older population cohorts by younger ones will in the future produce higher overall levels of support for democracy and the welfare state, and diminished support for laissez-faire capitalism.

But will the attitudes of the young in fact persist as they advance in age? This question, though vital for assessing future trends in support for capitalism and democracy, is difficult to answer. The crux of the problem is that one cannot be certain whether the differences in attitudes among age groups represent generational differences or life-cycle differences. In other words, do the differences between young and old represent differences in the prevailing values at the time they came to political maturity (and which they presumably carry forward into succeeding years), or do they represent changes that develop as individuals

Table 9–11   Effect of age on attitudes toward capitalism, democracy, and the welfare state[a]

	Ages 18–30 (N = 217)	Ages 31–45 (N = 284)	Ages 46–65 (N = 278)	Ages 66+ (N = 153)
Democracy	57	38	21	11
Capitalism	16	30	39	43
Welfare state	47	32	32	26

Source: Opinions and Values of Americans survey, 1975–77.

a. Cell entries are percentage of each age group scoring high on each scale.

advance in age? Today's generation of older Americans, for example, attained political maturity during an era in which democratic values were less widely accepted than they are now, when the welfare state activities of the federal government were minimal or just beginning, and when private enterprise was still largely unfettered by regulatory laws. Today's generation of young adults, by contrast, attained political maturity in the aftermath of the civil rights and civil liberties activism of the 1960s, in a period in which laissez-faire capitalism had been superseded by the mixed economy of the modern welfare state. If (in keeping with the generational explanation) we assume that both young and old have been most deeply influenced by the values prevalent in their formative years, and subsequently reinforced by their age cohorts, the attitudes of the young would be bound to differ from those of their elders in ways consistent with the findings in Table 9–11. However, the findings reported in Table 9–11 are also consistent with a life-cycle explanation, which would argue that people become less liberal and less democratic as they grow older.

The two explanations, then, are not mutually exclusive: both are plausible and can be defended, and both appear to be at work. From the available evidence, we have reason to believe that the attitudes learned by the younger generation toward democracy, capitalism, and the welfare state will in some measure be carried forward into the next decades—even if they are somewhat attenuated by life-cycle changes. Studies of public attitudes toward freedom of speech and racial equality, as we noted in earlier chapters, have documented a dramatic rise in popular support for these values over the past two decades. These studies, moreover, have attributed a substantial part of this rise to generational replacement—that is, to the dying out of an older, less well educated, less tolerant generation and its replacement by younger, better educated, and more tolerant generations.[15]

Unfortunately, no comparable studies of age-related differences have been conducted on attitudes toward capitalism or the welfare state. It seems highly unlikely, however, that Americans will in the foreseeable future favor a return to laissez-faire capitalism or countenance the dismantling of the welfare state. Our data on elite opinions offer little evidence that political leaders would be sympathetic to a sustained conservative shift of this kind. Moreover, to judge from our findings, most Americans have become thoroughly accustomed to, and dependent on, the services of the welfare state—including unemployment insurance, government controls of pollution, consumer protection services, old age and health insurance, federal savings insurance, and dozens of other such regulations and services. Since elderly citizens benefit greatly from many of these programs, there will be little incentive for Americans to turn against "welfare capitalism" as they advance in age.

In sum, our data provide reasons to expect that, ceteris paribus, the process of generational replacement will lead to higher levels of popular support for democratic values, as well as continued and possibly greater support for some form of the welfare state.

The popularity of democratic values in the nation's political culture, which we have now documented in a variety of ways, takes on particular significance in light of the potential conflicts between the values of capitalism and democracy. That is, the high standing of democratic values suggests that any conflicts that arise are likely to be resolved in ways that are more favorable to democracy than to capitalism. But what are the chances that serious conflicts *will* arise between capitalism and democracy in the future? And if such conflicts do develop, what kinds of modifications in American institutions are likely to result?

In regard to the first question, the intensity of conflict between the two traditions in the past has depended mainly on the performance of capitalist institutions. When capitalism has been associated with a relatively broad distribution of economic opportunities and a fair measure of social equality—as it was in the early nineteenth century—conflict between the two traditions, while by no means absent, has not been severe. At times, however, capitalism has produced—or has seemed to produce—dramatic inequalities between the rich and the poor, attempts by the business classes to dominate the government, and a narrow range of opportunities for debtors, workers, small farmers, and the unpropertied classes generally. Under such circumstances, democratic values have been invoked in order to justify reforms of the free enterprise system.

If the American private enterprise system performs fitfully in the future, exacerbating rather than reducing the serious social and economic inequalities that still exist, further efforts are likely to be made to modify capitalism, even at the expense of violating some of its most cherished values. And even if capitalism performs fairly well, providing a comfortable standard of living for most people but failing to provide adequately for the disadvantaged, pressure for economic reform would, in our view, still exist. In keeping with the growing strength of the egalitarian elements of the ethos, Americans are increasingly reluctant to ignore completely the needs of the poor, or to dismiss some members of society as simply not worth worrying about. As we saw earlier in the book, 78 percent of the public affirm that "all people are equally worthy and deserve equal treatment," while only 7 percent say that the poor "don't have much to contribute to society."

We are not suggesting, of course, that the favored economic classes are about to become crusaders for economic justice and a redistribution of wealth. That is an unlikely prospect. Our belief, rather, rests on what we have discovered about the attitudes of opinion leaders. With the exception of conservative elites, virtually every elite subgroup we have been able to study exhibits a strong commitment to the values of democracy and the welfare state but tempers its support for the values of capitalism by deep-seated skepticism about what private enterprise can accomplish when left unregulated by government.[16] Many members of the opinion elite, moreover, regard the existence of a sizable underclass of impoverished citizens as a standing indictment of the economic system that has produced them. When, as a result of normal swings in the nation's mood and voting tendencies, some of these liberally inclined elites come to power, they will attempt to mobilize public support for a renewed assault on the poverty and cultural deprivation that the private enterprise system has been unable to eliminate on its own. In view of the widespread support for egalitarian values that we have been able to document in this study, there is reason to believe that such appeals for economic reform will meet with a fair degree of success.

Having argued that the future of capitalism depends on its effectiveness in producing and equitably distributing the goods and services Americans expect, we should nevertheless add that it is difficult to know exactly how well capitalism must perform in order to forestall major efforts at economic reform. Judgments about "how good is good enough" are obviously subjective—and liberals and conservatives, laissez-faire capitalists and socialists, will reach different conclusions when making those judgments. Objective indicators of the performance of capitalism—indexes of inflation, unemployment, levels of productivity, income distribution, and the nation's standard of living—are bound to affect judgments about the necessity for economic reform. But in the end, the decision about how well capitalism must perform in order to forestall significant changes will be a political judgment, with all the uncertainty that such assessments entail.

If the performance of the capitalist economy appears to falter, and if efforts are therefore made to reform it, what kinds of changes are likely to result? One probability is that even if capitalism falters badly, Americans will be reluctant to press for the abolition or wholesale transformation of the economic system. As we have seen, most Americans continue to support the basic values of the capitalist economy and strongly reject recommendations for change along socialist lines, such as wage leveling or public ownership of the means of production. A second point, easy to overlook, is that given the nation's political traditions, the impulse to economic reform might initially result in pressures for "more capitalism" rather than less. As the Reagan administration has demonstrated, one approach to a faltering economy is to prescribe a return to laissez-faire. For some, this prescription is an appealing one: it preserves the basic features of capitalism, diminishes the size of government, promises to lower taxes, and reduces government intervention in economic affairs.

If, however, the free enterprise system fails to deliver on the promises made by its proponents, new efforts to modify it seem inevitable. These efforts are likely to take the form of renewed pressure for some version of welfare capitalism—a system in which the basic institutions of private enterprise are retained, but in which government plays a major role in regulating the economy and redirecting resources to individuals, groups, and even business enterprises in need of help. We say this because our data make it plain that Americans favor most of the specific programs associated with welfare capitalism. Study after study has shown that while Americans continue to express distaste for big government, they nonetheless repeatedly call upon government to alleviate the problems that arise when capitalism is left to operate on its own. This attitude, as we have seen, is especially prevalent among liberal and democratic elites. These opinion leaders, though for the most part committed to fundamental capitalist values, believe that government has a moral responsibility to correct whatever inequities and abuses arise from the workings of the private enterprise system.

Popular expectations that government will intervene to correct social and economic injustice and to ensure at least minimum standards of personal well-being have continued to rise among the American public for the past half-century. Over time, they are bound to rise even further in response to the play of democratic forces and the competition among elites for public favor. As the size of the attentive, educated, and democratically oriented public expands and becomes increasingly articulate in its demands, a freely elected government cannot help but respond. Notwithstanding the efforts of conservative administrations to scale back the welfare state and to reinstate laissez-faire, pressure from both elites and the general population for the reestablishment or expansion of government services to which several generations have become habituated is likely to prove irresistible. Our argument, then, can be summarized as follows: conflicts between capitalism and democracy remain a recurrent feature of American life; when these conflicts surface, they are likely to be resolved in ways predominantly favorable to the democratic tradition; and some type of welfare capitalism is the institutional form this resolution is likely to take.

Appendixes

Notes

Index

Appendix I
Empirical Methods

Since the data reported in this study have been drawn mainly from our Opinions and Values of Americans (OVS) and Civil Liberties studies, a brief comment should be made about the question format employed in these studies. Each item (as will be evident in some of the tables) is essentially a sentence-completion question. Each was designed to be short, concise, and easy to read. In each case the respondent was offered two alternative answers, devised so as to encompass the fundamental differences of opinion that prevail on that particular issue. Wherever possible, the terms employ language that is moderate and neutral in flavor, free of hyperbole, slogans, clichés, rhetoric, or inflammatory phrases that are likely to invite heedless rather than carefully deliberated responses. The format is designed to place the respondent under mild stress in that he is asked to choose between alternatives that are, *mutatis mutandis,* equally plausible, but that exact a "cost" for choosing one alternative and rejecting the other. Respondents who do not find either response acceptable can choose to answer "Neither" or "Undecided." This item format, we believe, requires respondents to weigh carefully devised alternatives and to deliberate before responding. It has the additional advantage of avoiding certain problems of response style, such as acquiescent response set—the tendency of some respondents to agree or disagree with statements regardless of their content. The items, we might add, are simple to score and easy to cumulate for purpose of scale construction.

A further word should be said about the three measures that bear the principal burden of the argument in this book. The capitalism and democracy scales are fairly lengthy (28 and 44 items, respectively), and the same is true for the political sophistication index (23 items). Tests for internal consistency on each of these measures have shown them to be highly reliable, a result, in part, of their length and of the care with which their items were selected.*

The items in the capitalism and democracy scales were designed to survey a variety of controversial issues relating to the two traditions. The capitalism scale, for example, includes questions about the use of property, the merits of competition, the profit system, the fairness of the private enterprise system, the efficacy of hard work, the rights of business and labor, and the levels of wages and salaries to which labor and management are entitled. The democracy measure assesses support for the rights and liberties of various groups, attitudes toward equal rights and other aspects of equality, and sympathy for the rights of privacy and due process of law, as well as other values listed at the beginning of Chapter 1. A complete list of the items in the capitalism and democracy scales is included in Appendix II.

The political sophistication measure is a linear combination of three variables—a 13-item political knowledge index, a 9-item political participation index, and a six-level education variable. A factor analysis performed on these three measures was used to extract a principal factor accounting for 61 percent of their variance. The factor scores obtained from this procedure, which were approximately equal, were used to combine the three variables into a single political sophistication measure.† The items included in this measure are also listed in Appendix II.

The OVS survey, a mailback instrument, was distributed to a national area probability sample of some 1,500 Americans and to several samples of opinion leaders. The cross-section sample con-

---

* For an analysis of the reliability of these measures among elites and within various segments of the general public, see Dennis Chong, Herbert McClosky, and John Zaller, "Patterns of Support for Capitalism and Democracy in the United States," *British Journal of Political Science,* 13 (October 1983), pp. 401–440.

† Note that education is used as one measure of political awareness rather than as a measure of social status. Where appropriate, we introduce a separate control for social status.

sisted of respondents who had participated in personal interviews conducted by the Gallup Organization. The rate of return of usable questionnaires, after four follow-ups, was approximately two-thirds for the elite samples and 61 percent for the general public.

Our book also draws data from a large-scale national survey conducted in 1978–79. Although primarily concerned with orientations toward civil liberties, this survey, like the OVS survey, contained some 340 self-administered items and various other questions covering a broad range of political and social-attitude clusters, cognitive capacities, and psychological dispositions. The usual battery of demographic questions was, of course, also included. The items were cast in the same format as those in the OVS survey. Return rates for both the elite and the mass samples were approximately two-thirds.

Like most surveys, the OVS and Civil Liberties studies tended to overrepresent some groups in the population and to underrepresent others. Respondents to these surveys were, on average, better educated, more affluent, and older than the American population as a whole. Whites also had substantially higher response rates than blacks. Although these differences in response rates have not, in our judgment, affected any of the substantive conclusions we report in this book, the issue bears discussion.

Consider first our hypothesis, developed most fully in Chapter 8, that better informed (and usually better educated) respondents tend to support the clear norms of the political culture more strongly than do the less informed and less educated. In order to conduct a test of this hypothesis, one must compare the attitudes of well-informed respondents with those of poorly informed respondents. Yet, as we have suggested, many of the least informed members of the public failed to respond to our survey. As a result, our sample contains too many people who are either moderately well informed or very well informed, and too few who are very poorly informed. Hence any differences we find between the most and least informed individuals *in our sample* are likely to be smaller than the actual differences between the most and least informed individuals *in the general public*. Thus, if response rates to our surveys had been higher, our findings on differences in the attitudes of the most and least sophisticated—though already quite strong—would have been still stronger, and our hypotheses concerning the effects of information on political attitudes would have been even more strongly supported.

In a few cases the effects of differential response rates pose more potentially serious problems. We have, for example, too few black respondents in our sample to undertake meaningful analyses of differences in the attitudes of black and white Americans. Accordingly, we have not reported such analyses. Another problem arises in connection with attitudes toward economic issues. Differential response rates by age, income, and race raise the possibility that our sample might lead us to overestimate the economic conservatism of the public. To compensate for this, we have relied more heavily than usual on data from other independent surveys (by Gallup, Harris, and so forth) in gauging popular attitudes toward the economic system (see Chapter 5).

We do not mean to exaggerate the seriousness of the problems we have raised. In cases in which we have been able to check our data against the findings of other surveys or, better still, against an external criterion, we have found the level of correspondence to be quite acceptable. For example, in a ballot initiative in California in 1978, an anti–gay rights initiative was defeated by a popular vote of 57 percent to 43 percent. In our mailback survey of 600 Californians (using a questionnaire which closely resembled the surveys we report here in format and length, and which was delivered for us by the California Poll), we found that 58 percent opposed the measure, 37 percent favored it, and the remainder were undecided.

In sum, while the effects of differential response rates are complex and difficult to estimate precisely, we have been alert to the problem and are satisfied that although the absolute magnitudes of certain percentage figures may have been somewhat affected, the direction of the results and the substantive conclusions we have drawn remain intact.

Appendix II
Three OVS Scales:
Capitalist Values,
Democratic Values,
and Political Sophistication

OVS Capitalist Values Scale

1. When it comes to making decisions in industry: workers should have more to say than they do now / the important decisions should be left to management. ["Neither" and "Undecided" response alternatives were also provided for each item in the democratic values and capitalist values scales.]

2. The profit system: teaches people the value of hard work and success / brings out the worst in human nature.

3. The private enterprise system: is generally a fair and efficient system / mostly leads to depression and widespread poverty.

4. A lumber company that spends millions for a piece of forest land: has the right to cut down enough trees to protect its investment / should, nevertheless, be limited by law in the number of trees it can cut.

5. If the system of private industry were abolished: most people would work hard anyway / very few people would do their best.

6. The poor are poor because: they don't try hard enough to get ahead / the wealthy and powerful keep them poor.

7. Unskilled workers (such as janitors, dishwashers, and so on) usually receive wages that are: about right, considering the amount of skill required / much too low for the dirty work they do.

8. Workers and management: have conflicting interests and are natural enemies / share the same interests in the long run.

9. Getting ahead in the world is mostly a matter of: ability and hard work / getting the breaks.

10. Trade unions: have too much power for the good of the country / need the power they have to protect the interests of working people.

11. A person's wages should depend on: how much he needs to live decently / the importance of his job.

12. When people fail at one thing after another it usually means: they are lazy and lack self-discipline / they weren't given a good enough chance to begin with.

13. Under a fair economic system: all people would earn about the same / people with more ability would earn higher salaries.

14. The way property is used should mainly be decided: by the individuals who own it / by the community, since the earth belongs to everyone.

15. Public ownership of large industry would be: a good idea / a bad idea.

16. Most businessmen: do important work and deserve high salaries / receive more income than they deserve.

17. Private ownership of property: is as important to a good society as freedom / has often done mankind more harm than good.

18. The use of strikes to improve wages and working conditions: is almost never justified / is often necessary.

19. Men like Henry Ford, Andrew Carnegie, J. P. Morgan, and John D. Rockefeller should be held up to young people as: models to be admired and imitated / selfish and ambitious men who would do anything to get ahead.

20. When businesses are allowed to make as much money as they can: everyone profits in the long run / workers and the poor are bound to get less.

21. The land of this country should be: turned over to the people / left in the hands of private owners.

22. Government regulation of business: usually does more harm than good / is necessary to keep industry from becoming too powerful.

23. Working people in this country: do not get a fair share of what they produce / usually earn about what they deserve.

24. Can you depend on a man more if he owns property than if he doesn't? Yes / No.

25. When people don't work hard on a job it's usually because: they just don't care about doing an honest day's work / their job is dull, unpleasant, or unimportant.

26. When it comes to taxes, corporations and wealthy people: don't pay their fair share / pay their fair share and more.

27. The free enterprise system: survives by keeping the poor down / gives everyone a fair chance.

28. Competition, whether in school, work, or business: leads to better performance and a desire for excellence / is often wasteful and destructive.

OVS Democratic Values Scale

1. The employment of radicals by newspapers and TV: is their right as Americans / should be forbidden.

2. If a speaker at a public meeting begins to make racial slurs, the audience should: stop him from speaking / let him have his say and then answer him.

3. For children to be properly educated: they should be protected against ideas the community considers wrong or dangerous / they should be free to discuss all ideas and subjects, no matter what.

4. Which of these opinions do you think is more correct? Like fine race horses, some classes of people are just naturally better than others / All people would be about the same if they were treated equally.

5. When a criminal refuses to confess his crimes, the authorities: are entitled to pressure him until he does / have no right to push him around, no matter what.

6. Meetings urging America to make war against an enemy nation: are so inhuman that we should not allow them to be held / have as much right to be held as meetings that support peace.

7. The use of federal agents to spy on radical organizations: is necessary for national security / violates their right to political freedom.

8. Most of the people who are poor and needy: could contribute something valuable to society if given the chance / don't have much to offer society anyway.

9. A radio or TV station that always speaks for the rich and

powerful against the poor and oppressed: should be required by law to present a more balanced picture / should have the right to favor or oppose any group it chooses.

10. "Crackpot" ideas: have as much right to be heard as sensible ideas / sometimes have to be censored for the public good.

11. Should a community allow the American Nazi Party to use its town hall to hold a public meeting? Yes / No.

12. In enforcing the law, the authorities: sometimes have to break the rules in order to bring criminals to justice / should stick to the rules if they want other people to respect the law.

13. Giving everyone accused of crime the best possible lawyer, even if the government has to pay the legal fees, is: necessary to protect individual rights / wasteful and goes beyond the requirements of justice.

14. A newspaper has a right to publish its opinions: only if it doesn't twist the facts and tell lies / no matter how false and twisted its opinions are.

15. Which of these comes closer to your own view? Nobody has the right to decide what should or should not be published / To protect its moral values, a society sometimes has to forbid certain things from being published.

16. If minorities aren't receiving equal treatment in jobs or housing: they should try to act better so that they will be accepted / the government should step in to see that they are treated the same as everyone else.

17. Our laws should aim to: enforce the community's standards of right and wrong / protect a citizen's right to live by any moral standard he chooses.

18. The freedom of atheists to make fun of God and religion: should not be allowed / is a legally protected right.

19. Tapping telephones of people suspected of planning crimes: is necessary to reduce crime / should be prohibited as an invasion of privacy.

20. When it comes to free speech, extremists: should have the same rights as everyone else / should not be allowed to spread their propaganda.

21. Prayers in the public schools should be: permitted / forbidden.

22. Laws protecting people accused of crime from testifying

against themselves should be: strengthened / weakened or abolished.

23. Is it a good idea / a bad idea for the government to keep a list of people who take part in protest demonstrations?

24. A person who holds a position of great responsibility, such as a doctor, a judge, or an elected official: is entitled to be treated with special respect / should be treated the same as everyone else.

25. On issues of religion, morals, and politics, high school teachers have the right to express their opinions in class: even if they go against the community's standards / only if those opinions are acceptable to the community.

26. Teaching that some kinds of people are better than others: goes against the American idea of equality / only recognizes the facts.

27. Censoring obscene books: is necessary to protect community standards / is an old-fashioned idea that no longer makes sense.

28. Requiring policemen to tell a suspect that he has the right to remain silent: prevents the police from doing their job properly / is necessary to a fair system of law enforcement.

29. Complete equality for homosexuals in teaching and other public service jobs: should be protected by law / may sound fair, but is not really a good idea.

30. In dealing with crime, the most important consideration is to: protect the rights of the accused / stop crime even if we have to violate the rights of the accused.

31. When the country is at war, people suspected of disloyalty: should be watched closely or kept in custody / should be fully protected in their constitutional rights.

32. Freedom in sexual conduct between adults should be: left up to the individual / regulated by law.

33. Books that preach the overthrow of the government should be: banned from the library / made available by the library, just like any other book.

34. Keeping people in prison without trial: is never justified, no matter what the crime is / is sometimes necessary when dealing with people who are dangerous.

35. An American citizen: should not mind having his record

checked by patriotic groups / is entitled to have his privacy respected, no matter what he believes.

36. Searching a person's home or car without a search warrant: should never be allowed / is sometimes justified in order to solve a crime.

37. How do you feel about movies that use foul language or show nudity and sexual acts on the screen? They should be banned / They have as much right to be shown as other films.

38. The right of a minority family to move into a particular neighborhood: should depend on whether the neighbors want them or not / should be the same as that of any other family.

39. If a person is found guilty of a crime by evidence gathered through illegal methods: he should be convicted no matter how the evidence was collected / he should be set free.

40. If some minorities haven't succeeded in business or the professions the main reason is that: they don't have the natural ability / they haven't been given enough training and opportunity.

41. Efforts to make everyone as equal as possible should be: increased / decreased.

42. If an employer is forced to lay off some employees, he should: let the women go first, especially if they are married / treat men and women employees exactly the same.

43. The laws guaranteeing equal job opportunities for blacks and other minorities: should be made even stronger / sometimes go too far.

44. Government efforts to bring about racial integration have been: too fast / too slow.

OVS Political Sophistication Scale

Information Items

1. The Fifth Amendment to the American Constitution mainly guarantees citizens: protection against forced confessions / freedom of speech.

2. Traditionally in the American political system the job of interpreting the Constitution is mainly exercised by: the President / the Supreme Court.

3. The "fairness doctrine" of the FCC (Federal Communica-

tions Commission) was intended to make sure that: both sides on controversial political issues can be heard on radio and television/newspapers print the truth.

4. Usually in American elections, most of the big city vote goes to: the Democrats/the Republicans.

5. The Bill of Rights in the American Constitution mainly: protects the rights and liberties of citizens / describes the rights of Congress, the President, and the courts.

6. The United States never joined the Common Market because: it was designed to include European countries only / the United States didn't want to give up its independence.

7. The stock market goes up and down mostly because: the confidence of investors changes from time to time / there are few government regulations of the stock market.

8. The use of primary elections in the United States to choose candidates was mainly introduced by: party "bosses" who can use them to control nominations / reformers who wanted the voters themselves to choose party candidates.

9. When people talk about "civil liberties" they usually mean: the right to vote and run for office / freedom of speech, press, and assembly.

10. One of the differences between democracies and dictatorships is that democratic governments: allow private property / allow citizens to choose their representatives freely.

11. Under the American Constitution: Congress can make any law it wants to, as long as the President also approves / Congress can make laws regulating certain things but not others.

12. Tariffs are usually favored by: consumer groups who benefit most from them / producers (business and labor) who want to cut down on foreign competition.

13. Inflation occurs when: people have more money while there are fewer things to buy / there is an increase in both unemployment and production.

Participation Items

1. Have you ever voted in national or local elections?

2. Have you ever helped in a political campaign by wearing a button, contributing time or money, etc.?

3. Have you ever joined an organization mainly concerned with public or political issues?

4. Have you ever discussed candidates or political issues with friends or neighbors?

5. Have you ever followed political news through the press or television?

6. Have you ever tried to solve some community problem by writing letters, attending meetings, joining with others, etc.?

7. Have you ever taken part in a peaceful demonstration, protest march, or sit-in?

8. I find most of the political news on television and in the newspaper: fairly dull / fairly interesting.

9. When people start talking about politics and the latest news from Washington or City Hall: I find it very boring / I usually enjoy it.

Education

1. How far did you go in school?

Appendix III
Clear and Contested Norms

A norm may be said to be "clear" when opinion leaders are highly united in their support for it. A norm is "contested" when they hold conflicting positions on it and attempt to solicit public support for their respective positions. Ideally, the determination of clear and contested norms would rely on an extensive and systematic content analysis of the views expressed by the nation's opinion leaders (politicians, the press, and so forth). Since such an analysis is beyond the scope of this book, we have followed an alternative procedure. First, we selected those items which, on their face, seemed clearly to exemplify our conception of a clear norm or a contested norm. Second, we used opinion data from our elite samples to check these judgments. Before including an item in one of our lists of clear norms, we required that at least 75 percent of elite members expressing an opinion support the norm. (In almost all cases, the ratios of support were actually about eight or ten to one.) Before an item was included in one of our lists of contested norms, elites had to differ sharply on the item. In addition, self-identified liberal and conservative elites had to disagree by 30 percentage points or more in their responses to it. (For an alternative method that employs strictly empirical criteria for determining clear and contested norms, see appendix III of Dennis Chong, Herbert McClosky, and John Zaller, "Patterns of Support for Democratic and Capitalist Values in the United States," *British Journal of Political Science*, 13 [October 1983], pp. 401–439.)

The items included in our final measures, along with information about their statistical properties, are reported below. (A

Neither/Undecided response alternative was included for each of these items but has been omitted here to conserve space.)

Clear Democratic Norms

1. Free speech should be granted: to everyone regardless of how intolerant they are of other people's opinions / only to people who are willing to grant the same rights of free speech to everyone else.

2. Freedom to worship as one pleases: applies to all religious groups, regardless of how extreme their beliefs are / was never meant to apply to religious cults that the majority of people consider "strange," fanatical, or "weird."

3. All systems of justice make mistakes, but which do you think is worse? To convict an innocent person / To let a guilty person go free.

4. Forcing people to testify against themselves in court: is never justified, no matter how terrible the crime / may be necessary when they are accused of very brutal crimes.

5. To be realistic about it, our elected officials: would badly misuse their power if they weren't watched and guided by the voters / know much more than the voters about issues, and should be allowed to make whatever decisions they think best.

6. In a democracy, must the party that wins the election respect the rights of extreme opposition parties to ridicule and attack the way things are being run? Yes, because the right of opposition parties, no matter how extreme, can never be abolished / No, because extremist opposition can prevent the majority from doing its job.

7. When making decisions about public affairs, the majority: should be able to do whatever it wants to / has a duty to respect the rights of the minority.

8. Teaching children that all people are really equal: recognizes that all people are equally worthy and deserve equal treatment / teaches them something that is obviously false.

9. A minority family that wants to move into a particular neighborhood: shouldn't have to check with anyone / would be well advised to find out whether the neighbors want them to or not.

Mean acceptance score: 12.95
Standard deviation: 2.98

Contested Democratic Norms

1. Which of these comes closer to your own view? The government has no right to decide what should or should not be published / To protect its moral values, a society sometimes has to forbid certain things from being published.

2. When a TV station reports secret information illegally taken from a government office: it's just doing its job of informing the public / the station owners should be fined or punished in some way for reporting such information.

3. Selling pornographic films, books, and magazines: lowers the community's moral standards and therefore victimizes everyone / is really a victimless crime and should therefore be left unregulated.

4. If a police officer stops a car for a traffic violation, he should: be allowed to search the car if he suspects it contains narcotics or stolen goods / be limited to dealing with the traffic violation and nothing else.

5. If a person on welfare becomes pregnant and wants an abortion, should the government pay for it? Yes, she should not be penalized for being poor / No, it would be an improper use of our federal tax money.

6. For the most part, local ordinances that guarantee equal rights to homosexuals in such matters as jobs and housing: damage American moral standards / uphold the American idea of human rights for all.

7. When a law goes against a person's conscience, he should: be allowed to disobey it so long as he has good reason and doesn't hurt anyone else / be required nevertheless to obey it, or else all law will lose its meaning.

8. Laws requiring employers to give special preference to minorities when filling jobs are: necessary to make up for a long history of discrimination / unfair to qualified people who are not members of a minority.

9. The laws guaranteeing equal opportunities for blacks and other minorities: should be made even stronger / sometimes go too far.

Mean acceptance score: 6.37
Standard deviation: 3.71

Clear Capitalist Norms

1. The private enterprise system: mostly leads to depression and widespread poverty / is generally a fair and efficient system.

2. Workers and management: have conflicting interests and are natural enemies / share the same interests in the long run.

3. Under a fair economic system: all people would earn about the same / people with more ability would earn higher salaries.

4. Public ownership of large industry would be: a good idea / a bad idea.

5. The land of this country should be: turned over to the people / left in the hands of private owners.

Mean acceptance score: 7.5
Standard deviation: 2.1

Contested Capitalist Norms

1. A lumber company that spends millions for a piece of forest land: has the right to cut down enough trees to protect its investment / should, nevertheless, be limited by law in the number of trees it can cut.

2. Most businessmen: do important work and deserve high salaries / receive more income than they deserve.

3. The use of strikes to improve wages and working conditions: is almost never justified / is often necessary.

4. Government regulation of business: usually does more harm than good / is necessary to keep industry from becoming too powerful.

5. When it comes to taxes, corporations and wealthy people: don't pay their fair share / pay their fair share and more.

Mean acceptance score: 3.55
Standard deviation: 2.25

Notes

1. The Foundations of the American Ethos

1. Louis Hartz, *The Liberal Tradition in America* (New York: Harcourt, Brace, 1955), p. 89.

2. Clinton Rossiter, *Conservatism in America: The Thankless Persuasion* (New York: Vintage Books, 1962), pp. 67, 71.

3. Richard Hofstadter, *The American Political Tradition* (New York: New Vintage Edition, 1972), p. xxxviii.

4. Samuel P. Huntington, *American Politics: The Promise of Disharmony* (Cambridge, Mass.: Harvard University Press, 1981), p. 23.

5. Huntington, "Postindustrial Politics: How Benign Will It Be?" *Comparative Politics* (January 1974), p. 188. Huntington also emphasizes the importance of the anti-authoritarian elements in the American democratic tradition. This orientation, he argues, makes it difficult for Americans to justify strong government action: "What justification is there for government, hierarchy, discipline, secrecy, coercion, and the suppression of the claims of individuals and groups within the American context? In terms of American beliefs, government is supposed to be egalitarian, participatory, open, noncoercive, and responsive to the demands of individuals and groups. Yet no government can be all these things and still remain a government ... The more intensely Americans commit themselves to their national political beliefs, the more hostile or cynical they become about their political institutions" (Huntington, *American Politics,* p. 41).

While Huntington has obviously identified a crucial characteristic of the American political tradition, it should also be noted that certain components of the ethos have been used at times to justify *strong* government action. Examples of such components include the concern for national security and the defense of property, which motivated the Constitutional Convention of 1787, and an egalitarian concern for the well-being of the poor and socially disadvantaged, which has motivated the New Deal and the growth of the American welfare state. As we discuss more fully in later sections of this study, the American political culture, though once strongly antigovernment, is now obviously ambivalent in its attitude toward government.

6. Thomas Jefferson, *Notes on Virginia* (Chapel Hill: University of North Carolina Press, 1955), p. 163.

7. Gunnar Myrdal, *The American Dilemma* (New York: Harper and Row, 1944).

8. Arthur Okun, *Equality and Efficiency, The Big Trade-Off* (Washington, D.C.: Brookings Institution, 1975), p. 1.

9. Survey on Political Affiliations and Beliefs, 1958.

10. Milton Friedman, *Capitalism and Freedom* (Chicago: University of Chicago Press, 1956).

11. V. O. Key, "Public Opinion and the Decay of Democracy," *Virginia Quarterly Review*, 37 (1959), p. 49.

12. The findings bearing on civil liberties are reported in Herbert McClosky and Alida Brill, *Dimensions of Tolerance* (New York: Basic Books, 1983).

13. Donald J. Devine, *The Political Culture of the United States: The Influence of Member Values on Regime Maintenance* (Boston: Little, Brown, 1972).

14. Gabriel A. Almond and Sidney Verba, *The Civic Culture: Political Attitudes and Democracy in Five Nations* (Princeton, N.J.: Princeton University Press, 1963); Lucien W. Pye and Sidney Verba, *Political Culture and Political Development* (Princeton, N.J.: Princeton University Press, 1965).

15. The anthropological literature is voluminous. For a general review, see Robert Keesing, "Theories of Culture," in *Annual Review of Anthropology,* ed. B. Siegel, A. Beals, and S. Tyler (Palo Alto, Calif.: Annual Reviews, Inc., 1974), pp. 37–98.

16. Ibid. See also Edward Lehman, "On the Concept of Political Culture: A Theoretical Reassessment," *Social Forces* (March 1972).

17. Insofar as possible, we shall adhere in this study to standard definitions of beliefs, values, and norms. *Beliefs* refer to an affirmation of what the believer takes to be factual statements. Many Americans, for example, believe that people will in fact work harder if they are in competitive situations than if they are not. *Values* are more normative in character and involve subjective preferences; they refer to standards of good and bad, right and wrong, desirable and undesirable. As such they furnish guides to principled conduct. A *norm* is a relatively specific rule or standard of conduct that embodies a given value. A norm of citizen participation, for example, might serve the value of popular sovereignty. In practice, of course, it is often difficult to tell whether an individual's attitudes or actions reflect beliefs, values, or norms. A person's commitment to an important value—say, equality—is likely to influence both his beliefs and normative preferences concerning that value. For example, someone who strongly values equality (1) might be led to believe that all people are in fact equal in their innate abilities; and (2) would be likely to favor the norm of equal opportunity in employment.

2. The Libertarian Tradition

1. Clinton Rossiter, *Conservatism in America* (New York: Vintage Books, 1962), p. 72.

2. Gallup release, May 21, 1982, Princeton, New Jersey.

3. See Bernard Bailyn, *The Ideological Origins of the American Revolution* (Cambridge, Mass.: Harvard University Press, 1967).

4. See J. Roland Pennock, *Democratic Political Theory* (Princeton, N.J.: Princeton University Press, 1979).

5. See Herbert McClosky and Alida Brill, *Dimensions of Tolerance* (New York: Basic Books, 1983).

6. There exists some scholarly disagreement over how tolerance ought to be conceptualized. For us, tolerance signifies a willingness to support the civil and political rights of a wide range of unconventional or nonconformist groups. We assume in this chapter that people may exhibit tolerant attitudes either because they have become indifferent or inured to certain forms of nonconformity, or because they believe they have a civic obligation to put up with groups, activities, ideas, and opinions which they continue to hate and fear. For a further discussion of this issue, see Dennis Chong, "New Limits of Tolerance in the United States," paper delivered at the 1984 annual meeting of the American Political Science Association, Washington, D.C. See also John L. Sullivan, James Piereson, and George E. Marcus, "An Alternative Conception of Political Tolerance: Illusory Increases 1950s to 1970s," *American Political Science Review*, 73 (1979), pp. 781–794.

7. Perry Miller, *Errand into the Wilderness* (Cambridge, Mass.: Harvard University Press, 1956), pp. 143–144.

8. Harris polls, cited in Hazel Erskine and Richard Siegel, "Civil Liberties and the American Public," *Journal of Social Issues*, 31 (1975), p. 26.

9. It was impossible to divide the public into even thirds on the religiosity scale in our Civil Liberties study, as the N's in Table 2–3 indicate.

10. Richard Morgan, *The Supreme Court and Religion* (New York: Free Press, 1962).

11. Engel et al. v. Vitale, 370 U.S. 421.

12. Paul L. Murphy, *World War I and the Origins of Civil Liberties in the United States* (New York: Norton, 1979), pp. 126, 225.

13. Ibid., pp. 130–132.

14. Cited in William Lockhart, Yale Kamisar, and Jesse Choper, *The American Constitution*, 3rd ed. (St. Paul, Minn.: Westbury, 1970), p. 522.

15. *New York Times,* January 18, 1981, p. E6.

16. Stouffer, *Communism, Conformity and Civil Liberties* (New York: Doubleday, 1955).

17. Clyde Nunn, Harry Crockett, Jr., and J. Allen Williams, Jr., *Tolerance of Nonconformity* (San Francisco: Jossey-Bass, 1978), p. 37.

18. See Nunn, Crockett, and Williams, *Tolerance of Nonconformity,* for a fuller report on changes in popular attitudes toward freedom of expression.

See also James A. Davis, "Communism, Conformity, Cohorts and Categories of American Tolerance in 1954," *American Journal of Sociology*, 81 (1975), pp. 491–513. For an opposing view, see Sullivan, Piereson, and Marcus, "An Alternative Conceptualization of Political Tolerance."

19. Quoted by Richard Hofstadter, *Anti-Intellectualism in American Life* (New York: Vintage Books, 1964), p. 78.

20. Stouffer, *Communism, Conformity, and Civil Liberties*, p. 220.

21. For a description of this measure, see McClosky and Brill, *Dimensions of Tolerance*, chap. 8.

22. New York Times v. Sullivan, 376 U.S. 254 (1964).

23. Whitney v. California, 274 U.S. 357 (1927).

24. Sullivan, Piereson, and Marcus, "Alternative Conceptualization of Political Tolerance."

25. Cited in George E. Probst, ed., *The Happy Republic* (New York: Harper and Row, 1962), pp. 108–110.

26. Stanley v. Georgia, 394 U.S. 557 (1968).

3. Egalitarianism

1. Alexis de Tocqueville, *Democracy in America*, trans. J. P. Mayer (Garden City, N.Y.: Doubleday, 1966), p. 9.

2. James Bryce, *The American Commonwealth*, vol. 2 (New York: Macmillan, 1923), p. 810.

3. Ralph Barton Perry, *Puritanism and Democracy* (New York: Vanguard Press, 1944), p. 354.

4. Bryce, *American Commonwealth*, p. 817.

5. Cited in John Higham, *Strangers in the Land* (New York: Atheneum, 1971), p. 277.

6. Ibid., p. 273.

7. Ibid., p. 137.

8. Cited in J. R. Pole, *The Pursuit of Equality in American History* (Berkeley: University of California Press, 1978), p. 224.

9. Ibid., pp. 240–241.

10. See ibid., chap. 8.

11. See S. M. Lipset and Earl Raab, *The Politics of Unreason* (New York: Harper and Row, 1970), pp. 354–355. See also Chapter 8 of the present volume.

12. Harris poll, cited in *Newsweek*, February 26, 1979. For a useful summary of the evidence concerning changes in American attitudes toward blacks, see Michael Corbett, *Political Tolerance in America* (New York: Longman, 1982).

13. Cited in George Abernethy, ed., *The Idea of Equality* (Richmond, Va.: John Knox Press, 1959), p. 185.

14. Richard Hofstadter, *The American Political Tradition* (New York: Vintage Books, 1972), p. 5.

15. Tocqueville, *Democracy in America*, p. 179.

16. Ibid., p. 51.

17. J. W. Prothro and C. M. Grigg, "Fundamental Principles of Democracy: Bases of Argument and Disagreement," *Journal of Politics,* 22 (1960), pp. 276–294.

18. Frank R. Westie, "The American Dilemma: An Empirical Test," *American Sociological Review,* 30 (1965), pp. 527–538.

19. John Adams, personal letter, cited in Abernethy, *Idea of Equality,* p. 159.

20. Herbert Croly, *The Promise of American Life* (Indianapolis, Ind.: Bobbs-Merrill, 1965), p. 181.

21. Sidney Verba and Gary Orren, *Equality in America* (Cambridge, Mass.: Harvard University Press, 1985), chap. 1.

22. Ibid.

23. For corroborating evidence, see Jennifer L. Hochschild, *What's Fair? American Beliefs about Distributive Justice* (Cambridge, Mass.: Harvard University Press, 1981); see also Everett Carl Ladd, Jr., "Traditional Values Regnant," *Public Opinion* (March/April 1978), pp. 45–49.

24. Hadley Cantril, ed., *Public Opinion 1935–1946* (Princeton, N.J.: Princeton University Press, 1951), p. 508.

25. Ibid., p. 988.

26. Ibid., pp. 509–510.

27. George Gallup, *The Gallup Poll, Public Opinion 1972–1977,* vol. 2 (Wilmington, Del.: Scholarly Resources, 1978), pp. 1135–36.

28. Westie, "American Dilemma."

29. William Leggett, cited in *Social Theories of Jacksonian Democracy,* ed. Joseph Blau (Indianapolis, Ind.: Bobbs-Merrill, 1954), p. 77.

30. *The United States Democratic Review,* October 1837, cited ibid, p. 27.

31. Cited in Richard Hofstadter, *Social Darwinism in American Thought* (Boston: Beacon Press, 1958), p. 123.

32. *Public Papers of the Presidents: Lyndon B. Johnson, 1963–64,* vol. 1 (Washington, D.C.: Government Printing Office, 1965), p. 376.

33. Whitney Young, Jr., *To Be Equal* (New York: McGraw-Hill, 1964), p. 29.

34. Verba and Orren, *Equality in America,* chap. 4.

35. Cited in Public Opinion (March/April 1978), p. 40.

36. *Public Papers of the Presidents: Lyndon B. Johnson, 1963–64,* vol. 2, pp. 842–843.

37. Cited in Pole, *Pursuit of Equality,* p. 172.

4. The Cultural Foundations of Capitalism

1. Cited in George E. Probst, ed., *The Happy Republic* (New York: Harper and Row, 1962), p. 7.

2. Our 1958 PAB study as well as the National Election Studies by the University of Michigan in 1972 and 1976 agree on the 35 percent figure. The percentage figure on attitudes toward big business comes from the 1976 NES

study. See also S. M. Lipset and William Schneider, *The Confidence Gap: Business, Labor, and Government in the Public Mind* (New York: The Free Press, 1983), pp. 81–88, 184–196, and passim.

3. Francis X. Sutton et al., *The American Business Creed* (Cambridge, Mass.: Harvard University Press, 1956), p. 3.

4. Perry Miller, *The New England Mind* (Cambridge, Mass.: Harvard University Press, 1963), p. 261 and passim.

5. Richard H. Tawney, *Religion and the Rise of Capitalism* (New York: New American Library, 1954).

6. Miller, *New England Mind*, pp. 42–43.

7. Max Weber, *The Protestant Ethic and the Spirit of Capitalism*, trans. Talcott Parsons (New York: Scribner's, 1958), p. 54.

8. Sutton et al., *American Business Creed*, pp. 275–276. For an excellent study of the evolution of American attitudes toward work, see Daniel T. Rodgers, *The Work Ethic in Industrial America 1850–1920* (Chicago: University of Chicago Press, 1978).

9. Alexis de Toqueville, *Democracy in America*, trans. J. P. Mayer (Garden City, N.Y.: Doubleday, 1966), p. 550.

10. Jerald G. Bachman and Lloyd D. Johnston, "The Freshman, 1979," *Psychology Today* (September 1979), p. 80.

11. The differences, though statistically significant, would doubtless be even larger if support for capitalist values were not so widespread to begin with.

12. *Oxford English Dictionary*, S. V. "individualism."

13. Tocqueville, *Democracy in America*, pp. 506, 508.

14. Yehoshua Arieli, *Individualism and Nationalism in American Ideology* (Baltimore: Penguin, 1966), p. 189.

15. Cited in John G. Cawelti, *Apostles of the Self-Made Man* (Chicago: University of Chicago Press, 1965), p. 9.

16. From "Self Reliance," in *Essays by Ralph Waldo Emerson*, ed. Irwin Edman (New York: Crowell, 1951), p. 53.

17. Cited in Arieli, *Individualism and Nationalism*, p. 331.

18. Cited in Irvin G. Wyllie, *The Self-Made Man in America* (New Brunswick, N.J.: Rutgers University Press, 1954), p. 9.

19. Ibid., p. 1.

20. S. M. Lipset, *The First New Nation* (Garden City, N.Y.: Doubleday, 1967), chaps. 1 and 2.

21. David C. McClelland, *The Achieving Society* (Princeton: von Nostrand, 1961).

22. Robin M. Williams, *American Society*, 2nd ed. (New York: Knopf, 1960), p. 417.

23. Wyllie, *Self-Made Man*, p. 12.

24. Tocqueville, *Democracy in America*, p. 621.

25. Wyllie, *Self-Made Man*, p. 9.

26. Ibid., pp. 72–73.

27. Daniel K. Yankelovich, *Changing Youth Values in the 1970s: A Study of*

American Youth (New York: John D. Rockefeller 3rd Fund, 1974), pp. 16, 18.

28. Kate L. Schlozman and Sidney Verba, *Injury to Insult* (Cambridge, Mass.: Harvard University Press, 1979), p. 202.

29. Cited in S. M. Lipset and William Schneider, "How's Business?" *Public Opinion* (June-July 1978), p. 42.

30. Cited in Richard Hofstadter, *Social Darwinism in American Thought* (Boston: Beacon Press, 1958), p. 57.

31. See, for example, E. van den Haag, "Economics is Not Enough: Notes on the Anti-Capitalist Spirit," *The Public Interest* (Fall 1976), pp. 109–126.

32. Cited in Michael Hill, *A Sociology of Religion* (London: Heinemann, 1973), p. 124.

33. *The Adams-Jefferson Letters,* ed. Lester J. Cappon (New York: Simon and Schuster, 1971), p. 551.

34. Daniel Bell, *The Cultural Contradictions of Capitalism* (New York: Basic Books, 1976), p. 477.

35. Ibid., p. 21.

36. Christopher Lasch, *The Culture of Narcissism* (New York: Norton, 1978), p. 53.

37. Irving Kristol, *Two Cheers for Capitalism* (New York: Basic Books, 1978), p. 262.

38. Bell, *Cultural Contradictions*, p. 84.

39. William Lawrence, "The Relationship of Wealth to Morals," *World's Work,* 2 (January 1901), p. 287.

40. Cited in Henry May, *Protestant Churches and Industrial America* (New York: Harper and Brothers, 1949), p. 54.

41. Ibid., p. 62.

42. Ibid., p. 69.

43. Bell, *Cultural Contradictions*, p. 21.

44. Theodore Caplow and Howard Bahr, "Half a Century of Change in Adolescent Attitudes: Replication of a Middletown Survey by the Lynds," *Public Opinion Quarterly* (Spring 1979), pp. 1–17.

45. Since the samples in the two surveys were somewhat different, the comparison of the results should be considered approximate. The 1939 survey was based on a representative sample of the nation's adult population; the 1976 survey was based on a sample of the work force, employed and unemployed. Data are cited from Kay Schlozman and Sidney Verba, *Injury to Insult* (Cambridge, Mass.: Harvard University Press, 1979), p. 220.

5. Capitalism as an Economic System

1. Joseph A. Schumpeter, *Capitalism, Socialism, and Democracy,* 4th ed. (New York: Harper, 1975 [1942]), p. 61.

2. In 1978 the book went into the eighteenth printing of its fourth edition.

3. Ibid., p. 154.

4. For a summary and analysis of recent trends, see Seymour M. Lipset and William Schneider, *The Confidence Gap: Business, Labor and Government in the Public Mind* (New York: Free Press, 1983).

5. Reprinted in Irving Kristol, *Two Cheers for Capitalism* (New York: Basic Books, 1978), p. 73.

6. Leonard Silk and David Vogel, *Ethics and Profits: The Crisis of Confidence in American Business* (New York: Simon and Schuster, 1976), pp. 71, 189.

7. See Marvin Meyers, *The Jacksonian Persuasion* (Stanford: Stanford University Press, 1960), passim.

8. Walter Lippman, *Drift and Mastery* (Englewood Cliffs, N.J.: Prentice-Hall, 1962, originally published in 1914), p. 17.

9. National Election Study, University of Michigan, 1976. See also Lipset and Schneider, *Confidence Gap,* chaps. 1 and 2.

10. Yankelovich, Skelly, and White, cited in Lipset and Schneider, *Confidence Gap,* pp. 181–183.

11. See Lipset and Schneider, *Confidence Gap.* For a related argument that distrust of authority is a deep-seated feature of American culture, see Samuel P. Huntington, *American Politics: The Promise of Disharmony* (Cambridge, Mass.: Harvard University Press, 1981).

12. The question of whether politically unsophisticated respondents understand the principles underlying capitalism (and democracy) is discussed briefly in the final section of Chapter 8, and at greater length in Dennis Chong, Herbert McClosky, and John Zaller, "Patterns of Support for Democratic and Capitalist Values in the United States," *British Journal of Political Science,* 13 (1983), pp. 401–440, especially pp. 424–433.

13. From a letter by Benjamin Franklin on the conditions in Ireland, in *Writings,* vol. 5, ed. Albert H. Smyth (New York: Macmillan, 1907), p. 368.

14. J. Hector de Crevecoeur, *Letters from an American Farmer* (New York: New American Library, 1963), p. 48.

15. Alexis de Tocqueville, *Democracy in America,* trans. J. P. Mayer (Garden City, N.Y.: Doubleday, 1966), p. 639.

16. For a general discussion of this issue, see William B. Scott, *In Pursuit of Happiness: American Conceptions of Property from the Seventeenth to the Twentieth Century* (Bloomington: University of Indiana Press, 1977).

17. Lippmann, *Drift and Mastery,* p. 46.

18. A. A. Berle, Jr., and Gardiner C. Means, *The Modern Corporation and Private Property* (New York: Macmillan, 1932), p. 297.

19. Ibid., p. 312.

20. The number of Americans favoring nationalization of big business, and especially of banking, seems to have declined somewhat over the past few decades. Doubtless the experience of the Great Depression and notably the memory of the bank failures of the 1930s made government ownership of banks and large corporations a more attractive idea than it was before or since. See Donald Devine, *The Political Culture of the United States* (Boston: Little, Brown, 1972), pp. 212–213.

21. Paul A. Samuelson, *Economics,* 10th ed. (New York: McGraw-Hill, 1976), p. 251.

22. See, for example, Sidney Fine, *Laissez Faire and the General Welfare State* (Ann Arbor: University of Michigan Press, 1956).

23. Yehoshua Arieli, *Individualism and Nationalism in American Ideology* (Baltimore, Md.: Penguin, 1966), p. 176.

24. For an extended discussion of public attitudes toward regulation, see Seymour Lipset and William Schneider, "The Public View of Regulation," *Public Opinion* (January 1979), pp. 6–13.

25. Cited in Richard Hofstadter, *Social Darwinism in American Thought*, rev. ed. (New York: George Braziller, 1959), p. 146.

26. Ibid., p. 134.

27. For an account of these developments, see Thomas C. Cochran, *Business in American Life* (New York: McGraw-Hill, 1972).

28. Lipset and Schneider, *Confidence Gap*, p. 238.

29. For data on mass opinion shifts, see *The Gallup Opinion Index*, Princeton, N.J., 1971, pp. 2295, 2315, 2321–22. The data on the shift among Republican business leaders are reported in Richard Wayne Parsons, "Political Attitudes of American Elites: Cleavage, Consensus and Conflict," (Ph.D. diss., Columbia University, 1976), p. 281. By chance, Nixon's announcement of support for wage and price controls occurred during the period in which Parsons' interviews were being conducted, thereby making it possible to estimate the effects of the announcement on elite opinion.

30. For additional discussion of this issue, see Chapter 8 and also John Zaller, "The Role of Elites in Shaping Public Opinion" (Ph.D. diss., University of California, Berkeley, 1984).

31. For information on the construction of this scale, see Chapter 1 and Appendix I.

32. It should be noted that the low-income respondents in Table 5–9 include many kinds of people, among whom are many elderly people on fixed incomes whose total wealth may be greater than their incomes alone might suggest.

33. Our finding that ideological variables have a larger impact on political values than do variables relating to self-interest has been confirmed in numerous other contexts. See Kay Schlozman and Sidney Verba, *Injury to Insult* (Cambridge, Mass.: Harvard University Press, 1979), especially chap. 8, "Economic Strain and Political Attitudes."

34. Cited in S. M. Lipset and W. Schneider, "How's Business?" *Public Opinion* (August 1978), p. 42.

35. Lipset and Schneider, *Confidence Gap*, p. 289.

6. Capitalism and Democracy in Conflict

1. For additional details on the construction of these indexes, including statistics on convergent and discriminant validity, see Dennis Chong, Herbert McClosky, and John Zaller, "Patterns of Support for Democratic and Capitalist Values," *British Journal of Political Science*, 13 (1983), pp. 401–440, especially pp. 424–433.

2. Milton Friedman, *Capitalism and Freedom* (Chicago: University of Chicago Press, 1956), pp. 108–109.

3. Robert Dahl, *Dielmmas of Pluralist Democracy* (New Haven: Yale University Press, 1982), p. 108.

4. Alexis de Tocqueville, *Democracy in America,* trans. J. P. Mayer (Garden City, N.Y.: Doubleday, 1966), p. 54.

5. It should be emphasized that our discussion in these pages refers mainly to white males, who dominated the economic and political life of this period. Equal opportunities, of course, were not available to slaves, Indians, women, or to the small number of free blacks.

6. John P. Kennedy, cited in George E. Probst, ed., *The Happy Republic* (New York: Harper and Row, 1962), p. 11.

7. See Joseph Blau, ed., *Social Theories of Jacksonian Democracy* (Indianapolis, Ind.: Bobbs-Merrill, 1954).

8. Werner Sombart, *Why There Is No Socialism in the United States,* trans. Patricia Hocking and C. T. Husbands (White Plains, N.Y.: Sharpe, 1976), p. 8.

9. Cited in Richard Hofstadter, *Age of Reform* (New York: Knopf, 1956), p. 228.

10. Campaign speech, June 27, 1936, cited in *The Public Papers and Addresses of Franklin D. Roosevelt,* vol. 5 (New York: Random House, 1938), pp. 230–236.

11. Charles Lindblom, *Politics and Markets* (New York: Basic Books, 1977), p. 356.

12. Dahl, *Dilemmas of Pluralist Democracy,* pp. 184–185.

13. F. A. Hayek, *The Road to Serfdom* (Chicago: University of Chicago Press, 1945), pp. 19–20.

14. It is worth noting that, when strong prodemocrats have reservations about a particular element of the capitalist creed, they tend to express their feelings by taking one of the nonsubstantive options ("neither" or "undecided") rather than by endorsing a notion clearly hostile to capitalism. See, for example, the first item in Table 6–2.

15. Cited in Kenneth Vines and Henry Robert Glick, "The Impact of Universal Suffrage: A Comparison of Popular and Property Voting," *American Political Science Review,* 61 (1967), p. 1078.

7. Ideology and the American Ethos

1. The literature on these subjects is voluminous. See, for example, Herbert McClosky, "Conservatism and Personality," *American Political Science Review,* 52 (1958), pp. 27–45; Glenn Wilson, *The Psychology of Conservatism* (New York: Academic Press, 1973). A fuller treatment can be found in Herbert McClosky and Paul Meehl, *Ideologies in Conflict* (forthcoming).

2. In making use of respondents from known or "criterion" liberal and conservative groups, we avoid for the moment the difficult problem of how one ought to measure ideology among members of the general public. We will

take up the problem of measurement in somewhat greater detail later in this chapter.

3. In fact, some of the items included in this table could be used (with suitable scoring and validation) as psychometric measures of such personality traits as misanthropy. The source of an individual's attitudes, of course, says nothing about the *wisdom* of the ideas that are at issue. That an opinion springs, in part, from a benevolent disposition does not necessarily make it correct. Nor are the personal dispositions we have described the sole source of the political beliefs with which they are correlated; many other influences are also at work.

4. Cited in Henry May, *The Enlightenment in America* (New York: Oxford University Press, 1976), p. 282.

5. *The Adams-Jefferson Letters,* ed. Lester J. Cappon (New York: Simon and Schuster, 1971), p. 334.

6. *The Political Writings of Thomas Jefferson,* ed. Edward Dumbauld (Indianapolis, Ind.: Bobbs-Merrill, 1955), p. 75.

7. Ibid., p. 118.

8. *The Political Writings of John Adams,* ed. George A. Peek, Jr. (Indianapolis: Bobbs-Merrill, 1954), pp. 199, 201.

9. *Papers of Thomas Jefferson,* ed. Julian Boyd (Princeton, N.J.: Princeton University Press, 1955), vol. 12, p. 15.

10. See Leonard Levy, *Legacy of Suppression* (Cambridge, Mass.: Harvard University Press, 1960).

11. *Political Writings of Thomas Jefferson,* p. 35.

12. The social change scale includes eight items, several of which are shown in Table 7–1. Among members of the general public, the alpha reliability of the scale is 0.51; among the opinion leaders it is 0.60; and among the ideological activists it is 0.79. For a discussion of why the reliabilities of attitude scales of this kind tend to be higher among elites than among members of the general public, see Dennis Chong, Herbert McClosky, and John Zaller, "Patterns of Support for Democratic and Capitalist Values in the United States," *British Journal of Political Science,* 13 (1983), pp. 401–410, especially pp. 424–433.

13. The social benevolence scale includes eleven items, several of which are shown in Table 7–2. It has an alpha reliability of 0.66 among the general public, 0.66 among the opinion leaders, and 0.77 among the ideological activists.

14. The faith in human nature scale contains four items. Its alpha reliability is 0.41 among the general public, 0.52 among the opinion leaders, and 0.70 among the ideological activists.

15. Because of the shortness of the scale measuring faith in human nature, it was necessary to use the twenty-third and eightieth percentiles as the cutoff points for the trichotomized version of the scale.

16. Philip Converse, a leading student of political attitudes, has estimated that fewer than 15 percent of the American public have a well-developed understanding of liberal and conservative principles, but that about 50

percent are able to use the terms *liberal* and *conservative* in a roughly serviceable fashion. See Philip E. Converse, "The Nature of Belief Systems in Mass Publics," in *Ideology and Discontent,* ed. David Apter (Glencoe, Ill.: Free Press, 1964), p. 222. Norman Nie, Sidney Verba, and John Petrocik put these figures a bit higher, but still within the same range as Converse's estimate; see *The Changing American Voter* (Cambridge, Mass.: Harvard University Press, 1976).

17. Respondents were asked the following question: "Many of us don't like to pin labels on ourselves. Our views are often too complicated to be described by a single label. Nevertheless, if you *had* to choose one word or phrase to describe your political beliefs, which of the following would you choose?" The choices were "far left," "strong liberal," "liberal," "middle-of-the-road," "conservative," "strong conservative," "far right," and "don't know." A very small fraction of the general public (about 1 percent) chose either the far left or the far right. Since the number of such people is small, and since in any case there are too few of them in our sample for reliable analysis, we have made no effort in the present study to investigate their views. See, however, McClosky and Meehl, *Ideologies in Conflict,* for a discussion of the adherents of far left and far right ideologies.

18. For example, we reported earlier that 98 percent of the respondents in Westie's Indianapolis study believed that all people ought to enjoy equality of opportunity.

19. Both reversals occurred on items that proposed limits on the editorial freedom of television stations. The first item proposed that a television station which "always speaks for the rich and powerful against the poor and oppressed" be required to present a more balanced view. The second item urged that a station which advocated "the use of military action against demonstrators" lose its license.

20. S. M. Lipset, *Political Man* (New York: Doubleday, 1960), p. 87.

21. See V. O. Key, Jr., *Southern Politics* (New York: Knopf, 1949).

22. See David B. Magleby, *Direct Legislation* (Baltimore: Johns Hopkins University Press, 1984), p. 185.

23. Charles Forcey, *The Crossroads of Liberalism* (New York: Oxford University Press, 1961), p. x.

24. Paul Samuelson, *Economics,* 10th ed. (New York: McGraw-Hill, 1976), p. 799.

25. Cited in Richard Hofstadter, *The Progressive Historians* (New York: Vintage Books, 1970), p. 438.

26. Daniel Boorstin, *The Genius of American Politics* (Chicago: University of Chicago Press, 1953).

27. Richard Hofstadter, *The American Political Tradition,* 2nd ed. (New York: Vintage Books, 1972) pp. xxviii-xxix.

8. Social Learning and the Acquisition of Political Norms

1. See Chapter 1 for a fuller discussion of this point.

2. S. M. Lipset and Earl Raab, *The Politics of Unreason* (New York: Harper and Row, 1970), pp. 355, 356.

3. The Civil Liberties study (CLS) contained our largest pool of democracy items, while the Opinions and Values survey (OVS) contained our largest pool of capitalism items. Accordingly, when studying the effect of exposure to politics on support for clear and contested democratic norms, we used data from the Civil Liberties study; when studying the effect of exposure to public affairs on support for clear and contested capitalist norms, we used data from the Opinions and Values study.

4. The OVS information scale contains thirteen items and has a reliability of 0.69; the Civil Liberties information scale has twelve items and a reliability of 0.65. The OVS participation scale has ten items and a reliability of 0.76; the Civil Liberties participation scale includes seven items and has a reliability of 0.69. The education variables in each study contain seven categories, ranging from "some grade school" to graduate or professional school.

5. The correlations were, however, somewhat reduced. The partial correlations (betas) for information, participation, and education with clear democracy were, respectively, 0.26, 0.18, and 0.21, all statistically significant; for clear capitalism, the betas were 0.32, 0.14, and 0.18, all statistically significant. The measure of support for clear democratic norms has a reliability of 0.47, and the measure of support for clear capitalist norms has a reliability of 0.59. When the partial correlation between information and measure of clear democratic norms is corrected for the reliabilities of the two measures, it becomes 0.47. The corrected partial correlation between information and support for capitalism is 0.50. The standard formula for calculating these corrected partial correlations is explained in George W. Bohrnstedt and T. Michael Carter, "Robustness in Regression Analysis," in *Sociological Methodology 1971,* ed. Herbert L. Costner (San Francisco: Jossey-Bass, 1971), pp. 118 146.

6. *Los Angeles Times,* October 13, 1978, p. II-6.

7. For a fuller treatment of the patterns of attitude change at the time of the Briggs campaign, see John Zaller, "The Role of Elites in Shaping Public Opinion" (Working Paper no. 63, Survey Research Center, University of California, Berkeley), 1982.

8. See the California poll, *San Francisco Chronicle,* October 5, 1978.

9. At high levels of information, the mean difference between prochange and antichange respondents is approximately one standard deviation on the contested democracy, contested capitalism, and clear capitalism measures; on the clear democracy scale, this difference is approximately 0.9 standard deviations. The regression analysis further indicates that at low levels of information, prochange and antichange respondents do not reliably differ from each other in their attitudes toward either clear or contested norms.

10. The principal participants in this disagreement include John L. Sullivan, James Piereson, and George E. Marcus, *Political Tolerance in America* (Chicago: University of Chicago Press, 1981); Mary R. Jackman, "General and Applied Tolerance: Does Education Increase Commitment to Racial Integration?" *American Journal of Political Science,* 22 (May 1978), pp. 302–324; and Paul M. Sniderman, Richard A. Brody, and James H. Kuklinski, "Policy

Reasoning and Political Values: The Problem of Racial Equality," *American Journal of Political Science,* 28 (February 1984), pp. 75–94.

11. For additional data pertaining to the question of whether the better educated are, in general, more tolerant, see Herbert McClosky and Alida Brill, *Dimensions of Tolerance* (New York: Basic Books, 1983), especially chap. 9.

12. Our measure of social benevolence produces results that are similar to—though slightly less pronounced than—those reported in Figure 8–1. In addition, we show in Chapter 9 that among respondents favoring social reform, increases in exposure to public affairs lead to greater support for welfare state programs, but among respondents favoring order and stability, increases in exposure lead to less support for the welfare state. At high levels of political sophistication, the difference between the two groups of respondents is approximately two standard deviations on the welfare state scale. (See Figure 9–1.)

The data reported in Figures 8–1, 8–2, and 9–1 involve twelve independent tests of our hypotheses concerning the effects of information on support for clear and contested norms. Although the coefficients obtained in some of these tests are not significant at the 0.05 level, all twelve coefficients have signs in the expected direction. The odds of obtaining such results by chance are about 1 in 4,000.

For other data indicating that when the elite norms are clear, the more politically informed members of the public tend to learn them, see the discussion of the "mainstream model" in William Gamson and Andre Modigliani, "Knowledge and Foreign Policy Opinion: Some Models for Consideration," *Public Opinion Quarterly,* 30 (1966), pp. 187–199; see also V. O. Key, *Public Opinion and American Democracy* (New York: Knopf, 1961), p. 341. For other data consistent with the notion that when elite norms are contested, increases in political sophistication are associated with a tendency toward ideological polarization among members of the public, see Angus Campbell et al., *The American Voter* (New York: Wiley, 1960), p. 208; George Belknap and Angus Campbell, "Party Identification and Attitudes toward Foreign Policy," *Public Opinion Quarterly,* 15 (Winter 1951), pp. 601–623; and the "consistency model" in Gamson and Modigliani, "Knowledge and Foreign Policy Opinion." For an attempt to integrate the findings reported in these and other studies, see John Zaller, "Toward a Theory of the Survey Response," paper delivered at the 1984 annual meeting of the American Political Science Association, Washington, D.C.

13. The central discussion of this problem remains Philip E. Converse, "The Nature of Belief Systems in Mass Publics," in *Ideology and Discontent,* ed. David Apter (Glencoe, Ill.: Free Press, 1964), pp. 206–261.

14. Although the measures of support for capitalism and democracy in the PAB and OVS studies are composed of different items, their general content is sufficiently similar to warrant the assumption that they are comparable measures of the same basic concepts. Since measures of political information and participation were not included in the PAB survey, we have relied, in Figure 8–5, on the best available indicator of exposure to public affairs, namely, education.

15. As a result of the way in which we constructed our classification scheme, we can draw no conclusions about the popularity of the nineteenth-century liberal pattern relative to the welfare state liberal and strong conservative patterns.

16. For a conservative writer's view of the value constraints on conservatives in the United States, see Clinton Rossiter, *Conservatism in America: The Thankless Persuasion* (New York: Vintage Books, 1962).

17. Slight discrepancies between the data reported in this chapter and the data in our *British Journal* article (see note 21) are due to the correction of a computational error in the earlier article.

18. Herbert McClosky and John Schaar, "Psychological Dimensions of Anomy," *American Sociological Review,* 14 (1965), pp. 14–40.

19. The inflexibility scale contains fifteen items and has a reliability of 0.54. The scale items are listed in Chong et al. (see note 21).

20. Philip E. Converse, "The Nature of Belief Systems in Mass Publics," in *Ideology and Discontent,* ed. David Apter (Glencoe, Ill.: Free Press, 1964).

21. For a more extensive treatment of the effect of political sophistication on the learning of attitude structures, see Dennis Chong, Herbert McClosky, and John Zaller, "Patterns of Support for Democratic and Capitalist Values in the United States," *British Journal of Political Science,* 13 (1983), especially pp. 423–434.

9. The Future of Capitalist Democracy in the United States

1. James Sterling Young, *The Washington Community* (New York: Harcourt, Brace and World, 1966), p. 250.

2. Thomas Jefferson, *Notes on Virginia,* ed. William Peden (Chapel Hill: University of North Carolina Press, 1955), p. 165.

3. See Joseph Tuckerman, *On the Elevation of the Poor* (Boston: Roberts Brothers, 1874; reprinted, New York: Arno Press, 1971).

4. Andrew Carnegie, *The Gospel of Wealth and Other Essays,* ed. Edward C. Kirkland (Cambridge, Mass.: Harvard University Press, 1962).

5. Cited in Sidney Fine, *Laissez-Faire and the General Welfare State* (Ann Arbor: University of Michigan Press, 1956), p. 257.

6. John Dewey, *Human Nature and Conduct* (New York: Holt and Company, 1922), pp. 21–22.

7. From Dwight D. Eisenhower, "Faith in the Individual," in *The Great Society,* ed. Glenn R. Capp (Belmont, Calif.: Dickenson, 1967), p. 34.

8. Richard Hofstadter, *Social Darwinism in American Thought* (Boston: Beacon Press, 1955), p. 11.

9. William G. Sumner, "Sociology," reprinted in *American Thought: Civil War to World War I,* ed. Perry Miller (New York: Holt, Rhinehart and Winston, 1954), p. 87.

10. Cited in Fine, *Laissez-Faire and the General Welfare State,* p. 82.

11. Carnegie, *Gospel of Wealth,* pp. 26–27.

12. F. W. Taussig, *Principles of Economics,* 2nd ed., vol. 2 (New York: Macmillan, 1915), p. 233.

13. *New York Times,* April 29, 1981, p. 7.

14. For discussions of whether it is reasonable to interpret the 1980 election as a "mandate" for conservative policies, see Stanley Kelley, Jr., *Interpreting Elections* (Princeton, N.J.: Princeton University Press, 1983); Warren Miller and J. Merrill Shanks, "Policy Directions and Presidential Leadership: Alternative Interpretations of the 1980 Presidential Election," *British Journal of Political Science,* 12 (1982), pp. 299–356.

15. See James A. Davis, "Communism, Cohorts, Conformity, and Categories: American Tolerance in 1954 and 1972–73," *American Journal of Sociology,* 81 (November 1975), pp. 491–513; D. Garth Taylor, Paul Sheatsley, and Andrew Greeley, "Attitudes toward Racial Integration," *Scientific American* (June 1978), pp. 42–50.

16. Obviously, one could locate vocational or ideological subgroups (for example, bankers, conservative activists) who would exhibit extraordinarily high levels of support for capitalist values. We believe, however, that the twelve occupational subgroups in the OVS and Civil Liberties studies are broadly representative of American elite opinion.

Index